Physical Evidence in Forensic Science

Third Edition

Henry C. Lee, Ph.D.
Howard A. Harris, Ph.D., J.D.

D0643048

 **Lawyers & Judges**
Publishing Company, Inc.
Tucson, Arizona

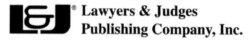

**Lawyers & Judges
Publishing Company, Inc.**

P.O. Box 30040 • Tucson, AZ 85751-0040
(800) 209-7109 • FAX (800) 330-8795
e-mail: sales@lawyersandjudges.com
www.lawyersandjudges.com

Library of Congress Cataloging-in-Publication Data

Lee, Henry C.
  Physical evidence in forensic science / Henry C. Lee, Howard A. Harris. -- 3rd ed.
    p. cm.
  Includes bibliographical references and index.
  ISBN-13: 978-1-936360-01-7 (alk. paper)
  ISBN-10: 1-936360-01-2 (alk. paper)
  1. Forensic sciences. I. Harris, Howard A. II. Title.
  HV8073.L39 2012
  363.25--dc23
                           2011030783

Printed in the United States of America
10 9 8 7 6 5 4 3 2 1

Contents at a Glance

Part III: Legal Aspects of Forensic Science

Appendices

Full Contents

Part I
General Concepts in Forensic Science

Chapter 1

Physical Evidence in Forensic Science

A combination of the importance and value of physical evidence in criminal, civil and national security investigations and the continuing advance of the applications of science and technology has caused the role of physical evidence to grow to unprecedented levels. As a result, most law enforcement agencies have become increasingly dependent on the fruits of forensic examinations to develop evidence not ordinarily obtainable by other avenues of investigation. It is important to realize that physical evidence transcends the simple concept of materials collected at the crime scene. Physical evidence may be found in many places, including emergency rooms, doctors' offices, a victim's body, a suspect's body, morgues, as records in computers or file cabinets, and a myriad of other locations.

Ironically, decisions about the extent of the use of physical evidence in criminal investigations traditionally are made not by forensic scientists, but by the investigating officers. In the crime scene search and initial investigative stages, police officers, detective investigators or crime scene technicians are usually the ones who decide what types of evidence will be collected, and how much evidence will be submitted to the forensic laboratory for analysis. At the adjudicative stage of cases, prosecutors or defense attorneys usually determine what physical evidence will be introduced in court, and the scope of forensic analysis that is to be presented at trial through expert testimony. In recent years many attorneys have felt pressured by the raised expectations of juries (as a result of a significant increase in exposure of forensic science by the media), the so-called "CSI Effect."

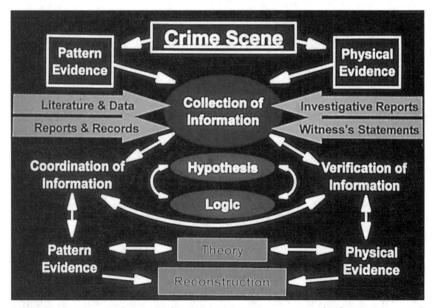

Figure 1.1 Steps in the complex investigation process, which requires coordination and cooperation. Forensic science expertise may be involved in every step of this process.

In many cases, forensic scientists do play a supportive role in the process of criminal investigation. With the rapid advances in forensic techniques, the value of forensic science in criminal investigation is increasingly recognized as significant or even critical. This is largely the result of the availability of databases of DNA profiles, expanded fingerprint searching capability and firearms image databases and their significant contribution to investigation. Thus the role of forensic scientists has shifted from passive to active. The forensic science profession has become an important element of the criminal justice team. Figure 1.1 depicts the role of forensic science in the criminal justice system.

1.1 Types of Physical Evidence at Crime Scenes

Virtually any material can develop significance as physical evidence. It may be something as small as a pollen particle, or as large as a train. It can be in the physical state of a gas, solid or liquid. It can occur in the form of patterns or a tangible physical object. Because of the diversity of physical evidence, it is virtually impossible to identify a single classification scheme which will be applicable in all cases. In general, physical evidence may be found at a crime scene in the following four forms: transient, pattern, conditional and transfer.

A. Transient Evidence

Transient evidence is any type of physical evidence which is temporary in nature and which can easily be changed or lost. The most commonly encountered types of transient evidence include the following:

- Odor—putrefaction odor, cooking odor, perfume odor, gasoline odor, cyanide odor, body odor, urine odor, burning odor, explosives odor, cigarette or cigar smoke odor.
- Temperature—the temperature in a room, the temperature of a car hood or engine, the temperature of coffee, tea or water in a cup, the temperature of water in a bathtub, the body temperature of a cadaver, the temperature of fire debris, and so forth.
- Imprints and indentations—moist footprints on hot or dry road surfaces, fingerprints on meltable material, tooth marks in perishable foods, tire marks on the beach at low tide, and footprints in snow are some examples.
- Markings—postmortem lividity marks before they become fixed, water soluble stains of markings at outdoor scenes, blood splatters on movable objects, a lip print on a smoldering cigarette butt, bloodstains on clothing immersed in water, and so forth.
- Biological stains—blood, semen, urine stains both wet and dried.

Transient evidence must generally be detected by the first responding officer or the first witness at the crime scene. It should be collected, recorded and documented as soon as possible. While preservation is often not possible, most transient evidence can be recorded by notes that are verified by other observers at the scene. Certain transient evidence can be recorded by photography or videotaping; other types can be collected and preserved with special care to prevent further change or loss.

B. Pattern Evidence

Pattern evidence is generally produced by forcible, direct contact between persons and objects, or an object with another object. A variety of physical patterns can be found at crime scenes. Most of these physical patterns are in the form of imprints, indentations, striations, markings, fractures or deposits. Pattern evidence has not attracted as much attention as it deserves, nor its potential value fully realized, since it has often been thought of as "not very scientific." However, pattern evidence at crime scenes is extremely valuable in the reconstruction of events. It can very often be used to prove or disprove a suspect's alibi or a witness' version of what took place, to associate or dissociate the involvement of persons or objects in particular events, or to provide investigators with new leads. Thus pattern evidence may play a significant role both during the investigation and afterwards during the prosecution of a case.

The following is a list of some types of pattern evidence commonly found at crime scenes. These pattern categories are discussed in more detail in Chapter 22, *Pattern Evidence*. In some incidents, multiple types of patterns may be present.

1. Blood spatter patterns
2. Glass fracture patterns
3. Fire burn patterns
4. Furniture position patterns
5. Projectile trajectory patterns
6. Track-trail patterns
7. Tire or skid mark patterns
8. Clothing or article patterns
9. Modus operandi patterns
10. Powder residue patterns
11. Material damage patterns
12. Body position patterns
13. Shoe or boot print patterns
14. Weave patterns
15. Pattern injuries on victim or suspect

The recognition of pattern evidence requires careful observation and a systematic, detailed approach in analyzing the crime scene. Proper documentation is also critical since this type of evidence can also be transient.

C. Conditional Evidence

The third type of physical evidence commonly encountered at a crime scene is conditional evidence. Conditional evidence is produced by a certain event or action. If not documented carefully, this evidence may be changed or lost. Conditional evidence is extremely important for crime scene reconstruction and to determine the set of circumstances leading up to an event. Some examples of conditional evidence commonly found at crime scenes include the following:

- Light, such as whether vehicle headlights were on or off prior to an accident, and lighting conditions at an indoor crime scene.
- Smoke, such as the color of the smoke, the direction of travel of the smoke, the density of the smoke, or the odor of the smoke.
- Fire, such as the color of the flames, the direction of the flames, the speed of the flame spread, the temperature of the fire, and the condition of the fire.
- Location, such as the location of a weapon or cartridge case in relation to a victim's body, the sequence and location of bloodstains on several objects, the location of a victim's vehicle, distribution of broken glass, and the location of injuries or wounds.
- Vehicle status, such as whether a vehicle's doors are locked or unlocked, whether a window is opened or closed, whether the radio is on or off and the station to which it is tuned, whether the ignition key is present, and the odometer reading.
- Body status, such as the degree of rigor mortis, the distribution of lividity, the degree of decomposition, body temperature, body position, and the types of injuries.

D. Trace and Transfer Evidence

Transfer evidence is the classical type of physical evidence. It is produced by physical contact between persons or between objects, or between person(s) and object(s). Transfer evidence can be classified according to many different criteria. However, no single classification scheme is completely satisfactory because no one can take into account all the different possible perspectives. Six different classification schemes for transfer evidence are described below. Each is useful in offering a different conceptual perspective for illuminating the varied nature of transfer evidence. Trace evidence may also be deposited at a scene or on other evidence by processes that do not require direct contact such as dust landing on a surface or gunshot residue being projected onto a surface.

E. Associative Evidence

Associative evidence includes major items that are left behind at a scene or taken away from the scene. These might include vehicles, clothing, identifiable jewelry, credit cards or other highly personal items.

1. Classification by type of crime

An obvious way of classifying physical evidence is by the type of crime from which it originates. Thus, there is homicide evidence, burglary evidence, assault evidence, rape evidence, and so on. Although this scheme has value in certain situations, remember that any type of physical evidence can occur in connection with virtually any kind of crime. Particular physical evidence types are not restricted to a defined crime classification. Bloodstains, for example, frequently occur in assault and homicide cases, but they may be just as important as evidence at a burglary scene or a hit-and-run. Similarly, semen stains are thought of as the primary type of evidence in rape and other sex crimes, but in some cases, a different type of physical evidence may prove to be even more important. There is some correlation between the type of crime and the type of evidence; these correlations should serve as reminders to investigators when searching for transfer evidence at crime scenes.

2. Classification by type of material

A second way of classifying evidence is by the nature of the material itself. Here, categories would include metallic evidence, fiber evidence, glass evidence, or plastic evidence, for example. This classification scheme, however, has limitations. A fingerprint found on glass, for example, is handled and examined in essentially the same manner as one found on plastic or other non-porous surfaces. Similarly, a toolmark on a metal surface would be examined and compared in the same way as one found in some other material, such as wood. In both of these cases, the nature of the material is less significant than the nature of evidence and its interaction with that material.

3. Classification by general nature of the evidence

Evidence can be classified as physical, chemical or biological; another possible scheme would be to classify the evidence as animal, vegetable or mineral in nature. Classifications according to the former scheme would include a firearm, a tool, a toolmark, or cartridge case as physical, while a drug sample would be chemical. Biological examples would include hair, marijuana, and bloodstains.

Table 1.1
Classification of Evidence by its General Nature

Biological	Chemical
Blood	Fibers
Semen	Chemicals
Saliva	Glass
Other Body Fluids	Soil
Hair	Gun Powder
Botanical	Metal
Bone	Mineral
Tissues	Controlled Substances
Urine	Drugs
Pollen	Paper
	Ink
	Paint

Physical (Patterns & Impression)	Miscellaneous
Fingerprints	Laundry Marks
Firearms	Voice Analysis
Handwriting	Polygraph
Printing	Photography
Number Restoration	Corneal Patterns
Footprints	Watermarks
Tire Marks	Profiling
Blood Spatters	
Typewriting	
Bitemarks	
Toolmarks	
Lip Prints	
Palm Prints	

Such schemes are of greatest value to an investigator to serve as a reminder for the most appropriate method of collection and preservation of physical evidence. Table 1.1 gives some examples of evidentiary materials classified according to this scheme.

4. Classification by the type of question to be resolved

Examples of classification by this scheme include whether evidence will be used to reconstruct an event, to provide an element of the crime, to link a suspect to a victim or to a crime scene, or to exclude or exonerate a suspect. Similarly, evidence can be classified according to whether it will be used to provide investigative leads, or as proof for use in a court of law.

5. Classification according to the way evidence was produced

The relationship of physical evidence to the act being investigated may also be used as a basis for classification. An important consideration when classifying evidence in this manner is the way in which the individuals involved have interacted with their environments, with each other, and the type of evidence produced by these interactions. Examination and interpretation of evidence allows the investigator or forensic scientist to offer an opinion as to the events which have taken place. For example, the discovery of tiny blood droplets on a suspect's boots would indicate presence at the time the blood was spattered, whereas a smear would indicate contact with blood already deposited. Physical evidence when viewed from this perspective is an unintentional, albeit somewhat imperfect, record of the interactions of the individuals involved in the activity and the environment at the crime scene. Considering physical evidence in this way can be extremely useful in a case investigation and reconstruction of a crime.

6. Classification according to the specific type of evidence

Physical evidence may be classified according to the specific nature of each type of physical evidence. This classification scheme includes the following:

1. Toolmarks
2. Fingerprints
3. Organic compounds
4. Glass
5. Tire tracks
6. Paint
7. Plastics
8. Wood
9. Dust
10. Semen
11. Paper
12. Soil
13. Fibers
14. Weapons
15. Construction materials
16. Documents
17. Metal
18. Hairs

19. Blood
20. Minerals
21. Inorganic compounds
22. Voice recordings

23. Videotapes
24. Digital evidence in the form of computers or other electronic devices

1.2 Stages in the Analysis of Physical Evidence and Types of Interpretation

The full value of physical evidence is realized only when the potential breadth of its use is understood. The application of physical evidence may concern the recognition, identification, comparison, individualization, interpretation and reconstruction of various types of conditional, pattern, transient, and transfer evidence. A very complex undertaking, indeed!

A. Recognition

The ability to separate important and potentially informative material from background and unrelated materials is extremely important, both to the investigator and to the laboratory analyst. Recognition involves pattern recognition, recognition of physical properties, field testing and information analysis. This is probably the single most important step in a forensic examination; without recognition there can be no further laboratory examination or scientific analysis. If evidence is not recognized, then proper collection and preservation will not take place, and the information that would have been provided from the analysis of this evidence would be lost.

B. Identification

Identification is the process of using class characteristics to identify a particular object. Identification generally involves one or more of the following methods:

1. Physical measurements
2. Physical properties
3. Chemical properties
4. Morphological (structural) characteristics
5. Biological properties
6. Immunological properties

In some cases, it is sufficient that a piece of physical evidence be identified; no further examination is necessary, for example, identification of a controlled substance or weapon. Usually, however, identification is the beginning of a more extensive forensic analysis which includes, in most cases, careful comparisons.

C. Classification

Classification is done by comparing the class characteristics of the evidence with those of a known standard. If all the measurable class characteristics are the same for both the evidence and the known samples, then the two could have come from the same source. When a significant difference between the two samples is noted, one may conclude that the questioned sample did not originate from the same source as the known. It is important to note that exclusion is considered absolute. It is also important to recognize that the classification process can go through many stages, each reducing the size of the class to which the evidence belongs. For example, an object could be classified first as a knife, then as a kitchen knife, then as boning knife, then as a certain brand of boning knife and so forth. Due to the inherent limitations, forensic analysis beyond the comparison stage is often not possible. Some methods used for the classification of physical evidence include simple visual, macroscopic, microscopic, chromatographic, spectroscopic, elemental composition or trace element content, immunologic and biochemical analyses.

D. Individualization

Individualization is the demonstration that the origin of an item of physical evidence is unequivocally determined to be uniquely related to some other object or particular source. Individualization involves the comparison of class and individual characteristics. The process of individualization is the most rigorous part of any forensic analysis, and true individualization may be possible only for some limited types of evidence. Methods of individualization include physical matching, pattern matching, genetic marker determination and composition matching.

E. Reconstruction

Physical evidence can also be used to help reconstruct a crime or to determine the sequence of events. This process is based on the results of crime scene examinations, laboratory analyses, deductive and inductive logic, statistical data, pattern analysis, and other types of information. Reconstruction of a crime can be very complex, involving the linkage of physical evidence, stain pattern information, analytical results, investigative information and other documentary and testimonial evidence into a single, complete entity. A more detailed discussion of this topic is given in Chapter 3, *Reconstruction.*

1.3 Role of Physical Evidence in Investigation and Resolution of Criminal Activity

The goal of physical evidence examination is to provide useful information for criminal investigators in solving crimes and for courts of law during the adjudication of these cases. The following are some types of information which physical evidence can supply.

A. Information on the Corpus Delicti

The corpus delicti (literally, the "body of the crime") refers to those essential facts which show that a crime has taken place. For example, toolmarks, broken doors or windows, ransacked rooms, and missing valuables would be important in establishing that a burglary has taken place. Similarly, in an assault case, the victim's blood, a weapon, or torn clothing could be important pieces of physical evidence.

B. Information on the Modus Operandi

Many criminals have a particular modus operandi, or MO, which is their characteristic way of committing a crime. Physical evidence can help in establishing an MO. In burglary cases, for example, the point of entry, the means used to gain entry, tools that were used, and types of items taken may all establish an identifiable method of operation. In arson cases, the types of accelerant used and the way the fires were set constitute physical evidence that helps to establish the "signature" of an arsonist. Analysis of physical evidence to establish an MO is one important way of linking cases in the investigation of a serial killer or rapist.

C. Linking a Suspect with a Victim

This linkage is one of the most common and important aspects that physical evidence can help to establish. Blood, hairs, clothing fibers, cosmetics and other items from the victim may be transferred to a perpetrator. Items found in a suspect's possession can sometimes be linked to a victim, for example through comparison of bullets with a weapon seized from the suspect. It is also possible that evidence can be transferred from a perpetrator to a victim; thus, the manner in which both victim's and suspect's clothing are handled and packaged is extremely important.

D. Linking a Person to a Crime Scene

This type of link is also one of the most vital in a crime scene investigation. Numerous types of evidence may be deposited by the person committing a crime, including fingerprints, blood, hair, fibers, and soil. In addition, the type of weapons or objects used may also leave evidence; for example, bullets and cartridge casings or toolmarks. Depending on the type of crime, various kinds of evidence from the scene may be carried away intentionally, as with stolen property, but also as transfers of trace evidence, such as carpet fibers or pet hairs on the criminal's shoes or clothing. These materials are extremely useful in linking an individual to a particular crime scene.

E. Disproving or Supporting a Witness' Testimony

Physical evidence analysis can often indicate conclusively whether a person's version of a set of events is credible, or whether an alibi is convincing. For example, the examination of a car which fits the description of a hit-and-run vehicle might reveal blood on the underside of the bumper. If the owner of the vehicle claims he hit a dog, laboratory tests on the blood can reveal whether the blood is from a dog or a human.

F. Identification of a Suspect

Possibly the best evidence for identifying a suspect is his fingerprints. A fingerprint found at a scene, and later identified as belonging to a particular person, results in an unequivocal identification of that person as having been at the scene. Similarly a DNA profile with sufficient matching markers is also now recognized as an identification. The term identification when applied to people really means "individualization" (identifying a single unique source).

G. Providing Investigative Leads

Physical evidence analysis can assist the investigator in pursuing a productive path, by providing clues from the characteristics of the physical evidence. In a hit-and-run case, for example, examination of a chip of paint found in the victim's clothing can be used to provide information on the color and possibly the model and year of the automobile involved. With the rapid emergence of searchable computer databases of fingerprints, cartridge case markings, bullet stria and DNA profiles, the ability of physical evidence to provide investigative leads has increased enormously.

H. Identification of a Substance

The results of examining a piece of physical evidence can provide information on the identity of a particular substance. As indicated above, this is a classification process. In its simplest form, such as in the identification of cocaine, heroin, LSD, morphine or any other type of drug, it meets the legal requirement for classification as a controlled substance. Laboratory analysis of fibers can sometimes yield information on the manufacturer of the fabric or garment. Simple identification of many types of physical evidence can provide critical information for use in the investigation or prosecution of a case. Further, in many civil actions identification of a substance can be every bit as useful in establishing or refuting the claims of one of the parties.

Chapter 2

Introduction to Forensic Science

Although a dictionary definition of *forensic science* may be generally stated as "science in the service of the law," common usage often narrows forensic science to the discipline of criminalistics. In recent years, however, the field of forensic science has grown tremendously, leading to a considerable expansion in forensic laboratories, both in size and scope of operations. The application of forensic science in both criminal and civil investigation has rapidly expanded, with the recognition that physical evidence occurs in many useful forms. This change has required a broader range of expertise, training and experience to deal with the growing variety of useful physical evidence. Forensic science now includes a diverse range of specialties, including criminalistics, forensic medicine, anthropology, odontology, psychiatry, toxicology, entomology, questioned documents examination, firearms examination, examination of computers or other digital evidence and fingerprint development and comparison.

2.1 Criminalistics

Criminalistics may be defined as a body of knowledge concerning the recognition, collection, identification, individualization, and evaluation of physical evidence using the techniques of natural science in matters of legal significance. Criminalistics also includes the reconstruction of events based on physical evidence analysis and crime scene pattern interpretation. At one time, a criminalist was considered a generalist, drawing upon a wide spectrum of scientific knowledge to analyze a variety of physical evidence. There are, however, many subspecialties within criminalistics. Although the general principles of the examination in each subspecialty are the same, the analytical approaches and techniques are sometimes quite different. As a result, there has been a movement toward more specialization. The following are some of the subspecialties currently practiced in the forensic science field.

A. Forensic Drug Analysis

Forensic drug analysts use standard methods of analytical chemistry to identify the presence of controlled substances and to quantitate these materials. In addition to the analysis of unknown powders, liquids, and vegetative materials, the drug chemist may also identify controlled substances in the form of pills, capsules and other dosage forms. Frequently, analysts must not only identify the active ingredient, but also determine the exact amount present, The forensic drug analysts are also called upon to assist with processing materials from clandestine laboratories and to develop important investigative information concerning country of origin or similarity of source from detailed chemical and physical examination of seized materials.

B. Forensic Chemistry

Forensic chemistry involves the identification and analysis of toxic substances, accelerants, gun powder residue, explosives, and other chemical substances. The forensic chemist uses both qualitative and quantitative methods to identify and determine amounts of unknown substances, and to make comparisons between known and unknown materials. The forensic chemist may also attempt to trace unknown substances to a specific origin. A wide variety of physical evidence can provide useful information when analyzed chemically. A small piece of shiny metal can be found to be lead, and further analyses to show that it is likely bullet lead, a lead fishing sinker, solder, etc.

C. Analysis of Trace or Transfer Evidence

The trace analyst combines the methodologies of microscopic, instrumental and chemical techniques in the examination of hair, fibers, glass, soil, plant material, minerals, and a wide variety of materials. These include both macro and microscopic materials present on seized evidence, usually in small quantities. While it is difficult to make absolute individualizations in these areas, the trace analyst can often make identifications with a high degree of certainty, and can in some cases establish partial individuality of a specimen. This is an area of analysis where confidence grows based on experience and a wide knowledge of analytical methods.

D. Firearms Examination

The firearms examiner conducts the examination of firearms, discharged bullets, cartridge cases, shotgun shells, unusual weapons, and ammunition components. Generally, a firearms examiner tries to answer at least these questions: (1) What kind of weapon fired the bullet? (2) Did this particular weapon fire this bullet or cartridge case? (3) What kind of ammunition was used? (4) What was the reconstruction of the path followed by the bullet? Many firearms examiners also perform toolmark comparisons. With increasing frequency, tools of many kinds are used as weapons or in the perpetration of crimes. Whenever a tool has been used, and the use results in marks on an object, it may be possible to individualize the tool to the mark, or at least indicate if a tool is consistent with the type of marks observed.

E. Latent Fingerprints

Latent fingerprint examiners are responsible for processing latent fingerprints on evidence submitted to a forensic laboratory from crime scenes. There are many chemical and physical methods for the detection and visualization of latent fingerprints. With the availability of Automated Fingerprint Identification Systems to virtually all law enforcement agencies, the investigative value of latent fingerprints has increased enormously, and as the value has increased it has driven the development of improved techniques for the visualization of latent fingerprints. After the latent fingerprints have been developed, the examiner compares them with known fingerprints submitted from the suspect, victim, or other individual involved in the case, and if necessary searches them through enormous databases. An absolute identification can often be made based on these fingerprint comparisons.

F. Forensic Serology

Forensic serologists apply the principles and techniques of biochemistry, serology, immunology, hematology, and molecular biology to the identification and individualization of blood and other body fluids. The questions which are generally answered by the examination are: 1) Is it a body fluid stain? 2) What type of body fluid was it? 3) What species does the stain belong to? 4) Does the questioned stain have the same blood groups and isoenzyme or DNA patterns as a certain known sample? 5) Can serological reconstruction be used to help individualize the sample in terms of origin?

G. DNA Analysis

Forensic biologists also apply the principles and procedures of molecular biology to the analysis of blood, semen, bones and other tissues, hair roots, and any material which contains nucleated cells. DNA methods allow for a virtual individualization and can be applied to a wide variety of samples. DNA analysis has been found to work well with many difficult stains, even where the sample is quite limited and the biological materials have partially degraded. The ability to separate the cellular material of spermatozoa from other types of cellular material makes successful results in sexual assault cases much more likely.

H. Impression Evidence

Criminalists who specialize in impression evidence are generally concerned with various types of two or three dimensional markings, such as footwear impressions, tire impressions, and footprints on smooth surfaces. Evidence impression marks are generally compared with known markings made by the object suspected of causing the imprint or impression. Some types of impression evidence, such as fingerprints and toolmarks, fall within the province of other subspecialties discussed above.

I. Questioned Document Examination

The questioned document examiner is involved in the scientific examination of handwriting, typewriting, printing, photocopying, or other mechanical production of written material. This discipline also includes the analysis of ink, paper, and other components of the document. Examinations can involve identifying the source or writer of a document, determining if a signature is authentic or forged, determining the age of the document, deciphering obliterated or erased writing, authenticating threatening letters, detecting alterations, and examining indented writing and burned or charred documents. It is now recognized that document examination can be a particularly valuable tool in white collar crime investigations.

2.2 Other Forensic Science Specializations

There are a number of other specialty areas in forensic science that are not part of the traditional criminalistics activities, but are deeply involved in the collection and examination of physical evidence. Some of the most active of these are discussed briefly below.

A. Forensic Medicine

Forensic medicine is the application of a variety of medical and related specialties to legal problems. Laws in every state require that the investigation of unexpected and/or unattended deaths be overseen by either a coroner or a medical examiner. Coroners are usually elected officials, who are not typically required to have any medical training. In fact, if they are not pathologists themselves, they usually direct the investigation and rely on trained pathologists for the more technical medical examinations. Medical examiners are usually qualified as forensic pathologists, who through autopsy, toxicological analysis and other investigation determine cause and manner of death. Forensic pathologists are also sometimes consulted even when the victim survives, to examine and interpret pattern injuries resulting from violent crime or even accidents.

B. Forensic Anthropology

Physical anthropology is the study of the human skeleton, and how it has developed and evolved throughout the history of the human race. Forensic anthropologists are physical anthropologists who specialize in recovering and examining human skeletal remains where legal questions are involved. The examination of recovered bones can reveal whether the bones are human, the age and height of the person, the sex, injuries to the skeleton, the nature of wounds, and a history of accidents or injury, as well as information about medical conditions and childbearing history. Anthropologists can also tell whether the skeletal remains were deposited relatively recently or whether they belong to a person who died many decades or centuries ago.

C. Forensic Odontology

Forensic odontology, forensic dentistry, is the application of dental science to problems of human identification. Forensic odontologists most commonly perform two types of forensic examinations: (1) Comparison of the dental x-rays of an unidentified human remains with the antemortem dental records of known persons, in order to identify remains that are difficult or impossible to identify by more conventional means. These cases generally result from the discovery of skeletal remains, or from remains recovered from fires, explosions, accidents, or mass disasters. (2) Odontologists also locate, examine and compare bite marks. Criminals sometimes inflict bites on their victims during abuse and violent crimes; or they may leave potential bite mark evidence at a crime scene, impressed in food remains.

D. Forensic Toxicology

The forensic toxicologist identifies, analyzes, and studies the effects of drugs, environmental chemicals and poisons on the human body. Often toxicologists are required to identify the presence of an unexpected chemical substance in body fluids or tissues and to determine the quantity of that substance in the sample. Toxicologists are particularly important in driving while impaired or intoxicated cases and in a wide variety of other criminal or civil cases where toxic or illegal substances may have been ingested. Toxicological analyses of postmortem tissue and body fluid samples assist the medical examiner in determining the involvement of drugs, chemicals or poisons in a questioned death. Forensic toxicology has a significant role in public health by detection of contamination or tampering in consumer products by examination of the victim's body fluids. The civil role of toxicology has greatly increased in recent years in detecting impairment at work or banned substances in athletes.

E. Forensic Entomology

Entomology is the study of the life cycles and distribution of insects. After an organism dies, if it is exposed to insect attack, various insects use the body as a host for their offspring, laying their eggs on or in the body. Because the life cycle and behavior of most common insects has been carefully studied by entomologists, the waves of insect infestation of a human body follow certain predictable patterns and time intervals. The forensic entomologist is often called upon to identify the type of insect present on evidence or at a scene, and to note where these insects are in their life cycle. Forensic entomologists use this information to estimate the time since death in human remains that have not been discovered or protected for some days after death. Toxicology on the material found in the gut of insect pupa may give useful information on materials taken by the individual they have been feeding upon.

F. Forensic Engineering

Forensic engineers are involved in a variety of analyses which apply engineering principles to legal issues. These include reconstructing events involving materials failures, building and structure collapses, and vehicular accidents from the physical evidence record following the incident. They might also be involved in analyzing the causes of airplane or train accidents. Because of public safety and liability issues, a considerable number of forensic engineering cases are civil rather than criminal in nature.

G. Forensic Photography

Photographers who are trained specialists in photographic documentation of crime scenes, accident scenes and physical evidence are forensic photographers. Often associated with crime scene investigation teams or with full-service forensic science laboratories, forensic photographers are involved in photograph enhancement, specialized photography involving non-visible light photography, use of alternate light sources, macro and microphotography, photographic and video conversion or enhancement, and digital image processing and clarification.

H. Forensic Accounting

Forensic accounting is most importantly used in the investigation of white collar crime and both civil and criminal investigations of fraud. It plays the key role in unraveling the complex schemes used to hide and move illegally obtained monies. By their very nature such crimes use complex accounting subterfuges to hide the fact that money is being misappropriated. Forensic accounting also plays an important role in civil cases for estimation of damages and a variety of other important financial concerns.

I. Digital Forensics (Computer Forensics)

Digital forensics includes physical evidence containing information from activities, communication and even recreation, yielding valuable investigative information. This is one of the most rapidly expanding physical evidence processing areas. See Chapter 10, *Digital and Multimedia Evidence (Digital Forensics)*.

Virtually any scientific specialty can prove useful in some forensic context. Some practitioners who do forensic work and preface their specialty with the word *forensic* are: forensic accountants, forensic actuaries, forensic linguists, forensic meteorologists, forensic geologists, and forensic metallurgists.

Chapter 3

Reconstruction

Crime scene reconstruction is the process of determining the events and actions that occurred during the commission of a crime through analysis of the crime scene and the examination of other physical evidence. Reconstruction not only involves the scientific scene analysis, interpretation of scene pattern evidence and laboratory examination of physical evidence, but also involves the systematic study of related information, and finally, the logical formulation of a theory based on all available data.

Reconstruction is a combination of the inductive and deductive aspects of science, and some art. The steps and stages of reconstruction closely follow a basic scientific method approach. It involves consideration and incorporation of all investigative information along with physical evidence analysis and interpretation into a reasonable explanation of the crime and related events. Logic, careful observation, and considerable experience, both in crime scene investigation and forensic examination, are necessary for sound interpretation, analysis and, ultimately, reconstruction.

3.1 Types of Reconstruction

There are many types of reconstruction. The nature of the crime, the questions
which need to be answered, and the types of events that have taken place are all
factors to take into account when classifying a reconstruction. In general, there
are five common ways to classify approaches to reconstruction:

A. Reconstruction of specific types of incident
    1. Accident reconstruction
        a. Traffic accident reconstruction
        b. Other accident reconstruction, such as train, airplane, boat
            accidents
        c. Construction accident reconstruction: building and bridge collapses,
            and many others
    2. Specific crime reconstruction
        a. Homicide reconstruction
        b. Arson scene reconstruction
        c. Rape case reconstruction
        d. White-collar crime reconstruction
        e. Reconstruction of scenes of bombing and other explosive
            incidents
        f. Other specific crime scene reconstruction
B. Reconstruction of specific portions of the incident
    1. Sequence determination
    2. Directional determination
    3. Position determination
    4. Relational determination
    5. Conditional determination
    6. Identity determination
C. Scope of reconstruction
    1. Total case reconstruction
    2. Partial case reconstruction
    3. Limited event reconstruction
    4. Specific pattern reconstruction
D. Specific type of physical evidence reconstruction
    1. Biological fluid evidence reconstruction
    2. Firearms evidence reconstruction
    3. Shooting incident reconstruction
    4. Handwriting or document reconstruction
    5. Gunshot residue pattern reconstruction
    6. Injury pattern determination and reconstruction

7. Fingerprint position reconstruction
8. Footprints or shoe prints reconstruction
9. Tire mark reconstruction
E. Specialized types of determinations
1. Criminal profiling
2. MO, motive, and psychological determinations
3. Organized or disorganized crime scene determination
4. Primary scene or secondary scene determination
5. Scene profiling
6. Physical characteristics determination
7. Timeline analysis
8. Clarification and enhancement of images
9. Facial reconstruction and automated facial recognition
10. Use of credit card information to profile criminal activities

All of the above have in common the need to integrate large amounts of data. The more abundant and accurate the data, the more likely the reconstruction will be accurate and useful.

3.2 Crime Scene and Laboratory Procedures
A. Recognition
Any type of forensic analysis usually starts from recognition of the potential evidence and its separation from those items which have no evidential value. Unless the potential evidence can be recognized, no useful analysis or reconstruction can be carried out. Although the examination of a macroscopic scene or a microscopic scene is different, the general approach is the same. Once the evidence is located, personnel must use every effort and precaution to preserve, to document and to collect this evidence.

B. Identification
Examiners use analysis and comparisons of physical evidence to identify objects, substances, and materials. Identification is a process which takes advantage of class characteristics, and results in classifying an object, substance or material within a group of related objects. Examiners then compare those identified items of evidence with known reference materials or standards.

C. Individualization
By careful comparison between a questioned sample (scene) and the known samples, one can then attempt to individualize the evidence and to determine its origin. Such individualization must be more formal than just a casual comparison,

and should include careful systematic examination and comparison. The process of individualization is based upon the presence of individual characteristics. Two things may be shown to have a common origin (such as in cases of physically fitting one piece of evidence to another), or a piece of evidence can be shown to be unique among members of its class (such as in unique pattern matches, like a fingerprint match). In these cases, there is usually no doubt about the individuality of an object or item of evidence. So-called identification of persons is another type of individualization that can be done with virtual certainty in most cases. With many kinds of physical evidence, it is not possible to achieve true individualization. When evidence items that cannot be truly individualized are similar, or match with respect to various characteristics, useful statements about how similar they are can often be made. The degree of similarity of particular evidence or characteristics depends on many factors, and varies from being fairly easily calculated, as in the case of blood groups or DNA, to being limited to broad, experience-based estimates.

D. Evidence for Laboratory Submission

Submit all available scene photographs, autopsy photographs, videotapes, measurements, notes, reports, and physical evidence to the laboratory for thorough examination.

E. Crime Scene Examination

Whenever possible, it is most desirable to visit the crime scene as soon as possible after the incident and make direct observation of the scene and patterns. Complete and accurate documentation of a scene and the physical evidence will provide the best opportunity for later reconstruction analysis.

F. Reconstruction

Identification and individualization analyses of physical evidence, and the conclusions drawn from them, are important ingredients in a final reconstruction. The reconstruction of an incident should begin only after the crime scene analysis, after a review of all case reports and interviews, and after the results of laboratory examination of physical evidence are available.

3.3 Stages of Reconstruction

Reconstruction generally involves a sequence of actions which will develop the necessary information for the crime scene reconstruction. The following are the five separate steps commonly used in the process of reconstruction.

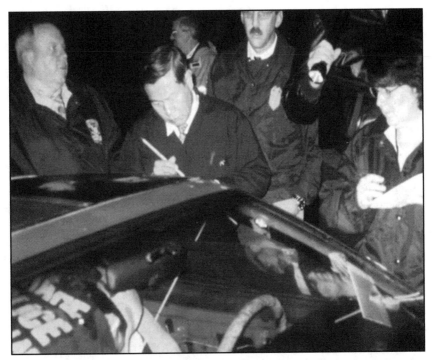

Figure 3.1 *Crime scene investigators reconstruct the bullet trajectories on a vehicle involved in a shooting.*

A. Data Collection

This step requires the accumulation of all information obtained at the scene, from physical evidence and from the victim. This includes the condition of the evidence, patterns and impressions, condition of the victim, and the relative positions of the victim and evidence. Investigators review and organize all of these pieces of information.

B. Conjecture

Before making any detailed analysis of the evidence, investigators may infer a possible explanation of the events involved in a crime. However, it is important at this stage that this possible explanation does not become the only explanation being considered at this time. In many cases there may be several possible explanations.

C. Hypothesis Formulation

Further accumulation of data is based on the detailed examination of the physical evidence, the continuing investigation, and additional reports. Scene examination includes interpretation of blood and impression patterns, gunshot patterns, fingerprint evidence, and analysis of trace evidence. As these findings become clearer and their interrelationships emerge, it will lead to the formulation of an educated guess as to the probable course of events, that is, a hypothesis.

D. Testing

Once a hypothesis is formulated, further testing must be done to confirm or disprove the overall interpretation or specific aspects of it. This stage includes comparisons of samples collected at the scene with known standards and alibi samples, as well as chemical, microscopic and other analyses, and additional testing, as necessary. Some of this "testing" is the mental exercise of careful re-examination and evaluation of the evidence in terms of the hypothesis.

E. Theory Formation

Investigators may acquire additional information during the investigation about the condition of the victim or suspect, the activities of the individuals involved, accuracy of witness accounts, and other information about the circumstances surrounding the events. Testing and confirming the hypothesis involves integrating all the verifiable investigative information, physical evidence analysis and interpretation, and the results of experiments. When it has been thoroughly tested and verified by analysis, the hypothesis can be considered a plausible theory. Complete reconstructions are often not possible; however, partial reconstruction, or reconstructing certain aspects of the events without necessarily being able to reconstruct all of them, can be extremely valuable. Information developed through reconstruction can often lead to the successful solution of a case.

These five stages in the reconstruction process parallel the steps in the scientific method. Like the scientific method, reconstruction must concentrate on the "testing stage." Only after exhaustive testing can one have confidence in the reconstruction.

3.4 Team Concept in Reconstruction

Investigators, laboratory personnel, medical examiner personnel in death cases, and other appropriate offices must cooperate and work together to document every important aspect of a scene, carry out analysis of the physical evidence, and conduct a thorough and unbiased investigation of a case in order to have all the necessary information for a sound reconstruction analysis. In addition, when special problems arise, forensic experts in the appropriate field should be consulted for the particular type of insight they can bring to the reconstruction.

Part II
Laboratory Analysis of Physical Evidence

Chapter 4

Arson and Fire Evidence

One important factor which can aid in the successful resolution of an arson case is the ability to recover physical evidence from the fire scene. If an accelerant (ignitable liquid) was used, its residues will generally be present at the point(s) of origin, or at areas near where the fire started. This is a considerable aid in making the decision concerning whether or not a fire was accidental or purposefully set. Therefore, considerable effort at a fire scene goes into locating the point(s) of origin of the fire and determining if any residual accelerant is present.

4.1 Nature and Types of Physical Evidence at Fire Scenes
A. Examination and Search of a Fire Scene

1. Documentation of the fire

The optimal situation is for the investigator to arrive at the scene before the fire is completely extinguished. This will allow for observation and documentation of the characteristics and condition of the fire. After the fire, photographs should be taken of all aspects of the scene, especially any destruction caused by the fire or overhaul operation. Nothing at the scene should be moved before the investigators complete the initial examination of the fire scene, unless absolutely necessary for safety reasons. The first priority at any fire scene is the safety of those present at the scene.

2. Determination of the point of origin

One major objective in the search of a fire scene is to determine the point of origin. The search should start from the area of least damage and move toward the most damaged location. Through observation of the level of destruction and the charring pattern, the investigator can follow the path of burning back towards the origin.

Electronic sniffers and specially trained dogs may assist by locating areas where higher vapor levels may indicate the presence of remaining ignitable liquid.

3. Fire burn pattern interpretation

Fire burn patterns often provide information on the various factors which lead to the cause of the fire. Detailed study of the burn patterns often help in determining the point of origin; direction of fire travel and the degree of damage by the fire can all provide clues to a possible arson. Burn pattern interpretation can be quite complex and is therefore best done by those with extensive training and experience. For a more complete listing of the patterns which may be found at a fire scene, see Chapter 22, *Pattern Evidence*.

4. Other evidence

Carefully examine any debris at or near the point of origin to determine if any physical evidence of the cause of the fire remains. In addition, other evidence found at the scene may assist in a determination of the fire as arson, or assist in the identification of a suspect. Other evidence includes:

- Odors—particularly petroleum odors that may remain from an accelerant or a mixture of flammable fluids.

- Delays—any device which is designed to ignite a combustible material at a time after the initiating action. The presence of timing or ignition devices or the remains of these objects should be considered.
- Trailers—any material designed to spread a fire from one point to another.
- Containers—any bottle, can, or box which an arsonist may have used to transport an accelerant.
- Ashes and debris—may contain traces of the accelerant or retain their original shape.
- Tools—the arsonist may leave behind any tools used to gain entrance to the structure or to start the fire. In addition, tools used to crack safes or to commit other crimes may sometimes be left behind.
- Documents—a mass of paper or books near the point of origin may have been placed there to destroy incriminating evidence and may still contain salvageable evidence.
- Ignition devices—such as matches, cigarettes, timing devices, explosives, candles, and other devices.
- Accelerants—such as gasoline, flammable liquid, flammable chemicals, and flammable gases.
- Imprints and impressions—such as fingerprints, footprints, tire tracks, toolmarks, or other impressions left by objects or persons.
- Biological evidence—such as bone and other tissues, blood, or hairs.

B. Examination for Accelerant Residue

The primary examination conducted on debris collected from fire scenes is the analysis at the laboratory for the presence of accelerants. These chemicals generally fall into two categories of flammable liquids:

1. **Petroleum distillates**—most accelerants fall into this category.
   a. Straight run products. Those complex mixtures of hydrocarbons found in crude oil which are separated by the distillation process and sold with little further processing. These include some lighter fluids, kerosene, gas oils, fuel oils, and others.
   b. Processed products. Extra steps in addition to the basic distillation process are necessary for the production of benzene, toluene, gasoline, mineral spirits, lubricating oils, and many other products.
2. **Nonpetroleum accelerants**—turpentine, alcohols, specialty solvents, or lubricants of vegetable or synthetic origin.

Figure 4.1 *A major fire scene located in an industry park.*

Figure 4.2 *Fire scene debris found near the point of origin.*

4.2 Collection and Preservation of Fire Scene Evidence
A. Evidence Packaging
An accelerant (ignitable liquid) is a substance that aids in the ignition and the development or spread of a fire. The investigator should collect suspected accelerants or debris as soon as conditions at the fire scene permit. By their very nature, accelerants will tend to evaporate quickly (flaming combustion requires fuel in the vapor phase); therefore, articles suspected of containing these chemicals must be placed in airtight containers as soon as possible.

1. Metal cans
A new metal paint can, free of volatile contaminants, is the preferred type of container for fire debris. The investigator must consider that the container is to remain airtight, and accelerants do dissolve plastic and rubber.

2. Glass jars
These are acceptable, if thoroughly cleaned, especially for liquid samples, but should be packaged to avoid breaking the container.

3. General guidelines
When choosing a container suitable for arson evidence, choose one that will allow head space within the container, allowing the accelerant to evaporate. Containers should be no more than two-thirds full. Often samples are taken from this head space for analysis at the laboratory. Never place arson evidence in ordinary plastic bags. There are specially constructed vapor-tight plastic bags that can be used for safe storage of arson evidence. Figure 4.3 shows some examples of well-packaged evidence.

B. Collection of Fire Debris Evidence

1. Accelerant evidence
Evidence for laboratory analysis should be collected from any likely point of origin indicated by the fire patterns or areas where accelerant may have pooled. It is possible that, due to the intensity of the fire or the nature of the accelerant, there will be no traces of the accelerant readily detectable on exposed surfaces. Absorbent materials, which include wood floors, carpeting, wall board, wood paneling, soil, fabrics, paper, and debris, should be collected from the point of origin. As indicated above, mechanical sniffers or trained dogs can be useful in selecting areas to sample for accelerant residues.

Figure 4.3 *Evidence from a fire submitted for laboratory analysis. Containers must be clean and airtight to prevent the evaporation of any accelerants which may be present.*

2. Other evidence

Package and secure ignition devices in a suitable box or container. Package fragile items accordingly to avoid breakage. Imprints and impression evidence, evidence for latent print examination, blood, hairs and so forth should be packaged according to the instructions in other sections of this book. Toolmarks found at a point of entry or other area should, as a rule, be cast with high resolution casting materials and properly packaged for forwarding to a crime laboratory.

4.3 Laboratory Analysis of Fire Debris
A. Macroscopic Examination
All evidence is quickly examined both macroscopically and microscopically for other types of physical evidence. Any materials found which may require further analysis should be properly documented and handled so that this evidence is not destroyed or altered.

B. Liquid Sample Analysis
Liquid samples are usually analyzed as obtained, but may need to be cleaned up at the laboratory before being analyzed. Liquid samples also include "empty cans" founds at or near the scene, since they often contain small amounts of residual liquid.

1. Gas chromatography (GC)
Because petroleum-derived materials are very complex mixtures often of hundreds of individual chemical compounds, they give characteristic complex patterns when separated into their components by gas chromatography. A small sample is injected into the instrument, and peak patterns and retention times are compared to known standards. (See Figure 4.4.)

2. Infrared spectroscopy
If the liquid is a pure sample, spectra are run and compared to known organic substances.

3. GC-IR or GC-MS
The gas chromatograph, interfaced with the infrared spectrophotometer or mass spectrometer allows for analysis of individual components separated by the GC. GC-MS analysis can also provide information to discriminate between interfering compounds, such as those produced due to the burning or thermal breakdown of synthetic building materials, those which fueled the blaze and those which could have been used as an accelerant. (See Figure 4.5.)

4. Determination of physical properties
Refractive index, boiling point, and flash point of liquid samples can be determined and are characteristic properties.

5. Thin layer chromatography (TLC)
Many liquids, such as gasoline, contain dyes which can be removed from the accelerant and separated on a thin layer chromatography (TLC) plate. Knowledge of the dyes present may help to identify the manufacturer of the accelerant.

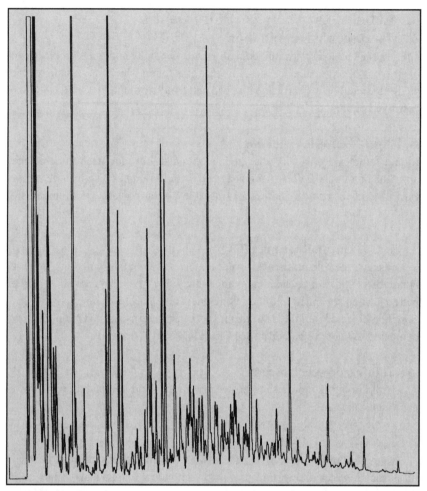

Figure 4.4 *Gas chromatogram of a mixture of gasoline and kerosene.*

C. Solid Debris

Recovery of accelerants from submitted solid samples (usually fire debris) is necessary for proper analysis using the gas chromatograph or other instruments. Once the accelerant has been recovered, analytical techniques would be similar to those described above for liquid samples.

1. Cold head space

A sample of the vapors above the specimen within the sealed container is withdrawn with a vapor-tight syringe and injected into the GC for analysis.

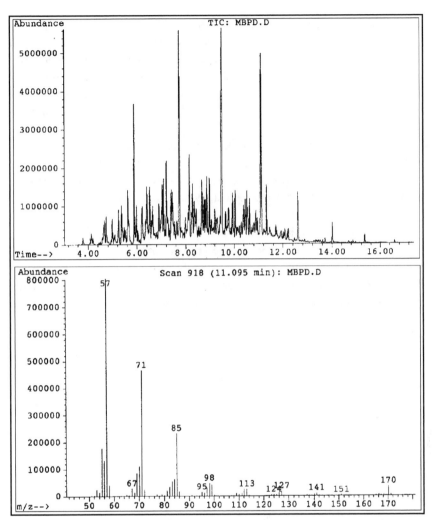

Figure 4.5 *GC-MS results obtained from fire debris. A total ion chromatogram of a medium boiling range petroleum distillate (top). An electron impact spectrum of an individual component of this chromatogram, dodecane (bottom).*

2. Heated head space

Sometimes after a cold head space sample is removed, the container is heated to 100°C, causing the release of more vapors into the atmosphere surrounding the debris. A sample of this vapor is removed and injected into the GC.

3. Carbon tube or strip adsorption

As in heated headspace, the container is heated to release vapors which are then swept from the container and passed through a charcoal tube which will absorb these components. This is usually done by passing a pure dry gas through the container over a period of time. Alternately, a piece of paper coated with a thin layer of activated carbon is hung inside the heated container to absorb any freed accelerant vapors.

Extraction from the carbon is then performed using a low boiling solvent and the absorbed components are recovered, concentrated by careful removal of some of the solvent and injected into the GC. The chances of finding even trace amounts of accelerant, if any are present, by this method is extremely high.

4. Solvent extraction

Debris is washed with a very low boiling solvent and the recovered solution is concentrated, by selective removal of the solvent, before injection into the GC. The solvent wash technique works best with non-hydrocarbon solvents, but a pure low molecular weight hydrocarbon can be used.

Chapter 5

Bite Marks

Bite mark evidence is usually encountered in crimes such as sexual assault, homicide and child abuse. Because bite marks are transitory, it is critical that the examination be prompt and complete. Each stage of examination—recognition, documentation, and collection of bite mark evidence—must be done with care to ensure a complete and accurate record of the bite mark pattern, and to obtain the full benefit of this potentially valuable evidence. Consideration also must be given to other analyses which may be carried out from samples of the bite mark area, such as standard serological and DNA testing.

5.1 Documentation and Collection of Bite Mark Evidence
A. Examination of the Bite Mark Area
If the bite mark is on skin, visual inspection of the skin of the victim must be made. Direct the light at right and oblique angles to the mark to bring out highlights of the mark. Laser or other alternate light source may also be used for examination of the bite mark area.

B. Photographic Documentation
Photograph the bite mark in both black and white and color. All photographs

should be taken with and without the ABFO No. 2 scale, a specially designed two-dimensional scale which aids in making the necessary measurements of the bite mark. Photographs should also be taken at right angles to the bite mark with a macro lens. If the victim is living, photographs should be taken for a period of several days following the attack to record skin color changes as the body's healing response to the bite mark continues. These color changes often allow detail to be seen which was not evident initially. Ultraviolet light photography may produce a latent bite mark on skin which was not evident under other light sources. Figure 5.1 shows a bite mark photograph taken under ambient light.

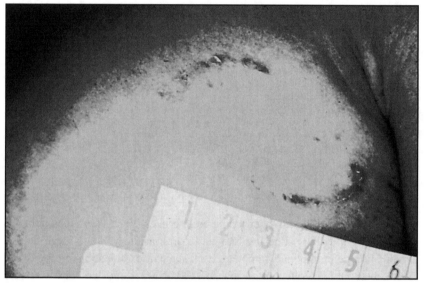

Figure 5.1 *A bite mark on the breast of a homicide victim.*

C. Swabbing the Bite Mark for Genetic Marker Testing

If the subject has not washed the area prior to examination, testing for blood group substances or DNA may be possible.

1. Moisten a sterile cotton swab with distilled water and gently wipe the periphery of the bite mark. Allow the swab to air dry, package in a clean paper and seal.
2. Moisten a second sterile cotton swab with distilled water and gently swab the center of the bite mark, air dry the swab, and package as above.

3. Repeat swab technique in another, similar area that does not have a bite mark. This sample will serve as a control swab.
4. If the victim is living, take a saliva sample using a sterile swab or a clean piece of filter paper. Air dry the saliva sample, package in a paper container, and label the sample appropriately.
5. Submit all samples to the laboratory as soon as possible after collection.

D. Collection of Bite Mark Impressions on Human Skin

Technicians should conduct the collection of impressions on skin according to the following steps:

1. Make a mix of powder and liquid acrylic and form a ring around the bite mark that extends 5 centimeters beyond the mark and let it harden.
2. Apply light-body vinyl polysiloxane, or other suitable high resolution casting material, to the bite mark area and carry it to the borders of the acrylic ring. Allow this mixture to set.
3. Apply heavy-body vinyl polysiloxane over the light-body material and let it set.
4. Apply an acrylic layer over the entire unit and allow it to set.
5. Remove the impression and acrylic frame and pour a mix of dental stone into the impression. Allow the dental stone to harden.
6. Separate the impression from the stone. This produces a stone model of the bite mark.
7. Record and label the model appropriately.

E. Excision of Bite Marks

At times it may be useful to remove the bite mark from a deceased victim's body, such as when the bite mark is in a location which is difficult to examine.

1. Make an acrylic ring to form a circle around the bite mark. There should be a 5 centimeter clearance between the ring and the bite mark.
2. When the ring is hard, remove it and apply cyanoacrylate to the skin upon which the ring will sit.
3. Cut the skin along the outer border of the acrylic ring. Mark the body and the cut portion with a pencil mark for orientation purposes prior to removal.
4. The excised tissue should be preserved in 4 percent formalin until examination.

5.2 Analysis of Bite Mark Evidence

A. Tracing Using a Photographic Negative

Place a sheet of white paper over the negative of a bite mark and direct the light source through the negative. Make a tracing of the incisal edges.

B. Transparent Bite Mark Overlays

1. Place stone dental models of the suspect on the glass of a photocopy machine with the incisal edges on the glass. An ABFO No. 2 scale is also placed on the glass. Cover the models with a white cloth and photocopy.
2. Place the photocopy upside-down on a light box. Trace the incisal edges of the teeth.
3. Place the paper with the incisal tracings face down on the photocopy machine. Place a sheet of Scotch Brand® 502 Transparency Film for plain paper copiers into the photocopy machine and make a copy. The copy is now a transparent overlay of the bite mark.

C. Wax Bite and Powder-type Amalgam Test

1. Press wax over incised edges of teeth and chill wax. Add powder-type amalgam to the resulting impressions in the wax.
2. Place the wax impression on an x-ray film cassette and expose to x-ray radiation. The developed x-ray will show the bite mark pattern.

D. Direct Imprint of Tooth Marks on Human Skin

Place dental stone model of the suspect on the skin. Press the incisal edges firmly against the skin. The resultant bite mark may be studied to make a comparison with the bite mark of unknown origin.

E. Transillumination of Bite Marks

Place excised tissue with the mark over a glass plate, and place the glass plate on top of a light box. By adjusting the light intensity, examination of the bite mark is possible.

F. Comparison of the Bite Mark with Known Samples

Using the described methods allows comparison of a bite mark with the models of known origin. These examinations and comparisons may result in an individualization of the bite mark's origin or an elimination of the suspect as the source of the impression.

G. Enhancement through Digital Imaging Technique

The intensity and clarity of bite marks can be significantly improved using digital imaging techniques. Photographic prints or large format negatives can be scanned into a computer using a flat bed scanner. If a digital camera of sufficient resolution is available, the digital image can be directly introduced into the computer. This presents the experienced digital image processor with very significant possibilities for assisting in the best possible visualization and comparison of bite marks. See Figure 5.2.

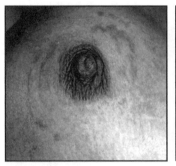 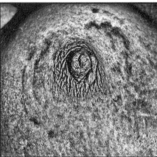

Figure 5.2
A bite mark on a breast that has been digitally enhanced to improve clarity.

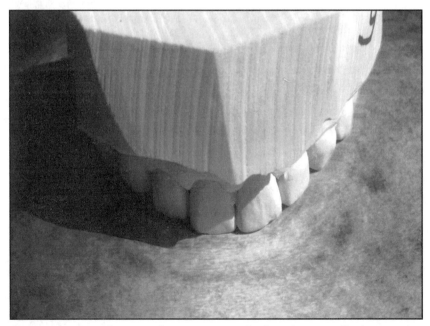

Figure 5.3 Reproduction of a suspect's teeth placed next to the bite mark for comparison.

Chapter 6

Blood

Crime scene personnel can encounter blood evidence in many types of cases, including burglaries and other non-violent crimes, but it is most often encountered in crimes of violence such as homicide, assault and sexual assault. The presence of blood of the suspect's type at the scene of a crime can be an important piece of associative evidence. Blood of the victim's ABO or enzyme type on the suspect's clothing, for example, can prove an invaluable link between the victim, the crime and the perpetrator. Further with the advent of routine DNA testing, blood is virtually always an unambiguous link to the donor.

6.1 Collection of Blood Evidence

Collection methods for blood evidence of various types, and on different types of surfaces, are listed in Tables 6.1, 6.2, and 6.3. The following are some general guidelines to follow with different types of evidence. Since the bloodstain patterns are important for reconstruction purposes, whenever collecting bloodstain evidence, make every effort to maintain the pattern itself and to document the pattern thoroughly before removal of any bloodstain samples.

A. Clothing

1. Clothing that is wet with blood or any body fluid should be allowed to air dry naturally.
2. Mark identification data away from stained areas on the garment.
3. Package all clothing in clean wrapping paper or paper bags. Always avoid folding garments through stained areas.
4. Under no circumstances should technicians place this type of evidence in any plastic or airtight container, since retained moisture will speed putrefaction of the biological stain evidence, often making it useless for analysis.
5. Do not shake out the clothing as it is packaged. If articles are found in a pile, note their order in the pile as they are picked up. They should be packaged individually since this information may aid in the reconstruction of the crime.
6. With living victims where it becomes necessary to cut the clothing off, avoid cutting through the pattern area or through holes that may have been caused by a bullet or weapon, as this will destroy valuable physical evidence.

B. Liquid Samples

If liquid blood is present at a crime scene, make every effort to collect a sample before it coagulates.

1. Take samples using a clean pipette or medicine dropper.
2. Place the blood in a sterile, stoppered test tube with EDTA ("purple cap") as anticoagulant and keep refrigerated but not frozen.
3. Deliver the sample to the laboratory as soon as possible.
4. An alternate method is to place a clean white cotton swatch in the liquid blood, allow it to dry, and then package it in paper.

Table 6.1
Collection of Whole Blood at Crime Scenes

Blood Condition	Collection Mode
Fresh, liquid blood	Use hypodermic syringe; put blood into EDTA vial.
	Use disposable glass pipette equipped with suction bulb; put blood into EDTA vial.
Fresh, wet, thick, clotting	Add an equal volume physiological saline to preserve red blood cells.
Whole blood from a living person	Have person drawing blood collect two tubes: one with EDTA or ACD (not NaF) anticoagulant; the other without any anticoagulant.
	Transport to lab immediately. Keep cold if overnight storage is necessary. Refrigerate only; do not freeze.

C. Dried Bloodstains

If possible, transport the entire item containing the stain to the laboratory. If not, cut the stain out of the article and then package in paper. In cases where the stain is on something solid and nonabsorbent, there are two methods of collection:

1. The stain may be scraped off the article onto a piece of paper. This paper is then folded into a "druggist fold" (see Appendix B) or placed in any non-airtight packaging such as an envelope, and sealed. Or, the dried blood can be tape lifted. The collection of solid dried blood provides a more useful sample than diluting it with a liquid.

2. The stain may be eluted onto cotton threads moistened with saline solution or distilled water by rubbing the thread on the stained area. A minimum of four threads should be used; however, a large number of threads or a piece of fabric is not recommended. The threads are then allowed to dry and are placed in a paper envelope, which is labeled and sealed. Alternately, moistened filter paper strips can be used.

3. Always obtain a control by repeating the same procedure in an area adjacent to the suspected bloodstain.

4. The use of cotton swabs for collection of bloodstains is not recommended.

Table 6.2
Collection of Bloodstains at Crime Scenes

Blood Condition	Collection Mode
Crusts of dried blood	1. Scrape into clean vial. 2. Scrape into paper, fold, then place in an envelope. 3. Tape lift from surface. *Collect material from surrounding area as a control.
Stained knives, rocks	Submit the item without sampling.
Upholstery, rugs (fabric)	Cut out section and submit. *An unstained area should be submitted as a control.
Stains on walls: small stains	1. Moisten unused $^3/_8$-inch cotton thread with water and swab stained area gently until thread has uniform deep red or brown color—collect as many threads as possible and air dry. 2. Tape lift dry. *Also collect a control sample.
Very small stains	Same technique. Use fewer threads or tape lift.
Large stains	Scrape the stains into paper fold, then place in an envelope.
Clothing	Air dry at room temperature; keep out of direct sunlight; put each item in a separate bag and staple shut—never use plastic bags.

D. Known Blood Standards

1. If it is possible, obtain two tubes of liquid blood sample from the victim, the accused, or other pertinent individual. The blood samples should be collected by a doctor or other qualified personnel.

2. One tube should contain EDTA and one tube should have no anticoagulant. This step should not be overlooked by the investigator, since the typing of liquid blood samples can provide information quickly to aid in the management and development of the case.

Table 6.3
Blood Evidence Field Collection Kit

Blood Collection Equipment	• Sterile bandage gauze • Cotton thread • 2 dozen disposable pasteur pipettes and 2 rubber suction bulbs • Small bottle of distilled water • 1 dozen EDTA Vacutainer blood collection tubes • 1 dozen blood collection tubes
Containers	• Scotch tape dispenser • Manila envelopes • 2 dozen of each four sizes: ($3\text{-}^{1}/_{8}$" × 6", 6" × 9", 9" × 12", $11\text{-}^{1}/_{2}$" × $14\text{-}^{1}/_{2}$") • 6 small screw cap vials • 2 dozen corked test tubes • Rubber bands • Pad of white paper (4" × 6")
Miscellaneous Supplies	• Large and small tweezers (plain, uncorrugated tips) • Scalpel and spare blades • Straight-bladed scissors • Disposable tissues • 1 package 3" × 5" cards

E. Blood Patterns

At times the pattern of the bloodstain is as important as the blood type. It is necessary to photograph and thoroughly document bloodstain patterns, regardless of whether the sample is liquid or dried, in order to provide invaluable assistance in reconstruction of the crime. In recent years interpretation of bloodstain patterns has been carefully studied and well-qualified experts can often provide considerable useful reconstruction information from well-documented patterns.

6.2 Field Tests for Blood (Chemical Screening Tests)

A positive reaction with any of the following test reagents will indicate the possible presence of blood. Suspect stains must then be subjected to confirmatory tests. If the chemicals have been tested on known standards of blood before testing the suspected bloodstains, the examiner can conclude that the lack of a reaction on the suspect stain means that blood is absent. A positive reaction only indicates the possible presence of blood and does not indicate the species of origin (i.e., it could be animal blood). Since all presumptive tests are subject to false positive results, experienced examiners should interpret these results and should perform confirmatory tests on any sample at the laboratory. If there is a question as to whether a sufficient sample is present at the scene for further testing, technicians should collect the entire stain without screening prior to submission.

The following are some commonly used chemical screening tests for blood:

- **Phenolphthalein (Kastle-Mayer reagent)**

  The test is conducted by rubbing a cotton swab that has been moistened in a saline solution on the suspected bloodstain. A drop of the phenolphthalein solution is added to the swab, and then a drop of hydrogen peroxide (3 percent). A positive reaction is a pink to red color on the swab within 15 seconds.

- **Leucomalachite green (LMG)**

  This test is performed in the same way as the phenolphthalein test above. A positive reaction is indicated by a greenish-blue color that will appear almost immediately on the area of the swab exposed to the suspected blood.

- **Ortho-tolidine**

  The ortho-tolidine test is similar to the other chemical screening tests described above. A positive reaction is indicated by an intense blue color. Some reports indicate that this reagent might be carcinogenic.

- **ABA Cards**

  In recent years a very stable and portable blood test has been developed called an ABA Card. This is an immunological (antigen/antibody) test that requires only the stain, a little pure water and the commercial test kit. It has quickly become widely accepted and a part of most crime scene processing kits.

- **Luminol**

  Part one of the test reagent (luminol) is sprayed onto the area to be checked for presence of suspected bloodstains followed by spraying with part two (sodium perborate). The area must be viewed in total darkness. In a positive reaction, bloodstains will become luminescent within 5 seconds. The luminol test works best to discover an area where an attempt has been made to clean up blood.

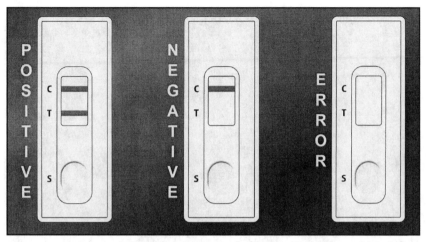

Figure 6.1 *ABA Card used for identifying body fluid samples as blood, semen or saliva.*

6.3 Laboratory Examination of Blood Evidence
A. Identification of Blood

1. Screening tests
Screening tests are based on the reaction of hemoglobin with chemical reagents, such as ortho-tolidine, phenolphthalein, luminol, tetramethylbenzidine, or leucomalachite green. The method of testing is similar to that described above for field tests.

2. Confirmatory tests
Confirmatory tests are not as sensitive as the screening tests, but are necessary to prove that the suspect stain is, in fact, blood.

- Microcrystal tests, although quite reliable in the hands of experienced examiners, are largely only of historical interest now.
- Immunological test uses anti-human hemoglobin. This test also confirms that the blood is human, and is often the test of choice to conserve a sample when testing.

B. Species Tests
These tests are used to determine whether a bloodstain is of human or animal origin. In the immunological precipitin test, antiserum for a particular species, such as anti-human serum, causes a visible hazy white area to develop at the interface

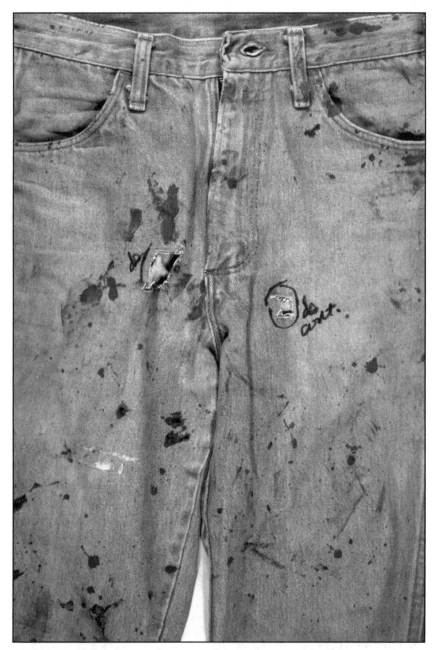

Figure 6.2 Blood-spattered pants with areas cut out for analysis.

between the suspected blood solution and the test reagent. Such a precipitation reaction is indicative of human serum proteins. Antisera for many different species or closely related species are also available to determine to what species of animal a non-human bloodstain belongs.

C. Blood Typing in Dried Bloodstains

Various blood group antigens and antibodies can be identified in dried bloodstain evidence. Factors such as the age and condition of the stain may affect testing.

1. Detection of ABO antibodies in serum (Lattes test)

Red blood cells of known type are agglutinated (clump together) if antibodies against them are present in the stain. This test is the bloodstain equivalent of "reverse typing" in whole blood.

2. Detection of blood group antigens

With the widespread availability of sensitive DNA tests, the testing of weak bloodstains for ABO group has been largely abandoned.

6.4 AIDS and Other Biohazards in Crime Scene Processing and Law Enforcement

The emergence of the HIV epidemic has increased the concern for exposure to various infectious diseases, such as AIDS, hepatitis B, and others. This has propelled the development of guidelines and precautions for law enforcement personnel. Today, with AIDS and other virus-caused diseases, such as hepatitis B, virtually epidemic, police officers, crime scene investigators and forensic laboratory examiners are more likely than ever to encounter these infectious agents in blood or other body fluids during routine activities. The following brief description of the infectious agents and methods of handling evidence represent general guidelines. Each department should have specific procedures for the handling and disposing of potentially infectious biohazardous materials. The only rational approach to this problem is to treat all unknown biological stain materials as potentially infectious.

A. Biohazards

1. AIDS

Acquired immune deficiency syndrome (AIDS) has presented a variety of manifestations ranging from asymptomatic, to some signs of illness (so-called AIDS-related complex, or ARC), to severe immunodeficiency and life-threatening secondary infections. The virus which causes the disease has been known

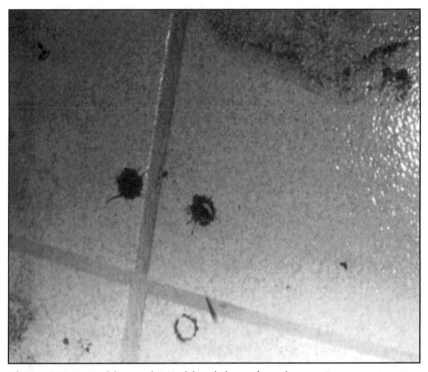

Figure 6.3 *Vertical low velocity blood drops found at a crime scene.*

by several names. It is currently referred to as human immunodeficiency virus (HIV or HIV-1). The AIDS virus is a "retrovirus" which invades the victim's own DNA and affects the immune system. The resulting gradual, irreversible destruction of the immune response mechanisms causes the patient to become highly susceptible to various infections (often called "opportunistic infections" because the infection-causing agents "seize the opportunity" to invade the person with a weakened immune-response system). Pneumocystis pneumonia is a common opportunistic infection in AIDS patients.

The AIDS virus has been isolated from blood, bone marrow, saliva, lymph nodes, brain tissue, semen, plasma, vaginal fluids, cervical secretions, tears and human milk. The mode of transmission generally involves direct contact of AIDS-contaminated blood or body fluids with the bloodstream or with mucous membranes. It is most frequently transmitted by direct sexual contact, through AIDS-infected semen or vaginal mucous, or by using a needle contaminated with the AIDS virus to make an IV injection. The latter route of transmission is common among the IV drug abuser population. However, exposure of any open cuts, wounds, lesions, or mucous membranes to AIDS-contaminated blood or body

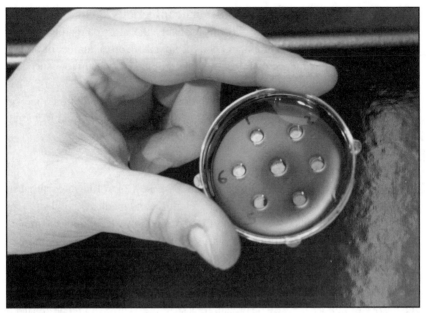

Figure 6.4 *Double immuno-diffusion plate used for species identification of bloodstains.*

fluids does carry a risk of possible infection. There is currently no cure for AIDS although newer treatments seem to prolong life. No vaccine is available, and thus far the disease has generally been fatal.

2. Hepatitis

Hepatitis is an infectious disease of the liver. Hepatitis B is so-called "serum hepatitis" which can result in jaundice, cirrhosis and, sometimes, cancer of the liver. It is caused by a virus that is transmitted by way of blood and body fluids in a manner very similar to HIV. The virus may be found in human blood, urine, semen, cerebrospinal fluid, saliva and vaginal fluid. Injection into the bloodstream and sexual contact with infected persons are well-known routes of transmission. Exposure of mucous membranes to infected droplets or dust, and exposure to infected body fluids through broken skin are also primary hazards. There is a vaccine currently available against hepatitis B. Another type of hepatitis, now called hepatitis C (formerly called "non-A non-B hepatitis"), is also caused by a virus which is transmitted via blood and body fluids. There is no vaccine at the present time for hepatitis C. Any form of hepatitis is a potentially serious (and sometimes even fatal) disease.

3. Other blood and body fluid-borne infectious agents

Although AIDS and hepatitis B are probably the most dangerous viruses that are transmitted through blood and body fluids, there are a number of others. Recently, a large resurgence of infectious tuberculosis has occurred, especially among the same "high risk" groups described above. This form of "TB" has proved highly resistant to traditional antibiotic treatments. In addition, medical science has identified other diseases transmitted by blood or body fluid including the herpes viruses that cause cold sores, and genital herpes lesions.

B. General Precautionary Measures

The U.S. Public Health Service Centers for Disease Control have established the following guidelines, based on current scientific and medical knowledge, for healthcare professionals. By practicing these precautions, laboratory examiners and police officers may perform their duties as required by law, while minimizing the risk of accidental infection, whether administering cardiopulmonary resuscitation (CPR) at the scene of an accident, collecting evidence at crime scenes, examining physical evidence at the laboratory, or dealing with individuals who are at high risk of being carriers. The precautions specified below should be enforced routinely, regardless of whether the persons or evidence involved are known to be AIDS or hepatitis B infected.

1. Consider all blood and body fluids infectious, whether wet or dry.
2. Handle all needles, syringes, blades, razor blades, knives and sharp instruments with utmost caution, and place in puncture-resistant containers.
3. Good personal hygiene is the best protection against infectious diseases. Wash hands with soap and water after each assignment.
4. Know your skin integrity. Keep all wounds carefully bandaged while on duty. Use a bandage which provides a completely impermeable 360-degree coverage. Change the bandage if it becomes soiled or dirty.
5. Wear latex gloves when handling blood specimens, body fluids, materials and objects that may be sources of contamination. Dispose of gloves after one use.
6. Wear gowns, masks and eye protection when your clothing may be soiled by blood or body fluids, or when performing procedures which may involve extensive exposure to blood or potentially infectious body fluids (such as the transport of the victim's body, laboratory examination specimens, and postmortem examinations).
7. Avoid all hand-to-face contact, including eating, smoking, and drinking, where the possibility of transmission exists.

8. Wash hands and skin area immediately and thoroughly if they accidentally become contaminated with blood or body fluids.

9. Clean up contaminated surfaces and objects with a solution of one part household bleach to nine parts water (1:10 dilution). An alcohol pad or soap and water can be used as a subsequent cleaning solution and to remove the odor of bleach.

10. Constantly be alert for sharp objects. When handling hypodermic needles, knives, razors, broken glass, nails, broken metal, or any other sharp object bearing blood, use the utmost care to prevent a cut or puncture of the skin.

C. Specific Guidelines for Crime Scene Investigators

1. Crime scene investigators should wear latex gloves and coverall gowns when conducting crime scene searches.

2. Wear surgical masks if aerosol or airborne particles may be present (e.g., blood droplets, dried blood particles, and so forth).

3. Use double latex gloves, surgical masks and protective eyewear when collecting or handling liquid blood, body fluids, dried blood particles, blood-contaminated evidence, or bodies of the deceased.

4. Wear latex gloves, eye-coverings, surgical masks and a gown when attending an autopsy.

5. When processing the crime scene, constantly be alert for sharp objects and broken objects or surfaces.

6. When conducting a search, do not place your hands in areas where you are unable to see.

7. Under no circumstances should anyone at the crime scene be allowed to smoke, eat, or drink.

8. When liquid blood and body fluids are collected in bottles or glass vials, these containers must be prominently labeled "Blood Precautions."

9. Dry and package blood and body fluid stained clothing and objects in double bags and label properly. If evidence is collected from a possibly infected person or scene, label the package "Caution—Potential AIDS (Hepatitis) Case."

10. If practical, use only disposable items at a crime scene where infectious blood is present. Decontaminate all nondisposable items after each use.

11. Destroy any reports, labels or evidence tags splashed with blood; copy the information on clean forms.

12. After completing the search of a scene, investigators should clean their hands with diluted household bleach solution and with soap and water solution. Properly dispose of any contaminated clothing and footwear.

Chapter 7

Body Fluids Other Than Blood

Synopsis
7.1 Collection and Preservation of Evidence
   A. Clothing
   B. Known Samples Collected from Victim or Suspect
      1. Known saliva and DNA standards
      2. Urine and/or fecal material
      3. Vaginal materials
      4. Nasal mucous
   C. Body Fluids or Tissues on Other Items
      1. Foreign objects
      2. Saliva
      3. Bite mark evidence
      4. Skin tissue
7.2 Laboratory Examination of Body Fluids
   A. Identification
      1. Saliva
      2. Urine
      3. Fecal material
      4. Gastric fluid
      5. Perspiration
      6. Epithelial cells and tissues
   B. Classification or Individualization
      1. ABO blood group substances
      2. Isoenzymes
      3. DNA testing

Crime scene personnel may encounter body fluids, such as semen, saliva, urine, vaginal secretions, perspiration, fecal material and nasal mucous on the victim's body or at scenes. Body fluid evidence is most commonly associated with sexual assault cases. The laboratory can identify these fluids and test for the ABO blood group substances, isoenzymes, and DNA that may be present. This information is then used to include or exclude any individual as a donor of these samples. The analysis of semen is discussed in more detail in Chapter 24.

7.1 Collection and Preservation of Evidence
A. Clothing

All evidence potentially containing body fluid evidence should be handled with gloved hands to protect the collector and to reduce the possibility of contamination of the evidence.

1. It is of primary importance that clothing that is wet with body or other fluids be allowed to air dry at room temperature prior to packaging. The item is then packaged in paper bags or wrapped flat in paper.
2. Under no circumstances should this evidence be packaged in plastic bags or other airtight containers. As with bloody evidence, putrefaction of the body fluid stains may occur, rendering them useless for most laboratory testing.
3. In order to preserve the trace evidence that may be present on the item, avoid excessive handling of clothing.

B. Known Samples Collected from Victim or Suspect

1. Known saliva and DNA standards

Obtain oral swab samples of known origin from rape victims and suspects to determine their secretor status. Saliva standards should also be collected if bite mark evidence or other physical evidence involving possible deposits of saliva is encountered.

1. Collect the sample after the donor has rinsed the mouth of food residues with water.
2. The donor should be asked to swab the inside of her mouth and cheek with cotton or other sterile applicator.
3. Air dry the specimen, then package in a paper envelope. Label the envelope appropriately and submit it to the laboratory as soon as possible after collection.
4. If it is necessary to collect a liquid sample (suspicion of oral sex), collect undiluted liquid saliva in a clean specimen jar. This sample must be kept in the refrigerator and delivered to the laboratory immediately.

2. Urine and/or fecal material

These samples may be collected in a clean specimen jar. Label accordingly and refrigerate until submission to the laboratory.

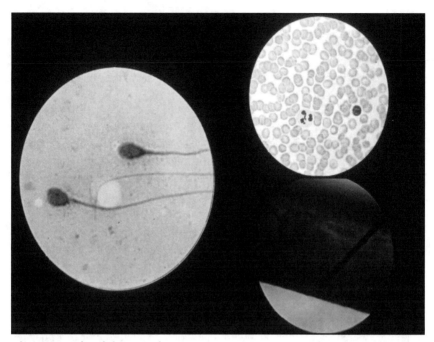

Figure 7.1 *Blood, hair, and sperm are common types of evidence found in rape cases.*

3. Vaginal materials

Vaginal materials are usually encountered in connection with a sexual assault case. Most often these samples are included in the sexual assault evidence kit and should be collected according to kit directions. Any fluids collected for analysis should be air dried, packaged in paper, and submitted to the laboratory as soon as possible after collection.

4. Nasal mucous

Nasal mucous is occasionally found at crime scenes on clothing, a handkerchief or tissue, or on a body. These materials should be air dried and packaged in paper.

C. Body Fluids or Tissues on Other Items

Forensic scientists sometimes encounter various types of items that may contain body fluid evidence or tissues for laboratory analysis. Package these materials with a minimum of handling.

1. Foreign objects

If a foreign object is used in committing a sexual assault, submit this item to the laboratory. The detection of epithelial cells could indicate the presence of a residue from vaginal materials. This object should be air dried and packaged in paper.

2. Saliva

Saliva may also be encountered at crime scenes on cigarette butts, chewing gum, toothpicks, beverage containers, and similar items. Collect these samples with forceps or gloved hands to avoid contamination. Package these items in a paper envelope or specimen jar (never put gum in paper!) and label accordingly.

3. Bite mark evidence

If evidence of a bite mark is found, collect a swabbing of the bite mark area as described in Chapter 5, *Bite Marks*.

4. Skin tissue

Skin and tissue may be present under the fingernails. Package fingernail scrapings, which should be taken with a new orange stick, file or other device, in paper and properly label. The evidentiary importance of fingernail scrapings has greatly increased since the advent of the routine availability of forensic DNA analysis.

7.2 Laboratory Examination of Body Fluids
A. Identification

Various tests may be conducted to identify the source of a body fluid stain. These tests identify characteristic cellular or chemical components.

1. Saliva

The presence of a starch-digesting enzyme called amylase is the basis of tests for saliva. Amylase is found in high concentrations in saliva, and the detection of this enzyme indicates the presence of saliva. An immunological test in the form of an ABACard test similar to the blood test is now available.

2. Urine

The identification of urine is based on its characteristic color and odor, as well as the presence of characteristic chemical components, such as creatinine or urea.

3. Fecal material

Fecal material usually has a characteristic color and odor. Chemical tests for the presence of urobilinogen are also conducted to identify feces.

4. Gastric fluid

The identification of gastric fluid or stomach contents (vomit) occurs through chemical and microscopic analysis in addition to the detection of digestive enzyme activity.

5. Perspiration

Perspiration is often present on clothing or other items that are submitted to the laboratory for examination. Its presence must be considered when analyzing evidentiary material for the presence of other body fluids. When testing articles of clothing, whenever possible test a control sample to ensure that contamination from perspiration is not a factor. This is especially important if tests for blood group substances or forensic DNA analysis will be conducted.

6. Epithelial cells and tissues

Microscopic examination is conducted of samples containing cellular materials. The morphological characteristics of epithelium and other tissues are used for their identification. Any nucleated cell has the potential for yielding DNA useful for analysis.

B. Classification or Individualization

Various genetic markers may be present in the body fluids tested. The tests conducted depend on the type of fluid detected and the amount of sample present.

1. ABO blood group substances

Approximately 80 percent of the population are secretors, therefore ABO blood group substances can be detected in the body fluids of these secretors. The laboratory can determine the secretor status of donors by testing their body fluid specimens. Investigators can determine information as to the inclusion or exclusion of a suspect or victim by comparison of known specimens to questioned samples in a particular case. A technique called absorption-inhibition allows for the detection of ABO blood group substances in body fluid samples. This method will produce no detectable level of antigens if an individual is a "nonsecretor."

2. Isoenzymes

Although levels of enzymes used for individualization are very low in most body fluids, some stains may yield information on Phosphoglucomutase (PGM) or Esterase D (ESD) type. The condition of the stain may also affect the ability to detect isoenzymes in a body fluid stain or mixture.

3. DNA testing

DNA may be obtained from the epithelial cells found in vaginal secretions, saliva, urine, nasal mucous, and even sweat. These results can then be compared to known samples from the victim or the suspect. As with blood samples, the sex of the donor or the body fluid may also be identified if sufficient DNA is present. DNA testing has greatly improved through more varied substrates and much higher sensitivity. Refer to Chapter 11, *DNA Analysis*, for more information on the analysis of body fluids.

Chapter 8

Bombs and Explosives

Explosions can cause extensive damage and destruction of property due to the force and heat produced as a result of the rapid exothermic (heat-producing) reaction. Explosive residues may be encountered in numerous forms, both unchanged explosive and the products of the explosive reaction. Because explosive materials have enormous stored potential energy, often in small amounts of material, even the smallest firecracker has the potential for great damage or injury under certain conditions.

8.1 Types of Explosives

Explosives are chemical substances that are unstable in their natural form. When heated, shocked or struck, they are capable of rapid decomposition, producing an explosion by the liberation of large quantities of heat and gas.

A. Low Explosives
Stable under ordinary conditions, violent explosions will occur if these explosives are confined and detonated. Examples are black and smokeless powders and many pyrotechnic materials (fireworks).

B. Primary High Explosives (Primer)
This type of explosive is sensitive to heat, spark or shock and used to initiate detonation of secondary high explosives. Blasting caps, "det cord" and nitroglycerine are examples of primary high explosives.

C. Secondary High Explosives
Explosive materials that are much less sensitive to heat, shock, spark or friction, are used as the primary charge. Common secondary explosives are TNT, RDX, dynamite, ammonium nitrate, and monomethylamine nitrate. These materials make up the bulk of most high explosive devices. They may be supplemented by other energetic materials used to further boost the power of the explosion.

D. Improvised Explosive Devices (IEDs)
An explosive device has three primary components: an igniter, a primer or detonator, and a main charge. Those who make improvised explosive devices often do not have easy access to commercial or military explosives. As a result, they have to use materials widely available or easily synthesized from readily available starting materials. The most common explosives used are ammonium nitrate (fertilizer), ANFO (ammonium nitrate plus fuel oil), urea nitrate, and triacetonetetraperoxide. Such individuals may resort to such crude materials as match heads or chemicals used in fireworks (pyrotechniques). See Figure 8.1.

8.2 Collection of Explosives Evidence
The most important aspect of detecting and identifying explosive residue is the collection of samples from the scene after the initial emergency of a bomb or explosive incident is under control. The scene must be systematically searched to recover the remains of the detonating device and explosive. It is also important to remember that an explosion scene is still a crime scene. It should be examined for all types of evidence such as shoeprints, blood, toolmarks, fingerprints and not just remains directly associated with the explosive device.

Figure 8.1 *Two pipe bombs (IEDs) in place at a scene, discovered before they were detonated.*

A. Location of the Origin of the Blast

Generally a crater will be present at the origin of the blast. Explosive residues will be found on debris near the origin while the detonating devices and the explosive containers will be found away from this area in a circular pattern.

B. Documentation

As with any other type of physical evidence, the bomb and explosive evidence should be photographed in color with a scale, prior to collection. Notes, diagrams, and videotape should also be used to document the evidence. Because of the transitory nature of some explosive byproducts, odor and other observations should be noted immediately upon arrival at the scene and documented if possible.

C. Collection of Physical Evidence

Evidence of bomb debris, bomb devices, explosive debris, explosive devices electrical devices, timing devices, wiring, connectors, and any items that seem strange or foreign to the setting should be collected as evidence.

D. Safety Considerations

Any undetonated devices should be exploded or rendered safe by the bomb squad before submission to a laboratory for analysis.

E. Packaging

Items collected should be packaged in jars, cans, or special vapor barrier plastic bags and carefully marked as to item, date collected, location and initials of the investigator. Flammable or hazardous items must be packaged in metal paint-type cans with metal covers and be well marked.

8.3 Laboratory Analysis of Explosives
A. Macroscopic Examination

By the visual examination of the debris and residues present from the explosion site, the experienced investigator and laboratory examiner will be able to determine what type of explosive was most likely used. This allows the examiner to proceed with the best technique for the analysis of the explosive residues.

Table 8.1
Color Test Reagents and Reactions for Explosives

Explosive Component	Color Reaction			
	Griess	Diphenylamine	J-acid	Alcoholic KOH
Chlorate	no color	blue	orange-brown	no color
Nitrate	pink to red	blue	orange-brown	no color
Nitrite	red to yellow	blue	orange-brown	no color
Nitrocellulose	pink	blue-black	orange-brown	no color
Nitroglycerine	pink to red	blue-black	orange-brown	no color
PETN	pink to red	blue	orange-brown to red	no color
RDX	pink to red	blue	orange-brown	no color
Tetryl	pink to red	blue	yellow to orange	red
TNT	no color	no color	no color	red violet

B. Microscopic Examination

Soil and debris are examined for the presence of unexploded or partially burned explosives and explosive residues. Any parts of timing devices, electrical devices, plastic, wires, or other bomb components should also be examined microscopically.

C. Extraction

Residues of explosives and explosive components are extracted for laboratory analysis. Usually these chemical materials are removed from the explosion debris first using an acetone wash followed by a water wash. The extracts are then filtered and evaporated to recover any explosive residue.

D. Chemical Tests

Residues and extracts are tested with various chemical tests to detect characteristic chemical structures or components.

1. Chemical color tests

Various reagents will give characteristic color reactions when the extract is tested. Some common color tests and their reactants are given in Table 8.1.

2. Microcrystal tests

Small quantities of residue or extract are added to chemical reagents. The resulting crystals are characteristic of explosive components and can be identified microscopically.

E. Thin Layer Chromatography

Acetone solutions of the residue are spotted on a TLC plate, developed, and compared to known explosives or common explosive residues on the same plate.

F. Instrumental Analysis

Detection of various explosive components using instrumental techniques is often successful.

1. Organic components

Infrared or mass spectra of a residue can be compared to known standards to identify an explosive from the specific organic components present in the residue.

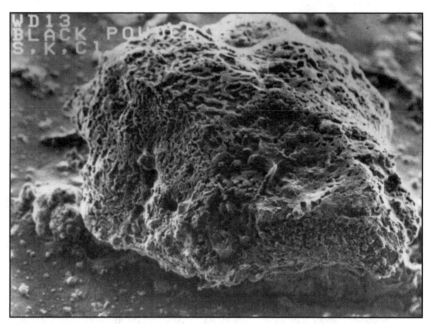

Figure 8.2 *A particle of black powder residue collected from an explosion as seen on the SEM. Major elemental composition as determined by EDX analysis is also listed.*

2. Inorganic components

Atomic absorption or emission, x-ray fluorescence and x-ray diffraction, as well as infrared spectra, can aid in the detection and identification of inorganic substances present in the residues. In addition, the scanning electron microscope (SEM) with EDAX analysis can be employed with great benefit even to microscopic particles of residue (see Figure 8.2).

3. Chromatography and Spectroscopy

Gas chromatography, liquid chromatography (HPLC), capillary electrophoresis and ion chromatography are used to separate the complex mixtures obtained. To aid in the detection and identification of explosives residues, the chromatographic techniques are often combined in one instrument with a spectroscopic technique such as mass spectroscopy, or infrared spectroscopy to allow identification of many of the separated compounds. Most laboratories use a combination of several of these techniques. Figure 8.3 is an infrared spectrum for identification of ammonium nitrate.

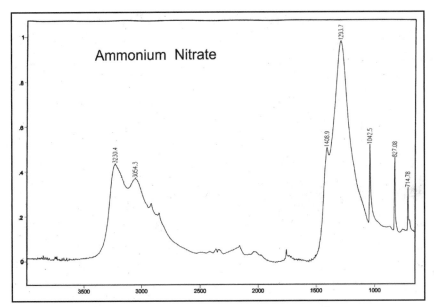

Figure 8.3 *Infrared spectrum suitable for identification of ammonium nitrate, a common component of improvised explosive devices (IEDs).*

G. Explosives Tagging Program

Some time ago, the U.S. Treasury Department's Bureau of Alcohol, Tobacco and Firearms instituted an exploratory explosives tagging program. Color-coded eight-layer plastic taggant particles were added to the explosive materials by selected manufacturers to enable tracing of the origin of explosives by recovery of the taggant particles from explosive incident crime scenes. Although this program indicated the technical feasibility of explosive tagging, tagging was never implemented by the explosives industry. If an explosive, produced as part of this program was used in an explosive incident, the taggant present would allow identification of the explosive source.

Chapter 9

Chemical Substances

Any unknown chemical substance found at a crime scene or otherwise associated with an investigation can be identified by chemical or instrumental techniques and may be considered chemical evidence. Presumptive field tests can detect many commonly encountered chemical residues, such as gunshot residue, accelerant residues, unknown powders, trace materials, and drugs. Crime scene technicians should collect these materials for further analysis at the laboratory. The chemical nature of these materials, their significance and their origin may become an important factor in solving or reconstructing a crime.

9.1 Nature of Chemical Evidence
A. Types of Chemical Evidence

Chemical evidence found at a crime scene may be composed of many different types of substances found in any of three physical states of matter.

1. Gas

Chemical evidence found in the form of a gas includes commonly encountered materials such as tear gas, propane, arson accelerant vapors and various household spray cans.

2. Liquid

Liquid substances may be pure liquids, mixtures or solutions, either in water or in other solvents. The most common liquids submitted to the laboratory for analysis include acids, gasoline and other types of accelerants, beverages, cooking fluids, poisons, cleaning fluids, and medications.

3. Solid

Any organic or inorganic chemical, or mixture of chemicals, can become physical evidence. The most commonly encountered solid materials in forensic cases are drugs, poisons, soil and minerals, residues of explosives, gunshot residues, and trace materials such as paint chips, plastic traces and even cleaning materials.

B. Field Tests

Crime scene technicians often use field tests to screen for chemical residues or components in blood, gunshot residue, semen, and drugs, for example. These tests will give some indication as to the nature of commonly encountered chemical substances, and may help to better define their location. Everyday materials may also contain the chemicals that affect or interfere with some field tests. Thus, false positive or ambiguous results may occur in some cases or environments. Any positive reaction, however, should lead to the collection of the material for subsequent laboratory testing. For specific information on the collection of commonly encountered materials, see the appropriate chapter.

9.2 Collection of Chemical Evidence
A. General Considerations

The chemical makeup of this type of physical evidence may be unknown until laboratory analyses can be conducted. Therefore, take care when handling these materials to prevent loss or contamination of the evidence. In addition, since the nature of the evidence is unknown, collect it with caution to prevent possible injury to persons handling the chemicals.

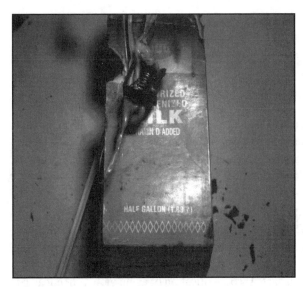

Figure 9.1 *This milk carton containing unknown chemical substances was collected from an explosion scene.*

B. Packaging of Chemical Evidence

The following are some general guidelines for the collection and appropriate packaging of chemical evidence encountered at a crime scene.

1. Packaged chemicals

Whenever possible, submit an unknown chemical in its original container if it is found packaged at the scene. Also submit any box, label, instructions, or forms associated with the chemical.

2. Containers

If only a portion of the unknown material can be taken, or if it is found unpackaged, use clean non-reactive, leak-proof containers when collecting such unknown materials (tins, vials, cans, etc.).

- **Gas**. Collect and submit any gas in its original container or draw a sample into an evacuated glass or metal device for transportation of gases.
- **Liquids**. Glass and certain plastics are suitable containers. Take care when transferring any liquid to a container that the chemical substance will not dissolve or react with the container, or leech material from the container. Bottles containing chemicals should be sealed and carefully packaged to prevent spillage and breakage.
- **Solids**. Place a representative sample of any unknown powdery material in a clean piece of paper made into a druggist fold, and then place that

paper packet in a labeled envelope. Never place powders directly into an envelope or plastic bag, and never place unknown solids in metal containers, since corrosion could occur.

3. Clothing

Lipsticks, cosmetics, and other types of powder or smeared chemical substances may be significant forensic evidence in crimes such as sexual assaults and homicides. These materials may be found as transfers on clothing, cigarettes or parts of the body. If possible, submit clothing or other object with lipstick or cosmetic stains to the forensic laboratory for complete examination.

9.3 Laboratory Analysis of an Unknown Chemical

The analysis and identification of unknown chemicals is a complex and intricate part of a forensic scientist's duties. One complicating problem often faced is the possibility of a mixed or contaminated sample, and a forensic scientist must understand and appreciate this fact. The identification of an unknown chemical can be a simple matter of a few moments examination, or a complex project requiring numerous instruments and several days to accomplish.

A. Preliminary Examination

1. Physical state

Observing whether the unknown is a solid, liquid or gas reduces the number of compounds under consideration. Macroscopic or microscopic examination may reveal additional physical characteristics. Odor, melting point or boiling point, color, pH and index of refraction are some of the physical characteristics that the examiner may determine during the preliminary examination of the sample.

2. Microscopic examination

Careful microscopic examination of a garment should be performed to locate trace evidence, or lipstick or cosmetic traces. Under the microscope, for example, a lipstick stain would show a greasy texture and some color. Once the material is visually located, carefully remove a sample for further analysis. Likewise, solid traces should be removed using fine forceps or a probe, or with solvent.

B. Chemical Tests

1. Solubility

A forensic scientist can also obtain information by examination of solubility properties. Solubility of inorganic materials is affected by the intrinsic nature of the compound, the nature of the solvent and, if a water solution, the acidity or basicity of the solution. Organic compounds differ in their solubility in water, dilute acid, dilute base, hexane, acetone, chloroform and other organic solvents. Asphalt, which might be encountered as a stain in a hit-and-run case, is much more soluble in chloroform than in acetone. Most inorganic or biological materials have some solubility in water, whereas many organic materials show little water solubility.

2. Microchemical analysis

Microchemical tests are a quick and inexpensive way to screen chemical substances that require only trace amounts of sample. Tests that produce characteristic color or crystal reactions can be applied to a wide variety of materials of potential forensic interest. There are numerous forensic applications for such spot tests, some of which are discussed in more detail in the respective chapter.

3. Chromatography—Separation Techniques

Chromatographic techniques are used to separate mixtures that cannot be easily separated using physical techniques or solubility. Chromatography involves the separation of mixtures by partition of the components between a mobile and a stationary phase. There are many variations on that theme such as thin layer chromatography (TLC), high performance liquid chromatography (HPLC), gas chromatography (GC) and capillary electrophoresis (CPE). These are excellent methods for separation of mixtures to aid in the identification of unknown samples and most effective when used in combination with spectroscopic techniques. The analysis of drug, explosive, ink, dye, and accelerant samples are all greatly improved through the use of chromatographic methods. Newer chromatographic methods, such as ion chromatography and capillary electrophoresis, also work to separate inorganic ions and other charged species.

C. Instrumental Techniques

The most powerful techniques for identifying organic unknowns involve the use of infrared, ultraviolet and mass spectroscopy or even nuclear magnetic resonance. The extent to which these are utilized depends on the forensic laboratory's equipment, the nature of the sample and the scientist's expertise.

1. Infrared spectroscopy

Infrared spectroscopy is most useful for qualitative identification of samples such as paints, fibers, explosives and drugs. It can often identify the major organic component(s) of the sample. For many forensic samples, a microscope sampling device, coupled with a Fourier transform infrared spectrometer (FTIR), can allow analysis of samples in the range of 10 × 10 microns (millionths of a meter) in size. This technique can also be used to determine the major organic components in smears or other microsamples. Figure 9.2 shows an FTIR instrument and the spectrum obtained from a fiber sample.

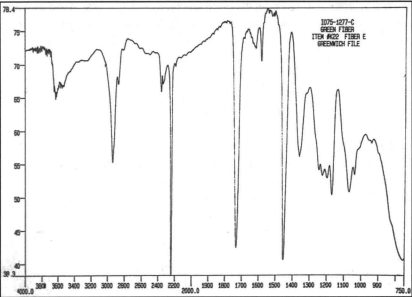

Figure 9.2 *The FTIR (top) spectrometer and the infrared spectrum of a green fiber sample obtained using this instrument (bottom).*

2. Ultraviolet (UV) and visible spectroscopy

UV and visible spectroscopy can provide useful screening information and, in some cases, can be used to gather quantitative information about drug and biological samples. In addition, scientists use these instruments to examine colored materials, such as dyes.

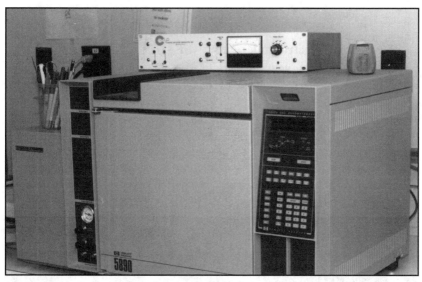

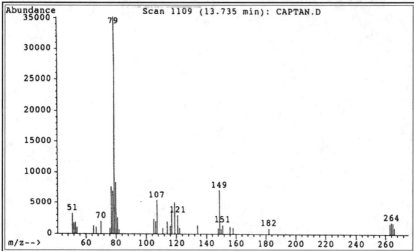

Figure 9.3 *The GC/MS instrument (top) and an electron impact mass spectrum of captan, a commonly used fungicide (bottom).*

3. Mass spectrometry (MS)

Mass spectrometry can be used to provide highly specific identifications of unknown samples, frequently quite rapidly. Because it normally requires a sample in the gas phase it works very well in combination with a gas chromatograph (GC/MS). Arson residue and drug samples are particularly well-suited to mass spectrometric analysis. A gas chromatograph mass spectrometer and typical mass spectrum are depicted in Figure 9.3.

4. Scanning electron microscope (SEM)

The scanning electron microscope (SEM) is an extremely powerful imaging device that can provide clear images of suitable objects at magnifications ranging from about 100 times to as much as several hundred thousand times. These instruments are usually equipped with an energy dispersive x-ray analyzer (EDX) that can be used to determine the elemental composition of anything they are imaging. They can provide useful information about the shape and composition of a wide variety of materials, from lipsticks to metal filings. Gunshot residue is a common type of forensic evidence analyzed by SEM/EDX.

Figure 9.4 *A photomicrograph shows the enlargement of the unknown chemical substances.*

Chapter 10

Digital and Multimedia Evidence (Digital Forensics)

A useful definition of *digital forensics* is: use of proven scientific methods in the seizure and processing of evidence that is stored in digital or can readily be converted to digital form. This can involve computers, mobile communication devices, digital storage media, internet and network transaction, digital images, analog images and audio data. Computers and other digital devices are now so widely used that they have become extremely important as evidence in both criminal and civil cases. Even where there is physical evidence, the real material of interest is the *information* recorded on or available through the evidence.

10.1 Collection of Computer Evidence

The gathering of computer evidence is a little more complex, both in terms of legal requirements and scene activities, than other types of physical evidence. Virtually all federal and state law enforcement agencies now have individuals, or an office that specialize in gathering and processing digital evidence. There may be different parties to handle the legal and technical issues, but they are usually in communication and can assist investigators in obtaining qualified assistance.

Once the legal requirements for seizure of the digital evidence have been satisfied, the first step is forensic imaging of the information on the evidence. Obtaining an accurate and complete digital image of the information sought is by no means trivial and one should never just turn a target computer or network system on or off, since system software may be booby-trapped or have programs that destroy or hide the desired information and important date in cache and temp files may be lost. Digital forensic specialists have the necessary knowledge and equipment to make a suitable image and avoid any such pitfalls.

It may not be practical to seize and remove an entire computer system and associated equipment, so the imaging may have to be done on-site rather than at the laboratory. It is important to document everything possible at the site in detail, with photographs and markings, the exact connections and full scope of any computer equipment or other evidence seized and its connections to a network or other communications media. A careful scene search is as important for a successful computer evidence case as it is for the more traditional crime scene. It is also important to be aware that equipment at a site or else where may be "wirelessly" connected to the system. The location of notes with passwords, printouts, backup disks and many other associated items may be the key to obtaining and processing the evidence to obtain useful evidence.

10.2 Processing of the Digital Evidence

There are now well-established protocols for identifying and preserving digital files as well as considerable well-proven software for assisting in recovering and interpreting digital data from computers, data storage devices and a myriad of other digital information and communication devices. In addition to what can clearly be seen, there are techniques for recovering information that has been deleted, hidden or encrypted or otherwise protected from intrusion. Often the digital forensic examiner must reach out to others to recover e-mails and other communications that are referred to but not on the seized evidence. Other materials gathered at the scene should also be carefully examined and checked to determine if they are of possible evidentiary value in the investigation.

Many laboratories have developed some sophistication in digital image clarification. Analog video images can also be readily captured and converted to digital format. This allows a variety of clarification techniques such as frame averaging, contrast enhancement, focus improvement and many others to be used on video evidence.

10.3 Some Other Digital and Analog Devices

Videotapes or digital video recovered at or near a scene may prove to be valuable evidence, particularly bank or store security tapes that may document robberies in progress. Surveillance tapes from hidden cameras can, with proper processing, yield highly valuable evidence. Tapes should be submitted to a laboratory for examination or enhancement purposes. Tapes may be submitted for the determination of their authenticity, the sequence of taping, tampering with the tape or alteration of the videotape. Photographic documentation of specific frames on a tape or clarification or enhancement of poor quality images is frequently useful.

Audio tapes, either analog or digital, are frequently of considerable evidentiary value. It is usually possible to "clean up" the sound track of a video or audio tape by enhancing or eliminating background noise and other filtering techniques. This process may facilitate transcription of tapes, from body wires or answering machines. As discussed in Chapter 30, either electronic or human processing may allow identification of a speaker from such tapes.

Chapter 11

DNA Analysis

Since the nuclear DNA of all individuals, with the exception of identical twins, is undoubtedly unique, the testing of even a small portion of an individual's DNA can be highly individualizing. DNA typing has been applied in forensic laboratories for the analysis of many types of biological evidence, including blood, semen, hair roots, bone, and other biological materials that contain nucleated cells. Analysis of DNA evidence has proven extremely valuable in an enormous variety of cases such as rape, homicide, assault, hit-and-run accidents, identification of human remains, missing person investigations and paternity issues. As the explosive expansion of medical research involving DNA continues, forensic benefits will also follow. Non-nuclear (mitochondrial) DNA also has important forensic applications such as hair shaft and bone or other severely compromised DNA characterization.

11.1 Nature of DNA Analysis
A. Deoxyribonucleic Acid (DNA)

DNA is the biochemical compound in the nucleus of each cell that contains the genetic or inheritable material of the organism. DNA is present in all body fluids and structures that contain nucleated cells. Each cell contains approximately seven billion nucleotide pairs, the unit from which DNA is built. Half of the DNA of an individual is inherited from the mother and half from the father. Because of the randomized way the parental DNA is distributed to its offspring, each person's DNA is unique, including siblings, except for identical twins. Recent research now suggests that, in some instances, the DNA of identical twins may have some subtle differences, although these have not been utilized in analysis of forensic samples.

B. Types of DNA Analysis

1. Restriction fragment length polymorphism (RFLP)

Restriction fragment length polymorphism (RFLP) depends upon variations in the length (size) of specific DNA pieces (fragments) that are generated when DNA is digested (selectively cleaved into fragments) using restriction enzymes. The length variations are caused by different individuals having a different number of tandem repeats (VNTR) of a particular sequence. RFLP analysis requires DNA of relatively good quality (high molecular weight) and a sizable evidence sample and is seldom used on forensic evidence anymore.

2. Polymerase chain reaction (PCR)

The polymerase chain reaction (PCR), originally developed by scientists at the Cetus Corporation, results in the synthesis of millions of copies of a specific, selected portion of DNA where the original DNA is in very low quantity. PCR requires much less DNA than RFLP, and even somewhat degraded DNA can be amplified successfully. Thus PCR is the method of choice for analyzing small amounts of DNA and samples, such as a single hair root or the sloughed buccal cells in a saliva stain. In fact, virtually all DNA analysis testing done in forensic laboratories is now done using the power of PCR.

11.2 Collection and Preservation of Evidence for DNA Analysis
A. Evidence Suitable for DNA Analysis

Evidence that can be subjected to DNA analysis is limited to things that are biological in nature. The following is a partial list of the types of evidence from which DNA has been successfully isolated and analyzed:

1. Blood and bloodstains
2. Semen and seminal stains
3. Tissues and cells
4. Bones and organs
5. Teeth
6. Hairs with attached cellular material
7. Urine and saliva (which usually contain sloughed nucleated cells)

Other types of biological evidence, such as tears, serum and other body fluids that do not contain nucleated cells are not generally amenable to DNA analysis.

B. Collection of Biological Evidence

The ability to perform successful DNA analysis on biological evidence recovered from a crime scene or other evidence depends very much on the kinds of specimens collected and the methods used to preserve them. Thus, the technique used to collect and document such evidence, the quantity and type of evidence that is collected, the way the evidence is packaged, and how the evidence is handled, are all critical. In addition, unless the evidence is properly documented, collected, packaged and preserved, it will not meet the legal and scientific requirements for admissibility into a court of law.

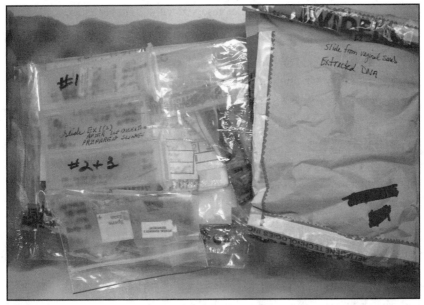

Figure 11.1 *Evidence from a sexual assault submitted for DNA analysis.*

1. Documentation of evidence

Documentation of evidence for DNA analysis should be thorough and follow the guidelines applicable to all physical evidence at crime scenes or otherwise legally obtained, as discussed above. Nothing should ever be disturbed until its original condition and position have been recorded. All specimens should be labeled with the case number, item number, date, time, location, and the evidence collector's name. Whenever possible, preserve blood or body fluid stain patterns when collecting biological evidence. If the collection process will destroy the pattern, then thoroughly document and photograph the pattern before collection.

2. Collection methods

In most cases, the handling of a bodily liquid or a stain from a bodily liquid is the same regardless of the origin of the liquid. The following outline gives a brief description of the basic techniques that should be employed in the collection and preservation of the evidence for DNA testing. As indicated elsewhere, the use of gloves for protection of the collector and to avoid contamination of the evidence is critical.

a. Liquid evidence. Collect liquids with a clean (preferably sterile) syringe or disposable pipette and transfer to a clean (preferably sterile) test tube. If a tube is unavailable, use a clean cotton cloth or gauze to soak up liquid. The cloth must be air dried and then placed in a paper envelope that is labeled and sealed.

1. Wet blood samples must be preserved with a suitable anticoagulant and kept in a refrigerator. Submit these specimens to the laboratory as soon as possible.
2. Samples found on snow or in water should be collected immediately to avoid further dilution. The largest possible quantity of these samples should be collected in a clean, suitable container, minimizing contamination. If possible, label and freeze the specimen; if no freezer is available, refrigerate the diluted sample and take to the laboratory as soon as possible.
3. Blood clots should be transferred to a clean test tube with a clean spatula or absorbed onto a clean cotton cloth. Areas containing only serum should be collected separately.

b. Evidence with wet stains on small objects. All clothing or small objects stained with blood or other body fluids which are still wet, must be air dried before packaging. When dry, package the garments or objects in paper bags or paper wrapping. Never package a wet or moist piece of evidence in a sealed, airtight container or plastic bag. This practice will retain moisture, which promotes bacterial growth and causes rapid sample deterioration.

c. Wet stains on large objects. Evidence that is large and cannot be removed from a crime scene should have the stain transferred onto clean cotton swabs. Air dry the cotton swabs before packaging in an appropriately labeled paper container.

d. Known samples. Liquid blood drawn from a person should be collected by individuals qualified and licensed to collect blood.

1. Two tubes of blood, about 5 ml each, should be collected in containers with EDTA as anticoagulant ("purple cap"). Label each tube with the subject's name, the date and time of collection, the location, the collector's name, the case number and the exhibit number.

2. Blood tubes should be refrigerated (NOT frozen) and submitted to the laboratory as soon as possible.

3. Since most DNA analysis is being done using polymerase chain reaction (PCR) based techniques, known control samples can be collected in a non-invasive way. Thus swabbings from the inside of an individual's mouth can provide an excellent sample for PCR base methods. This is done by rubbing a sterile cotton swab or other special collector on the inside of an individual's cheek to collect saliva and loose cells from the mouth. These swabs should be air dried and placed in a clean envelope or cardboard box and properly sealed. A typical collection kit is shown in Figure 11.2.

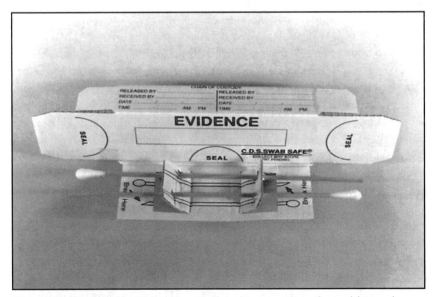

Figure 11.2 *Evidence Collection Kit for obtaining mouth swabbings for DNA known reference samples.*

e. Dried stains on evidence

1. Dried stains on movable items: Collect evidence on smaller objects such as garments, weapons, small items of furniture and so forth by seizing the entire item. Place each item in a separate paper container, seal, and label with appropriate case information.
2. Dried stains on surfaces of immovable objects: The location and pattern of each stain should be documented, sketched, and photographed before it is collected.

If the stain is on an object such as carpet or upholstery that can be cut, excise the stain area and a small area around it with a clean sharp instrument. Thoroughly clean or use a new instrument for each sample. Package each cutting separately and label accordingly. Collect and package an unstained portion of the item, close to the stained area, to provide a control sample.

If the sample cannot be cut out, the stained area can be scraped off onto a clean piece of paper and folded into a druggist fold. The paper packet should be placed in an envelope, sealed and labeled. Alternately, lift the stain with the pattern intact using a tape-lift method.

Thoroughly document dried stains on immovable objects where stains cannot be scraped or cut off. Then elute the stain onto clean cotton threads or a swab moistened with sterile physiological saline solution or distilled water. Use the smallest amount of liquid possible to elute these samples. Air dry the cotton swab and then place it in a paper fold packet. Always obtain a control by repeating the procedure on an adjacent, but unstained, area of the surface containing the stain.

Dried small spatters are often difficult to remove from their surfaces. It may be possible to collect them using the tape lift method. After proper documentation, use clean fingerprint tape to lift the spatter from its surface. Place each piece of tape into a large plastic container. Tape the ends of the tape lift in place to secure the lift. Suspend the tape with the spatter portion in the middle of the container, seal and label the container.

f. Seminal evidence from sexual assault victims. Sexual assault victims should always be examined in hospitals or clinics by trained forensic science or medical personnel. Physical evidence should be collected using established procedures and a standard sexual assault evidence kit. Medical personnel should collect specimens of vaginal, oral and anal evidence, as well as control samples, according to established protocols. Each item of evidence should be packaged, sealed and labeled.

g. Tissue, organ and bone

1. Each item of tissue or bone can be picked up with a clean pair of forceps or a gloved hand and placed in a clean container without a fixative.

2. Use caution not to contaminate any item with material from a second item. Carefully clean forceps after each specimen is collected, or preferably use different forceps for each. If no forceps are used, change gloves between the collection of each item.
3. Seal and label each container, and place in a freezer as soon as possible. Whenever possible, keep containers cold during transport to the laboratory.

h. Hair evidence

1. Pick up hair evidence using a clean pair of forceps.
2. Package each hair or group of hairs separately in a paper fold. Then place the paper fold in a paper package, seal and label.
3. Exercise care during collection so that any hair root tissue is not lost.

Hairs mixed with blood, tissue or other body fluids should be air dried before being placed in a clean container. The container should be appropriate for the type and condition of the material present with the hair. Evidence should be stored in a freezer.

11.3 Laboratory Analysis of DNA Evidence

Molecular biology techniques currently applied in forensic laboratories allow for the extraction of DNA from biological samples which contain nucleated cells, including blood, semen, bone, muscle, teeth, hair roots, and other tissues. The DNA obtained from these specimens is then analyzed. The technique chosen for each sample is dependent upon both the quality and quantity of the DNA present in the item submitted.

A. RFLP Analysis

Please note: this is included here primarily for historical interest, as it is seldom if ever done in forensic laboratories today.

1. Some terms used in describing RFLP analysis

Several steps are involved in obtaining DNA from a specimen and in the analysis and comparison of that DNA in the forensic laboratory.

- **Restriction enzyme**. Restriction endonucleases (restriction enzymes) are biological catalysts obtained from bacteria and have the ability to cut (digest) the DNA in specific locations determined by the base sequence.
- **Probe**. A DNA probe is a short portion of single-stranded DNA labeled in some way to allow later detection. DNA probes used in forensic RFLP analysis are chosen to detect specific regions where length polymorphism is known to occur.

- **RFLP patterns**. The pattern of DNA pieces that results after restriction enzyme digestion, electrophoretic separation, and detection with a specific probe is characteristic of a specific source of DNA.

2. Forensic RFLP analysis

Two approaches to RFLP analysis have been used in forensic science laboratories:

- **Single locus probes**. The repeating sequences probed for are located at only one location (locus) on each of a pair of homologous chromosomes. The result is then a one or two band pattern, in most cases. Thus, when single locus probes are used, multiple VNTR loci are often examined to achieve greater individualization.
- **Multi-locus probes**. The first forensic DNA work used multi-locus probes that recognize more than one location in the DNA at the same time. Their use results in a multi-banded pattern, similar to a bar code in appearance. These patterns were the genesis of the term "DNA fingerprint." They find little use in forensic DNA testing in the U.S.

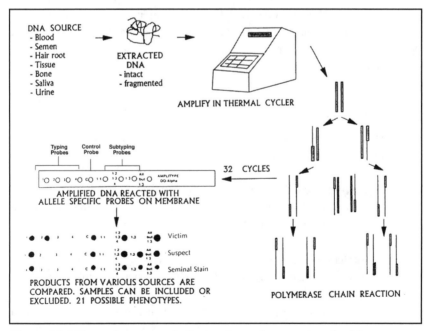

Figure 11.3 *The polymerase chain reaction scheme using dot blot visualization procedure.*

B. Polymerase Chain Reaction (PCR)

The polymerase chain reaction (PCR) portion of the analysis is not directly used to differentiate individuals, but is the first step in several different techniques. PCR is used to make large numbers of copies of a particular portion or portions of the DNA. By making many copies of selected areas of the DNA, scientists can then carry out probing techniques more easily, even on degraded or very small DNA samples. PCR-based methods have virtually totally replaced RFLP-based methods for forensic purposes.

1. Basis of PCR analysis methods

Like RFLP analysis, PCR-based methods exploit polymorphisms (variations) among individuals in the human population. Two types of polymorphism in human DNA have been used so far for forensic testing purposes: length polymorphism (discussed above in connection with RFLP) and sequence polymorphism.

a. Sequence polymorphisms. A single difference in the DNA sequence results in detectable variation.

b. VNTR. As described above, some portions of DNA exhibit polymorphisms due to the variable number of repeats of a particular DNA sequence. Specific amplification of the DNA in the region of these variable repeats allows the sizes of the repeat sequences to be determined. Many VNTR loci have been validated in forensic laboratories, including large repeat sequences similar to those used in RFLP analysis, and various "STRs" (short tandem repeats), which occur in large numbers in nuclear DNA.

The analysis of STRs now dominates forensic DNA analysis. A huge number of STR markers (loci) have been characterized and a sizable subset of STR markers has been validated for forensic DNA application. It is now possible to carry out PCR (amplification) on over a half dozen different STR markers at the same time, from the same forensic DNA sample. This makes it fast and efficient to look at over a dozen STR markers in either forensic evidence stains or convicted felon control samples.

As a result, this technology has been adopted for the creation of convicted felon databases (Figure 11.5). Although each individual STR marker does not have a great deal of power to differentiate individuals, when a dozen or more are compared and a complete correspondence is found, that virtually becomes an identification. The value of DNA evidence has exploded as laboratories have become highly proficient in STR analysis.

2. Sex determination by STR

Amplification of DNA sequences found specifically on the X or Y chromosomes using standard STR markers allows for the determination of sex of origin of biological samples. This procedure is useful for investigative purposes and it is useful to indicate mixed samples.

3. Y-STR Analysis

In addition to the sets of STR markers commonly used to characterize DNA samples, additional marker sets have been developed for specialized purposes. One of the most useful is a set of Y-STR markers that are designed to study only the DNA from the Y chromosome and therefore only work with DNA from males. This is particularly useful to study male heredity and to look for male DNA in a vast sea of female DNA, which may be the case in vaginal swabs with very few sperm cells.

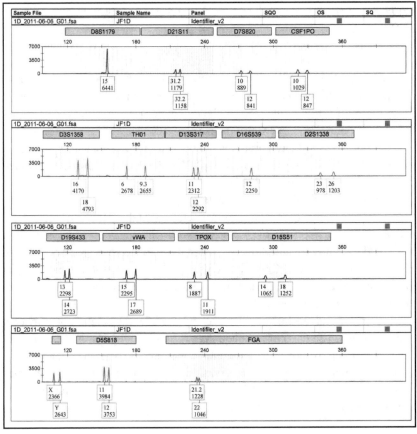

Figure 11.4 *Fifteen locus electropheragram of a forensic DNA sample.*

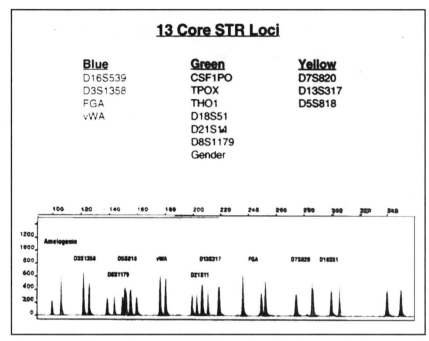

Figure 11.5 *Short tandem repeat (STR) markers (loci) currently being used for construction of convicted felon databases as well as case analysis.*

4. Mitochondrial DNA (mtDNA)

Mitochondria, inclusions in the cell outside of the nucleus, contain DNA that is useful as a marker for DNA analysis. Mitochondria can occur in numbers greater than 10,000 per cell and as a result one can often obtain such DNA from sources such as hair shafts and bone that do not have enough nuclear DNA for other DNA analyses. Variable regions of the mtDNA have been identified which show polymorphisms. These polymorphisms are detected by determining the exact base sequence of the variable regions of the mtDNA. Mitochondrial DNA typing methods are used in the analysis of biological evidence, especially of skeletal remains and hair shaft, where the normal STR techniques do not provide useful data.

5. Non-human DNA

DNA technology has been applied to identification of both plants and animals. This area is expanding and has already been used in a few cases. It is certain to play a significant role in investigation and prosecution in the future.

Chapter 12

Questioned Document Examination

Any written, printed, or typed material, whether on paper or on a wall, is considered a document. If the origin is unknown or the authenticity of the document is in doubt, the article can be considered a *questioned document*. Some common examples of documents submitted to forensic laboratories include checks, wills, business records, credit card charge slips, printed materials, ransom notes, robbery notes, suicide notes, letters, computer printouts, lottery tickets, extortion notes and others. Although document examination may be of most value in economic crimes, it is also often important in the investigation of cases such as untimely death, kidnapping, homicide, and sexual assault.

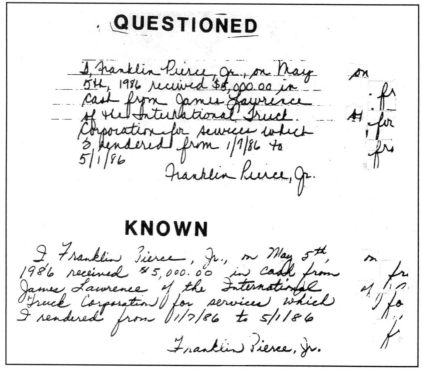

Figure 12.1 A handwriting comparison chart suitable for court use.

12.1 Types of Document Evidence Examinations
A. Handwriting Comparisons

Handwriting comparisons involve the detailed examination of exactly how the evidence document was written and a comparison to the class and individual characteristics of authenticated handwriting exemplars. Sufficient authentic handwriting standards must be either requested or collected to allow a full comparison. (See Figure 12.1.)

B. Comparison of Writing Materials

Experts can often determine the types of writing implement, ink, paper, and mechanical devices and compare them using a variety of physical and chemical techniques. These analyses may include procedures such as thin layer chromatography (TLC), infrared spectroscopy, infrared and ultraviolet luminescence and visible microspectrophotometric analysis.

C. Determination if a Document Has Been Altered

A variety of techniques from spectroscopic (IR, UV/VIS), to photographic, to mechanical can disclose erasures, additions, deletions, obliterations, and eliminations.

D. Determination of Common Origin or "Authorship"

Careful chemical and physical examination may determine the manufacturer of inks, papers, and the writing or copying device used to produce the document, and possibly the author.

E. Reconstruction

Charred or indented writing can be made legible using various techniques. Matching torn edges of a document with a portion found at the scene, on the victim, or in the possession of the suspect may also be of great value in investigations involving documents.

12.2 Collection and Preservation of Document Evidence
A. Questioned Evidence Samples

The investigator must exercise care in handling document evidence, particularly with regard to the presence of latent fingerprints.

1. The document must be handled as little as possible while being placed in a clear plastic envelope, which should then be sealed and initialed. The investigator or individual submitter should use forceps or tongs when directly handling the document to avoid leaving fingerprints on the evidence.

2. In some laboratories, document evidence is not automatically processed for fingerprints. If this is a consideration, the submitting agency should so indicate in its letter of transmittal. This letter should be affixed to the outside of the envelope containing the evidence. It is necessary to inform the laboratory of the dual processing as the chemical processing for latent prints may cause the paper to discolor and may also dissolve certain inks. Therefore, the document must be photographed by the laboratory before the application of any chemicals for fingerprint processing. In addition, document examiners often like to do the latent print work themselves to minimize any adverse effects on the document.

3. Where there is the possibility of body fluid on a document, it should be protected for possible DNA analysis

4. The investigator should make no additional folds, nor mark any identification data on the document itself.

B. Requested Known Standards (Often Subject to Court Order)

1. It is vital that the person obtaining a requested standard duplicate as closely as possible the conditions under which the questioned document was made. These conditions include writing instrument, type and size of paper, context of the written message, and writing type or style (printing versus handwriting).
2. The donor should be seated in a chair placed at a table to ensure comfort and natural writing conditions. The situation in which the donor has been placed is inherently stressful, since the sample is to be used in a police investigation; therefore efforts should be made to minimize additional stress.
3. The material of the writing sample should be dictated from a carefully prepared text. Dictation of standard writings is critical to preclude the donor seeing and imitating the questioned sample.
4. The known samples should be removed from view as soon as they are written and the dictation must make the donor write the entire requested text verbatim several times, if possible.
5. Continue the exercise until the dictator is satisfied that the subject is writing naturally and has been discouraged from attempting to disguise the sample. Where appropriate, the donor should be required to repeat the process using the unnatural hand.
6. For many purposes, the best known writing samples are well-authenticated existing writings that can be obtained in many places that individuals must write. Commonly they may be documents filled out in the usual courses of business such as mortgages, school records, etc. Refer to Table 12.1 for some suggested handwriting sources.

12.3 Laboratory Examination of Document Evidence
A. Analysis of Writing Materials

Examiners employ various chemical, microscopic, and instrumental techniques to understand and characterize the writing instruments, the inks and the type of paper used to produce a document. Many times the physical analysis of questioned document materials can provide unambiguous answers to questions about authenticity and a variety of other important characteristics of a questioned document.

Table 12.1
Where to Find Authentic Handwriting Samples

City Records	Building department permits.
	City auditor: canceled checks and office records.
	City clerk: licenses for peddler, tavern, special permits, and so on, and voter registration lists.
	Personnel department: civil service applications.
	Permits for dogs, building, parks and other city facilities, applications.
County Records	County clerk: civil service applications, claims for services or merchandise, fishing, hunting, and marriage licenses.
	Department of taxation: state income tax returns.
	Purchasing department: bids and contracts.
	Register of deeds: deeds, birth certificates, public assistance applications, and ID card applications.
	Selective service (local board): registrations and appeals.
Department Store Records	Credit applications.
	Receipts for merchandise.
	Signed sales checks.
	Merchandise delivery records.
Drug Store Records	Register for exempt narcotics or poisons.
	Signed prescriptions.
Hospital Records	Admission and release forms.
	Consent forms.
	Checks and payment records.
	Communications and letters.
Library Records	Applications for cards.
	Check out and reserve slips.
Education Documents	Applications for entrance.
	Athletic health waivers.
	Daily assignments.
	Examination and research papers.
	Fraternity or sorority records.
	Receipt for school supplies, i.e., laboratory and athletic gear.
	Registration cards and forms.
	Federal and state loan and grant applications.
	Scholarship applications.

Table 12.1 (continued)

Federal Records	Customs documents: immigration and naturalization records.
	Department of Justice (FBI): fingerprint cards, applications, and records.
	National fraudulent check file, checkwriter standards file, safety paper standards file, rubber stamp and printing standards file, and typing standards file.
	Military records.
	Patent office applications.
	Post Office department: P.O. box application, registered and special delivery receipts.
	Social Security administration: applications for numbers and benefits.
	United States Treasury: canceled payroll checks.
	Veterans administration: application for benefits for veterans and widows.
Social, Recreational, and Fraternal Documents	Civic organizations, clubs such as sports, luncheon, and so on, lodges, nonprofit groups, political groups, PTA organizations, and religious organizations.
Financial Documents	Canceled bank checks.
	Contracts and related correspondence.
	Credit applications, i.e., department store.
	Deeds.
	Deposit slips.
	Expense accounts.
	Insurance documents, including health and accident.
	Lease agreements.
	Loan company records.
	Microfilm bank records.
	Pension applications and checks.
	Promissory notes.
	Safety deposit vault register and applications.
	Bankruptcy proceedings, cash received slips, and withdrawal slips.
	Title company documents.
	Account applications.
	Stock certificates.
Real Estate Records	Property listing agreements.
	Purchasing contracts.

Table 12.1 (continued)

Public Utility Records (Corporate Documents)	Applications for service: cable television, internet, electricity, garbage removal, gas, telephone, and water.
	Book of accounts.
	Invoices.
	Minutes.
	Original telegram messages.
	Reports to intrastate and interstate commerce agencies.
Miscellaneous Documents	Administrator and estate.
	Airplane logs.
	Answers to decoy letters.
	Architect plans.
	Asylums.
	Auctions.
	Bail bonds.
	Building after-hour registers.
	Close associates.
	Complaint bureaus.
	Copyright applications.
	Death certificates.
	Decoys, delivery receipts, and return receipts for registered mail.
	Exchanges.
	Express company, cartage, and mover's receipts.
	Express records and receipts.
	Furniture contracts.
	Guardian.
	Janitors (wastepaper).
	Legal papers.
	Messenger receipts.
	Neighbors.
	Newspaper reporters.
	Notaries.
	Partner memos and records.
	Permit to open mail.
	Railroad passes.
	Rent receipts to tenants.

Table 12.1 (continued)

Military Documents	Bases and stations: Air Force, Army, National Guard, Navy, and Marines.
	General service related papers: tax exemption filings, lien, real estate, pension, medical, educational.
	Record depots (ex-service men).
	Selective Service (draft board) records.
	Leave records.
	Hospital records.
Motor Vehicle Documents	Applications for registration.
	Court documents relating to accidents.
	Credit card applications and invoices based thereon.
	Hotel and motel registration and reservations upon routes of travel, collected from credit purchases.
	Installment contracts on vehicle purchases.
	Insurance papers.
	Operator's and chauffeur's licenses and applications.
	Orders for service.
	Accident reports.
	Report of loss or theft.
	Tickets and fines.
On the Person	Contents of wallet, i.e., signed ID cards and photographs.
	Letters and postcards.
	Notebooks.
	Passports.
	Permits.
Personal Documents	Autograph albums.
	Automobile repair work order receipts.
	Back of photographs.
	Bank account books.
	Birth and baptismal certificates and records.
	Book contracts.
	Books in general.
	Canceled checks.
	Check stubs.
	Correspondence and postcards.
	Diaries.
	Family Bible.
	Greeting cards.
	Hospital and medical records.
	Insurance policies.
	Labeling on cans, bottles, and so on, in kitchen and workshops.

Table 12.1 (continued)

Household Documents	Memoranda about home and office, such as a note to a delivery person.
	Military service records.
	Pages of photograph albums.
	Passports.
	Personal notebooks.
	Prescriptions.
	Receipts, i.e., movers, credit, and rent.
	School yearbooks.
	Telephone and correspondence listings.
	Wills.
Police Department Records and General Criminal Documents	Complaints and reports to police, sheriff's departments, and district attorney's.
	Arrest records including fingerprint cards.
	Court of claims.
	Court clerk.
	Exemplars obtained incident to booking procedures.
	Jail and penitentiary records.
	Jury records.
	Juvenile court.
	Parole and probation reports.
	Receipts for returned property.
	Writings obtained by other agencies in prior investigations.
Relatives	Letters of all types.
	Greeting and gift cards.
State Records	Conservation files: boat, fishing, and hunting licenses.
	Corrections files: probation and parole reports.
	Incorporation documents filed with state agencies.
	Motor vehicle files: driver's license and title.
	Personnel files: Civil Service applications and examinations.
	Secretary of State: applications for notary public.
	State Treasurer: canceled checks.
	Taxation files: beverage and cigarette tax applications.

Table 12.1 (continued)

Vocational Documents	Account books.
	Applications for employments.
	Applications for professional and vocational licenses.
	Canceled payroll checks.
	Civil service papers.
	Client checks.
	Credit union paperwork.
	Employment bureau and personnel office papers.
	Labor union documents.
	Order blanks.
	Professional rolls.
	Public examinations, i.e., Civil Service.
	Receipt books.
	Receipted bills.
	Receipts for pay.
	Reports and surveys.
	Secretary.
	Stenographic and clerical memoranda.
	Time cards.
	Vacation and petty cash requests.
	Withholding exemption forms.

B. Handwriting Analysis

Class and individual characteristics of the handwriting on the questioned document and in the known standards are analyzed and compared. Document examiners are trained to understand the writing process and through extensive training and experience develop knowledge of what important characteristics to look for in making such comparisons.

Such comparisons are used not only to determine authorship but also to evaluate disguised writing. A writer's characteristics may often be discerned to attribute disguised writing (see Figure 12.2).

C. Typewriting and Printer Analysis

Questioned typewriting and other mechanical printing can be compared with known standards to determine the style, manufacturer, and possibly the individual source. Although typewriters are falling out of use, there is still an enormous amount of typewritten material that can be of consequence to an investigation. In addition, computer printers and other printing devices have characteristics that

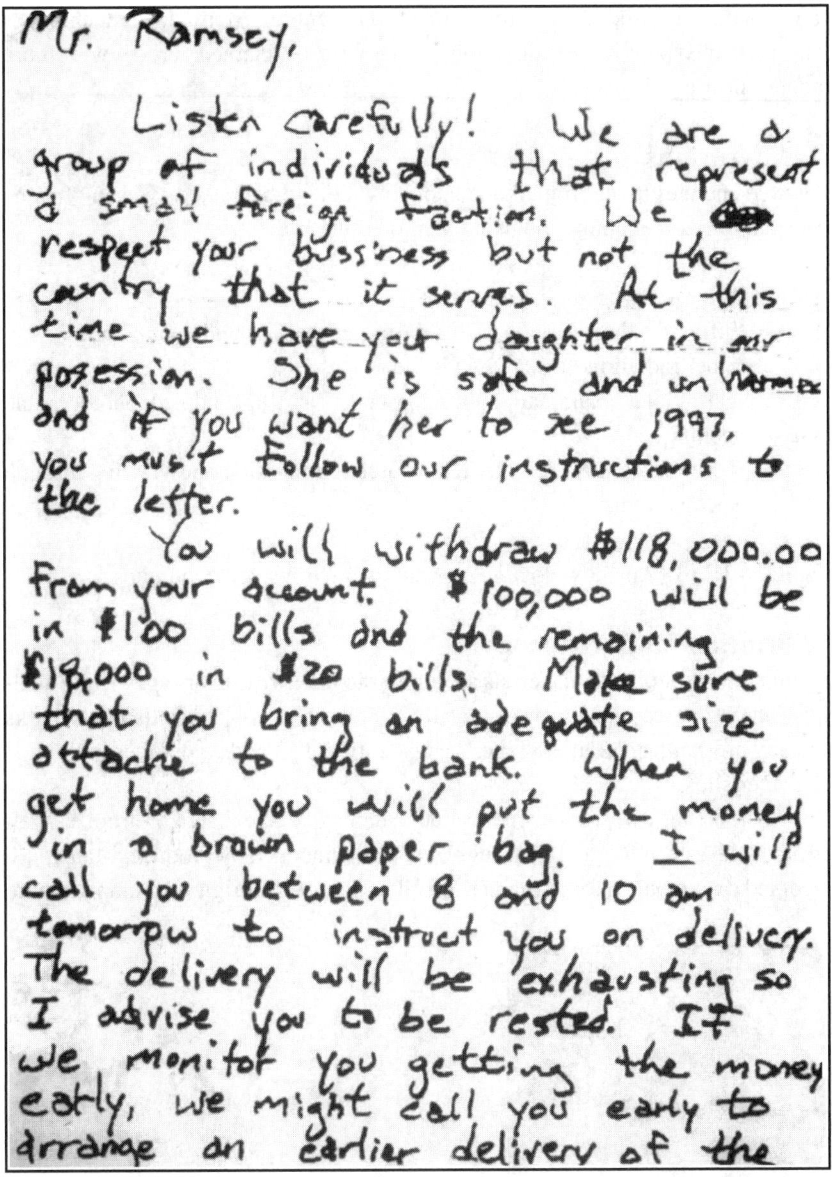

Mr. Ramsey,

Listen carefully! We are a group of individuals that represent a small foreign faction. We ~~do~~ respect your bussiness but not the country that it serves. At this time we have your daughter in our posession. She is safe and unharmed and if you want her to see 1997, you must follow our instructions to the letter.

You will withdraw $118,000.00 from your account. $100,000 will be in $100 bills and the remaining $18,000 in $20 bills. Make sure that you bring an adequate size attache to the bank. When you get home you will put the money in a brown paper bag. I will call you between 8 and 10 am tomorrow to instruct you on delivery. The delivery will be exhausting so I advise you to be rested. If we monitor you getting the money early, we might call you early to arrange an earlier delivery of the

Figure 12.2 First page of ransom note of JonBenet Ramsey homicide case.

can be fruitfully used in investigation and prosecution. Many of the techniques long used in typewriter examination can be used or adapted for use with more modern printing devices.

D. Alterations

Possible changes to an original document invisible to the naked eye can often be detected through examination using methods such as:

- Microscopic examination
- Infrared illumination, infrared luminescence, and examination with other radiation outside the visible range
- Ultraviolet examination, luminescence and specialized photographic techniques
- Laser and other alternate light source illumination and viewing through special filters

Figures 12.3 to 12.6 show documents examined with such techniques.

E. Printing and Photocopying

Examinations of printed materials are similar to handwriting or typewriting analysis. Through careful analysis of type fonts, imperfections, miscellaneous marks and any mechanical oddities, experts can identify class and sometimes individual characteristics.

Photocopies can produce marks due to damage to the platen or drum, as well as other class or individual markings on the documents they produce. Many photocopied documents may be made from all or part of the original, making it more

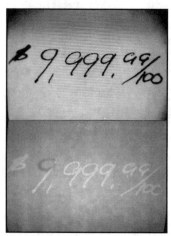

Figure 12.3 An alteration of the original document made visible by use of infrared luminescence. Top is normal light photograph and bottom is infrared luminescence photograph.

difficult to examine these types of evidence, since multigenerational copies may obscure the original marks. Examination of the type of toner and how it has been applied to the paper will often allow determination of the make, and sometimes even the model, of copier used.

F. Indented Writing

Impressions are sometimes left on a surface underlying the one upon which writing has occurred. Special techniques, such as oblique lighting, and so forth, are employed when this type of evidence is submitted for examination. (See Figure 12.5.)

The electrostatic detection apparatus (ESDA) is an instrument available for detecting indented writing. ESDA employs static electricity and a special powder to produce an image of any indented writing or impressions on documents on a clear piece of plastic. The ESDA is so sensitive that impressions, even several sheets down on a pad or in a multipage document, can often be clearly deciphered.

G. Charred Documents

If a document is difficult to read due to charring, the writing can sometimes be made visible by the use of non-visible illumination and special filters or photog-

Figure 12.4 A document as it appears under normal lighting conditions (top). Alterations to this document are made visible by photography using ultraviolet light (bottom).

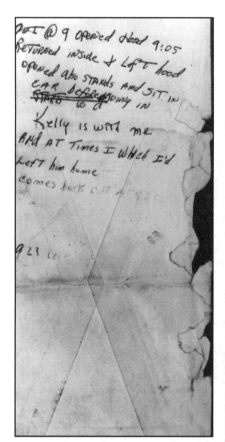

Figure 12.5 *Indented handwriting on the envelope (left) can be made visible through the use of oblique lighting techniques (right).*

raphy. (See Figure 12.6.) Charred documents often present more of a handling problem than a decipherment problem due to their fragility. Handling between glass, or gentle chemical techniques to soften the charred material, will usually be successful in skilled hands.

H. Determination of Document Age

Determination of age is carried out by analysis of the components of the documents such as ink type, style and paper. Perhaps the best indicator of a document being of an age different than it is purported to be is finding textual anachronisms or materials (ink, paper) in the document itself that were not available at the time it was purported to have been written.

Figure 12.6 *Restoration of a portion of the text on a burned document using infrared light and photographic techniques.*

I. Visible Microspectrophotometry

Visible light absorption spectra have been measured from minimal quantities of commonly encountered ballpoint and fiber-tip pen inks using any of several commercial visible light microspectrophotometers. Comparison of spectra of known and questioned samples may provide a degree of discrimination between inks which appear to be of a similar color.

J. Video Spectral Comparator (VSC)

The video spectral comparator (VSC) is a useful instrument developed by forensic document examiners and now widely used in questioned document examination. It incorporates into one instrument the ability to illuminate a document with a wide variety of electromagnetic radiation and capture the image with a high resolution video camera. In addition there are a variety of filters built into the instrument that can filter the radiation in either or both illumination and image capture.

K. Image Enhancement

Computerized image enhancement systems are available for the examination of documents. They allow for viewing under alternate light sources and improvement of the image utilizing video techniques or digital imaging techniques. As computing power has become less expensive, the necessary processing power and speed to handle large digital image files has moved into the realm of desktop computers. Relatively inexpensive digital imaging software has also improved and become more useful to the non-specialist. Digital enhancement of contrast, color correction, sharpening algorithms, and many more are readily available to the document examiner.

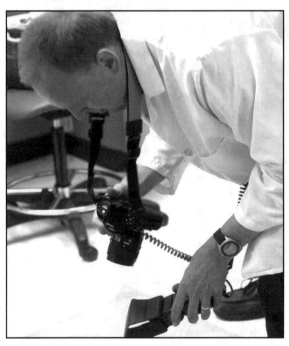

Figure 12.7 A document examiner photographs a questioned document.

Chapter 13

Drugs and Controlled Substances

Laboratories analyze controlled substances and other drugs of many types and in many forms. Most are seized during drug investigations or are incident to an arrest. Other drug evidence may be seized through burglary, robbery, traffic control, and internal affairs investigations or homicides. At times, investigators may submit chemicals used in the synthesis, purification, or processing of controlled substances for analysis as part of the investigation of a clandestine drug laboratory.

13.1 Types of Drug Evidence
A. Definition

A drug is any substance, natural or synthetic, which is used to produce a specific physiological or psychological effects on the body. Many substances can have such effects on the body and not be of forensic interest. One can narrow the practical definition by adding: the effect must be detectable by the consumer and come reasonably promptly after consumption. Drugs include both legal substances and illegal controlled substances.

B. Classification of Forensic Drug Evidence

1. Opiates (analgesics)

Opiates are drugs which have the effect of reducing sensation, particularly pain, and often inducing a euphoric sleep-like state. Common opiates are morphine, heroin, codeine, percodan, demerol, fentanyl and methadone.

2. Stimulants

Substances that stimulate the sympathetic nervous system and result in symptoms such as decreased appetite, inability to sleep, agitation, high energy and excitement are called stimulants. Physiological effects may include elevated blood pressure, increased heart rate, and rapid breathing. Amphetamine, methamphetamine and cocaine are some common examples of stimulants.

3. Hallucinogens

Hallucinogens significantly affect an individual's perceptions and may result in illusions and visual or other sensory distortions. LSD (lysergic acid diethylamide), mescaline, phencyclidine (PCP) and marijuana are common hallucinogens.

4. Depressants

Depressants are drugs that depress the central nervous system, resulting in reduced blood pressure and respiration, loss of motor coordination, drowsiness or sleep, and other slowed responsiveness. Barbiturates, Valium and other benzodiazepines, anesthetics, and ethanol are all commonly abused depressants.

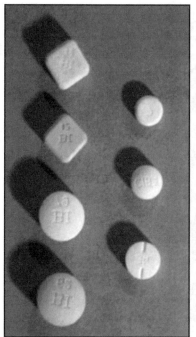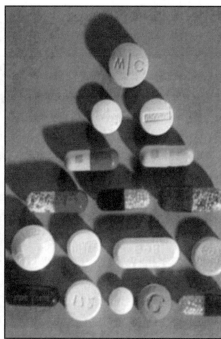

Figure 13.1 *Various forms of pills.*

Figure 13.2 *Different forms of Cannabis (marijuana): vegetable matter, hashish, and hash oil.*

5. Athletic performance enhancers

Steroids that are used to enhance muscle growth are the most commonly used drugs of this type, but hormones and even under certain conditions analgesics are also used for this purpose.

13.2 Collection of Drug Evidence
A. Blood Samples

Blood samples collected for testing of drugs or metabolites in serum must be obtained and stored to prevent contamination or deterioration of the sample.

1. Blood samples must be drawn by a licensed physician, nurse, or medical technician.
2. Use a disinfectant to clean the site where the blood sample will be drawn.
3. Two 10-mL (10-cc) tubes of blood should be collected.
4. Use gray top tubes (containing sodium fluoride as preservative) for collection.
5. The tubes should be sealed and properly labeled.

B. Urine Samples

1. The collection of a urine sample must be witnessed by an authority to prevent dilution of the urine sample with water from the tap or toilet.
2. The urine sample should be collected in a new plastic screw top jar used by hospitals for urine specimens or similar container.
3. Seal and properly label the urine container.

C. Plant Material

1. Submit plant materials suspected to contain illegal drugs to the laboratory for chemical analysis.
2. The most common drug derived from plant material is marijuana. Marijuana consists of the leaves, seeds, stems and flowers of the plant. Chemically laced cigarettes are also sometimes encountered.
3. Collect all of the plant parts in the evidence bag and air dry the plant materials before sealing the bag to prevent the growth of biological organisms.
4. If the plant materials already are in bags or containers, place the bags or container into a clean evidence bag to preserve fingerprint evidence on the original bags or container. Follow guidelines suggested for packaging fingerprint evidence described elsewhere.

5.   Seal and properly label the evidence bag.

D. Powders, Tablets, and Capsules

1.   Narcotics and other controlled drugs are often found in plastic or glass-ine bags, packets, cans, and other containers. Collect and preserve these containers for fingerprint evidence.
2.   Count and mark every drug package and container on the inventory sheet.
3.   Collect labels on bottles and containers of drugs or prescriptions as evidence.
4.   Seal and properly label each container.

E. Drug Paraphernalia

1.   Needles, syringes, spoons, cigarettes, foils, pipes, papers and other drug paraphernalia should be collected as evidence.
2.   Use appropriate containers for the collection of each type of evidence. An example of the safe packaging of a hypodermic syringe is shown in Figure 13.3.
3.   Exercise extreme caution when collecting drug paraphernalia and related items, as they may contain biohazardous materials which can lead to infection if they puncture or contact broken skin.
4.   Seal and properly label each container.

13.3 Investigation of Clandestine Laboratories
A. General Guidelines

The clandestine laboratory site should be treated as other potentially dangerous crime scenes — with caution and care. Evidence such as fingerprints, documents, money, records, computers and supplies could be extremely important for further investigation. Because the operations of an illicit laboratory are extremely varied in nature, use caution when seizing and handling any materials found.

If the clandestine laboratory appears to be active (material being heated, etc.), immediately call for the assistance of a chemist from a forensic laboratory to ensure that everything is shut down safely.

B. Safety Guidelines

The following general precautions should be taken when seizing any clandestine drug laboratory.

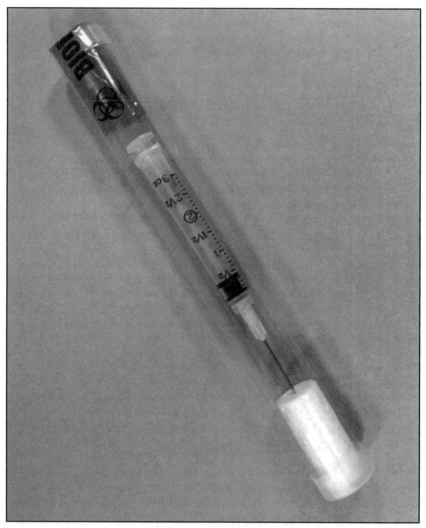

Figure 13.3 *The safe packaging of a hypodermic syringe.*

1. Chemical hazards

1. Maintain security until a qualified chemist reaches the scene to dismantle and shut down laboratory operations.
2. Never enter a possible clandestine laboratory without having a qualified chemist as technical advisor to the team. Call the forensic lab or toxicology lab for technical assistance.
3. Never smoke in the laboratory, and avoid bringing any possible sources of ignition into the laboratory or its immediate vicinity.

4. Do not dispose of or destroy anything by pouring into water or by pouring water into it.
5. Do not shut off any heaters, stirring motors or other mechanical or electrical apparatus.
6. Secure the clandestine laboratory and vicinity. Give no unauthorized or unnecessary personnel access to the premises.

2. Biological hazards

1. Never taste any material suspected of being a controlled drug.
2. Never smell materials suspected of containing a controlled drug.
3. Do not handle controlled drugs more than absolutely necessary.
4. Handle all chemical materials recovered with caution.
5. Wear gloves when handling liquid and powder forms of chemicals.
6. Wash hands thoroughly after handling any drug or chemical evidence.
7. Use particular care in searching a drug suspect, an automobile suspected of containing drugs, or any area where it is possible that hypodermic syringes or makeshift needles may be hidden.

C. Chemicals

An abbreviated list of chemicals which may be found at the site of a clandestine laboratory is given in Tables 13.1 and 13.2.

13.4 Laboratory Examination of Drug Evidence

Since the number of different drug substances used in modern society is enormous and their chemical nature highly varied, forensic chemists use a number of different methods to analyze controlled substances and other drugs. General techniques used in forensic laboratories for the analysis of commonly encountered drugs are outlined below.

A. Macroscopic Analysis

1. All drugs submitted to the laboratory must be weighed and catalogued. A careful description of the packaging and gross characteristics of the suspected drug sample must be recorded.
2. If the drug sample consists of pills or capsules, lab personnel should record the shape, color, any identifying markings, and the number of items or pills. This information can then be used for comparison to known standards or descriptions listed in the Physicians' Desk Reference (PDR), or for the investigation of drug trafficking patterns.

Table 13.1: Reagents for Specific Drug Syntheses

Chemical Reagent	Drug
Phenylacetone	Amphetamine, Methamphetamine
Formamide	Amphetamine
Methylformamide	Methamphetamine
Cyclohexanone	Phencyclidine – PCP
Piperidine	Phencyclidine – PCP
Piperanol	Heliotropine – MDA, MDMA
Nitroethane	MDA, MDMA
Isosafrole	MDA, MDMA
Indole	Dimethyltryptamine
Dimethylamine	DMT
Olivetol	Tetrahydrocannabinol
Ergotamine	LSD
Lysergic Acid	LSD
Benzoyl Chloride	Cocaine
Succinaldenhyde	Cocaine
Diphenylacetonitrile	Methadone
Phenylacetonitrile	Methylphenidate
2,5-Dimethoxy-e-methylbenzaldehyde	STP
3,4,5-Trimethoxybenzoic acid	Mescaline

Table 13.2: Reagents for General Synthesis and Associated Hazards

Chemical	Hazard
Acetic Acid	Caustic
Acetone	Flammable and toxic
Benzene	Flammable and toxic
Boron Triflouride	May inflame on contact with water
Chloroform	Toxic
Ethanol/Ethyl Alcohol	Flammable
Ethyl Ether	Highly flammable (even explosive)
Lithium Aluminum Hydride	Inflames and may explode on contact with water
Magnesium Metal	Flammable
Methanol/Methyl Alcohol	Flammable and toxic
Sodium or Potassium Hydroxide	Caustic

Table 13.3
Common Color Tests for Drugs

Drug	Reagent	Color Reaction
Amphetamine	Mandelin Marquis	gray-green red-brown
Barbiturate	Dille-Koppanyi	purple
Cocaine	Cobalt Thiocyanate Mandelin	blue precipitate orange
Codeine	Mandelin Marquis	green purple
Heroin	Mandelin Marquis Nitric Acid	brown purple yellow-green
LSD	Marquis Erlich Van Urk	dark purple pink-purple blue-purple
Marijuana	Modified Duquenois	blue
Methadone	Cobalt Thiocyanate Marquis	blue yellow-pink
Morphine	Mandelin Marquis Nitric Acid	orange-brown purple orange
Psilocin and Psilocybin	Weber test	red to blue
Benzodiazepines	Janovsky	orange

B. Chemical Tests

Chemists often use color tests as screening tests in the analysis of drugs. Certain drugs will react with selected chemical reagents to give characteristic color changes or precipitates. Some commonly used drug screening reagents and their characteristic reactions are shown in Table 13.3. These tests are used both by officers on the street to gain a preliminary idea of what they have, and in the laboratory to guide the chemist toward the proper analytical scheme.

C. Microscopic Analysis

1. Microscopic examination of seized materials

Often, much useful information can be gained from examining seized materials under magnification. If the material is a mixture it can sometimes be separated by noting the different appearance of the solid materials present. It can usually be easily determined if vegetable matter contains marijuana or if it has other crystalline drug matter added to it. An experienced eye can tell a great deal about a material from microscopic examination.

2. Microcrystal tests

As a rule, the chemist will place a small portion of the suspected drug powder on a clean microscope slide and add a drop of a chemical reagent. The slide is placed on the stage of a microscope and the chemist observes the drop in the microscope field. Specific chemical reagent solutions, when added to a mixture containing a drug, will result in the formation of microscopic crystals which can then be identified by their characteristic shapes. These reactions are more specific than the color tests, particularly in the hands of experienced examiners.

D. Thin Layer Chromatography

1. A sample of the drug is dissolved in a solvent and spotted on a TLC plate; samples of known drugs are also applied to the same plate.
2. The plate is developed by placing it, spotted side down, in a container with a small amount of a solvent or solvent mixture. The solvent travels up the plate by capillary action, causing different drugs to move different distances up the plate.
3. Compare of the Rf value (a characteristic measure of how far a substance travels on a TLC plate relative to the solvent in a given solvent separating system) of the unknown drug with Rf values of the known drugs.

E. Instrumental Analysis

A number of instrumental techniques may be employed as confirmatory tests in the analysis of drugs. Selection of which instrument to use is dependent on what instruments are available and the nature of the drug being examined.

1. Infrared spectroscopy (IR)

A relatively pure drug sample can be analyzed by IR. In most cases, the spectrum obtained is specific and unique for that substance. (See Figure 13.4.)

2. Gas chromatography-mass spectrometry (GC-MS)

By linking a gas chromatograph with a mass spectrometer, drug preparations can be separated into components, and each component of the mixture analyzed and identified. The identification of a drug is based on comparison of the mass spectrum produced by the unknown drug with the reference spectra of known drugs. Mass spectra, like infrared spectra, are usually highly specific for a particular substance. Derivatives and metabolic products of drugs which may be found in blood serum or urine can also be analyzed by GC-MS. The mass spectrum of cocaine is shown in Figure 13.5.

3. High performance liquid chromatography (HPLC)

High performance liquid chromatography (HPLC) is a separation technique which helps in the identification of a drug or separation of a particular drug from other materials with which it has been mixed. Identification is based on retention time with the particular solvent system and must usually be confirmed by some spectroscopic method. HPLC systems can also be linked to a MS (HPLC-MS) for identification of mixture components. As with GC-MS, a "separation instrument" and an "identification instrument" provide a powerful combination.

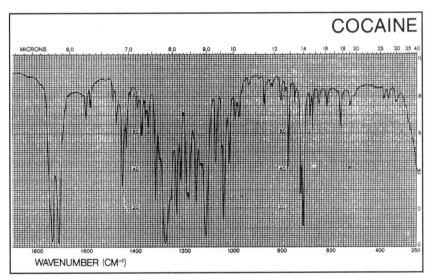

Figure 13.4 The infrared spectrum of cocaine.

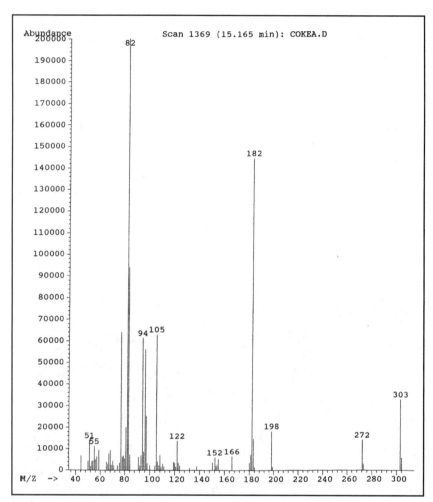

Figure 13.5 *The mass spectrum of cocaine.*

Chapter 14

Fibers

Fibers are among the most common types of trace and transfer evidence encountered at a crime scene. Fibers often will be transferred to clothing, shoes, bodies, head hair and other physical evidence when an individual or object comes in contact with a fabric or other fiber source. Factors such as the type of fiber, weave of the fabric, amount of loose fiber available, mode of physical contact, the degree of contact and various environmental factors will all affect the amount of fiber transfer which takes place. It should be remembered that although a fiber is transferred to a different surface, it may not stay there very long. The nature of the receiving surface and the forces subsequently applied to that surface are important factors in how long a transferred fiber will remain. Fibers suspended in fluids can also be transferred to pieces of evidence.

14.1 Nature of Fiber Evidence
A. Natural Fibers
These are formed from naturally occurring substances, including:

- plant fibers, such as cotton, ramie, jute, and hemp;
- mineral fibers, such as asbestos, carbon, glass, and metallic wires; and
- animal fibers, such as silk, wool and other animal hairs used as fibers.

B. Synthetic Fibers
Synthetic fibers are man-made materials. Commonly encountered synthetic fibers include nylon, polyester, polyethylene, polypropylene, acetate, acrylic, and a wide variety of specialty fibers.

C. Derived or Regenerated Fibers
Regenerated fibers are manufactured by reprocessing natural materials. For example, rayon is prepared from cellulosic (plant) starting material.

14.2 Collection and Preservation of Fiber Evidence
A. Manual Collection
Collection of fibers as evidence is best accomplished by picking up the fibers with gloved fingers or with forceps. Picking up the evidence with forceps has the advantage that samples are not contaminated and can be singly handled in the collection process.

B. Vacuum
It is also possible to collect fibers through the use of a vacuum cleaner fitted with an in-line canister attachment in the hose. The canister must contain a filter that is changed with each use. Figure 14.1 shows a vacuum with a fiber collection attachment.

C. Tape Lift
A third method is to use tape to pick up this type of evidence. A clear cellophane tape, that is not too sticky, is most useful. Placing the tape against the surface is very efficient at removing loose fibers. This process can be a little too efficient if fibers are pulled out of the surface being taped. Placing the tape with any removed fibers on a piece of clean glass or clear plastic will protect the collected material and ease their examination.

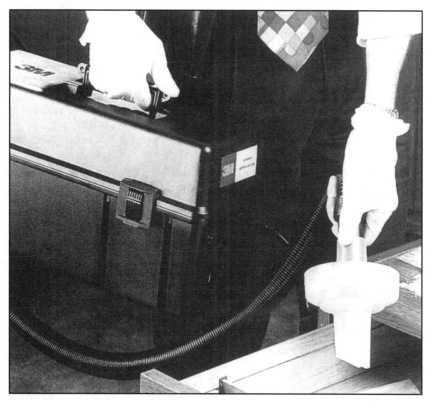

Figure 14.1 *Collection of trace evidence using a vacuum with a fiber collection attachment.*

D. Mechanical Dislodgment

Shaking or mechanical scraping over a clean piece of paper is also effective for collecting fiber and trace evidence in many cases. This technique is used in the laboratory, not at crime scenes and allows convenient processing of large objects such as bed sheets.

E. Packaging Fiber Evidence

1. Material recovered from vacuum processing

Place filters with materials recovered during vacuum processing in separate containers in accordance with their origin and label properly. Carefully seal these containers well, with no openings through which small particles can be lost. Do not use plastic bags for this purpose.

2. Individual fibers

If small amounts of individual fibers are picked up, place these in paper folded in the druggist fold (see Appendix B), which is in turn sealed in a paper envelope labeled with identification data. Label both the paper and the envelope.

3. Other fiber evidence

Collect materials composed of fibers to prevent damage or alteration to the evidence.

a. Cloth and cordage. Photograph as to location. Collect as evidence, package in paper bags or similar article, and label appropriately.

b. Fabric imprints. Collect the entire article and submit to the laboratory. If this is impossible, photograph the imprints with the inclusion of a scale, and oblique lighting or other specialized lighting necessary to make the pattern more visible. The fabric imprint should be thoroughly documented by describing, sketching, and photographing.

14.3 Laboratory Examination of Fibers
A. Physical Match

In cases where larger pieces of fabric are involved or cloth was torn, physical matching of two pieces of fabric material may be possible. Physical matching can be achieved through a direct fit-and-match method or an indirect pattern match method.

B. Microscopic Examination

Color, texture, shape, pattern, twist, cross-sectional appearance, and surface characteristics can be used to characterize fiber evidence. Microscopic examination is an important first step in the examination and comparison of fiber evidence. In fact, careful examination with a comparison microscope is perhaps the most important step in comparison of evidence and known control fibers.

C. Microchemical Tests

Various chemical reagents are available for testing the solubility of a fiber. These tests are destructive tests, but when done on a microscale, do not destroy significant amounts of sample, and can quickly yield useful information.

D. Determination of Physical Properties

Examiners may also measure physical characteristics such as melting point, density, ash formation, and tensile strength.

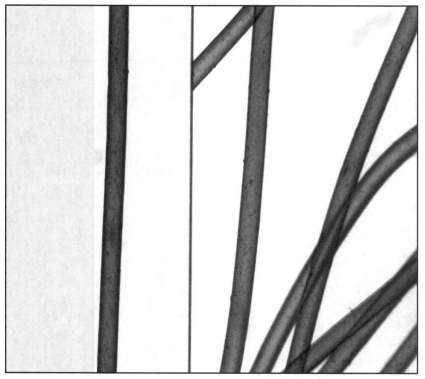

Figure 14.2 *Photomicrograph comparison of fibers: red fiber found in a victim's fingernail (left), and a known fiber sample removed from the suspect's sweater (right).*

E. Polarized Light Microscopy

Various optical properties such as birefringence, dispersion, extinction angle, optic sign, sign of elongation, and refractive indices can be determined using the polarizing microscope. Many fibers can be identified as to general class, by these techniques alone.

F. Instrumental Methods

Various instrumental methods may be used to determine the chemical composition of fiber evidence.

- **Infrared spectroscopy** has become the method of choice in examination of fibers. The advent of microscope sampling with a Fourier transform (Ft) IR spectrometer makes obtaining infrared spectra on even the smallest sample fairly rapid and straightforward. Figure 14.3 shows the FTIR spectra of two common synthetic fibers.

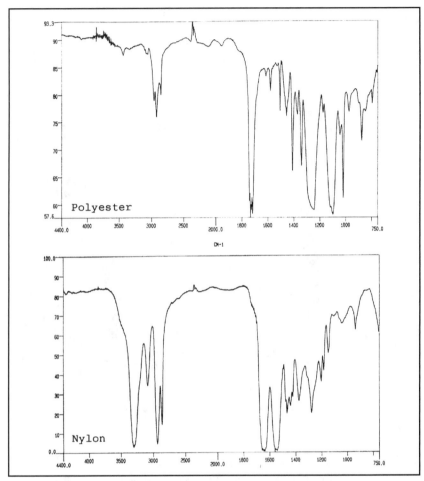

Figure 14.3 *The FTIR spectrum of polyester (top) and nylon (bottom).*

- **Gas chromatography/mass spectrometry (GC/MS)** is not well-suited
  for direct analysis of fibers, but by first pyrolysing the fiber in the injection port of a GC/MS, the fragments produced can be introduced into
  the chromatography column and their chemical nature ascertained from
  their retention time and mass spectra. This technique is very sensitive to
  very small differences in the composition of pyrolysed fiber.
- **Scanning Electron Microscope** with energy-dispersive x-ray (SEM-
  EDX) may be employed to analyze the morphology and elemental composition of the fiber evidence. Atomic absorption (AA) spectroscopy
  can also be employed for elemental composition, but is seldom used in
  forensic laboratories for this purpose.

- **Microspectrophotometer** can provide visible spectra of dyes present in fibers. (See Figure 14.4.) These spectra are then compared to those obtained from control samples to determine similarities in the dye components between evidence and control fibers. Further, since fibers are almost always colored with a combination of several dyes, another dimension is added to comparison when the dyes are extracted and separated into individual components using chromatography. Fibers with colors indistinguishable to the human eye have been found to have been dyed with different dye combinations.

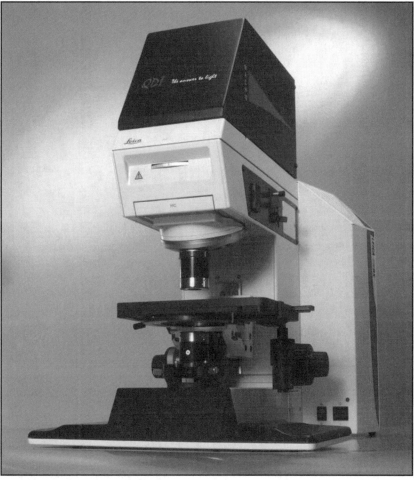

Figure 14.4 The UV and visible light microspectrophotometer.

Chapter 15

Fingerprints

Fingerprints are among the oldest and most valuable types of physical evidence in criminal investigations. The fingerprints of the offender are often found at scenes in connection with a variety of crimes, ranging from larceny or burglary to homicide. Besides their use in linking a suspect to a scene, investigators also use fingerprint comparisons to determine previous arrests, to apprehend fugitives, and to identify unidentified bodies, amnesia victims, and mass disaster victims.

There are three fundamental facts that have made fingerprints good evidence for personal identification and well accepted by the courts:

1. An individual's fingerprint ridges are formed during fetal life, between 100 and 120 days of development, and remain unchanged for the remainder of a person's lifetime.
2. It is generally accepted that fingerprints are unique. No two persons, even identical twins, have identical friction ridge characteristics.
3. Classic fingerprint classification systems and automated fingerprint identification systems (AFIS) allow the development of files containing systematically classified fingerprints. These systems allow for the rapid retrieval of a particular fingerprint card, and AFIS systems allow searching a single latent fingerprint against the ten print cards on file.

In addition, dermal skin will virtually always reform the same friction ridges after being damaged through accident or on purpose. Individuals have inflicted considerable pain on themselves trying to remove their fingerprints with generally disappointing results.

15.1 Nature and Classification of Fingerprint Patterns
A. Fingerprint Patterns
The general ridge patterns observed in fingerprints can be divided into eight basic fingerprint types. (See Figure 15.1.)

1. Loop
The ridges flow inward and then recurve in the direction of the origin. A single delta-shaped divergence must be present in front of the recurving ridges.

*   **Radial loop**—ridges flow from the recurve toward the radius or thumb side of the hand, approximately 5 percent of all fingerprint patterns.
*   **Ulnar loop**—friction ridges flow from and recurve toward the ulna or little finger side of the hand, approximately 60 percent of all fingerprint patterns.

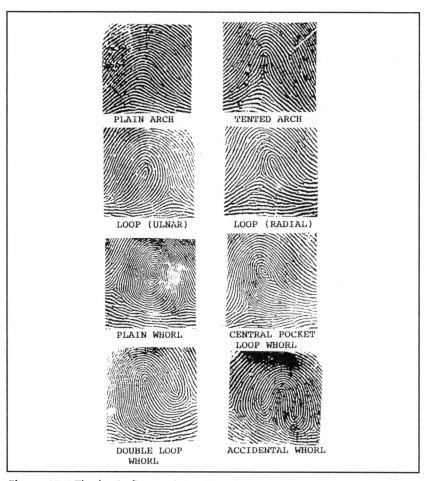

Figure 15.1 The basic fingerprint pattern types.

2. Arch

Ridges enter on one side of the impression and tend to flow out the other side with a rise in the center.

- **Plain arch**—ridges enter, wave or rise, and exit smoothly.
- **Tented arch**—ridges in the center thrust upward to give an appearance similar to a tent. Both types of arches combined comprise approximately 5 percent of all fingerprint patterns.

3. Whorl

At least two delta-shaped divergences are present with recurving ridges in front of each. Whorls comprise approximately 29 percent of all fingerprint patterns.

- **Plain whorl**—one or more ridges form a complete revolution around the center.
- **Central pocket loop whorl**—some ridges form a loop pattern which recurves and surrounds a central whorl.
- **Double loop**—two separate loops are present, which sometimes surround each other.
- **Accidental**—any pattern which does not conform to previously described patterns.

B. Types of Fingerprints

1. Inked fingerprints

Ridge impressions are taken by inking an individual's finger or palm and rolling it across a card, or other smooth surface. It is now becoming common to take so-called live scan fingerprints for control purposes. The finger is placed on a platen and scanned, with the result being an electronic image of the print. This electronic image is generally directly compatible with computerized fingerprint matching systems.

2. Visible (patent) prints

Patent prints are ridge impressions formed by the transfer of a material on the skin, such as paint, blood, ink, or other colored substances, to a receiving surface.

3. Plastic prints

Plastic prints are ridge impressions that are indentations (three-dimensional) and found in soft material such as putty, wax, clay, or other deformable surfaces.

4. Latent prints

Latent fingerprints are finger ridge impressions that are deposited on a surface by the transfer of natural body secretions and which are not readily visible. Latent prints are among the most common type of fingerprint evidence found at crime scenes and must be chemically or physically processed to enhance visibility.

15.2 Collection and Preservation of Fingerprint Evidence

The determination of whether to process an article of evidence for latent fingerprints at the crime scene or to package that article and submit it to the laboratory is largely dependent on the surface involved. Other factors which affect this decision may include the location of the evidence, the environmental conditions where the investigator is working (e.g., outside or inside), the size of the item being processed, and the materials available to the investigator at the scene. The following describe some of the basic procedures used for processing latent fingerprints at a crime scene.

A. Dusting of Nonporous Surfaces

The following procedure outlines the steps for the processing of a nonporous surface using standard fingerprint powder techniques:

1. **Powder**. Choose a fingerprint powder of a contrasting color to the surface being processed. For example, choose Chemist Gray for dark colored surfaces, glass, mirrors or chrome, and black powder for light colored surfaces. Pour a small amount of the powder from the jar onto a piece of paper to ensure that the rest of the powder does not get contaminated.

2. **Brush**. Use a fingerprint brush for initial processing after first shaking out any retained excess powder, dip the brush into the fresh powder and apply the brush to the object. Move the brush it in a rotary motion to pick up the circular patterns of the fingerprints. You will be aided in this process if a flashlight is held to the side and at a low angle to the area being processed. The fingerprint may be enhanced by brushing out excess powder between the friction ridges with a feather duster or fiberglass fingerprint brush.

3. **Numbering**. Number each latent print in sequence using a grease pencil or marker and record that information, as well as careful location of the print, in notes. Photographs should then be taken using both one-to-one (actual size) and overall photography to show the location relative to the object containing the print. With the move towards digital photography, one-to-one has lost its cache; therefore, a close-up high resolution image is fine.

4. **Tape lift**. Position transparent fingerprint tape so that it picks up the grease pencil markings and powdered fingerprint and then it will yield the print's identification number on the completed lift. Lift the fingerprint with the tape and place it on a backing of a contrasting color to the powder. In many instances, a second lift may provide better quality minutiae reproduction than the original lift.

5. **Labeling**. Initial and label all latent lifts. The package label should include the following information: case number, lift/item number, location of the print, date, time, and person lifting the latent print.

B. Alternate Processing Methods

Many techniques are now available for use at the crime scene which extends the capability of the scene investigator.

1. The "super glue wand" for cyanoacrylate fuming

The "super glue wand" is a portable system which allows for fuming of larger items, such as automobiles, and surfaces on nonmovable objects at a crime scene. If used with appropriate safety procedures at the scene, this method offers the advantages of super glue processing which often provides latent print development superior to dusting. Thus the portable wand allows the use of the super glue technique on objects not easily moved to the laboratory in some cases. If, however, the object can be moved, laboratory processing is preferred. Figure 15.2 shows a fuming process using the wand.

2. Alternate light source

Portable alternate light sources, with appropriate filters, used in conjunction with fluorescent chemicals and powders may make it easier to locate latent prints on certain surfaces. Use of an alternate light source to examine an item for latent prints is shown in Figure 15.3.

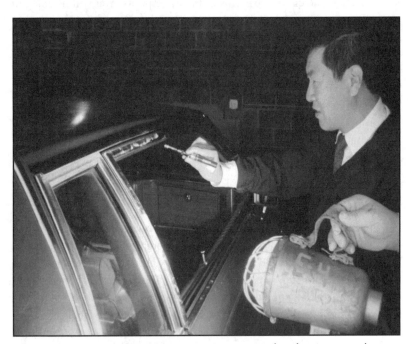

Figure 15.2 *Fingerprint examiner using super glue fuming wand process on a vehicle searching for latent fingerprints.*

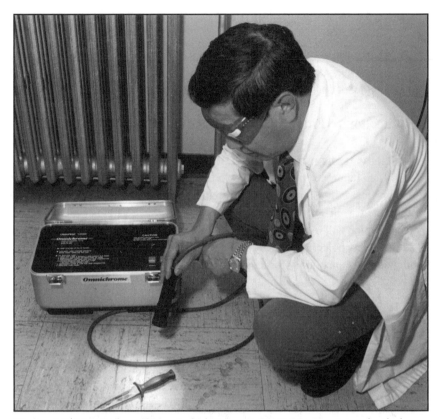

Figure 15.3 *Use of an alternate light source (ALS) to examine a knife for latent fingerprints.*

C. General Recommendations

1. Do not dust visible prints, such as those formed from paint, grease or blood. It will not make them any clearer and may destroy them. Do photograph them and transport the whole article to the laboratory, if possible.
2. Do not use the side of the dusting brush as it will smear the latent print. Use only the end of the brush.
3. Do not dip the brush directly into the bottle containing the fingerprint powder. Do pour a small amount on paper, and dip the brush on that to ensure that the whole bottle does not get contaminated with debris.
4. Do not process wet items. Let them air dry naturally or submit these to the laboratory immediately for special processing.
5. Do not use heat lamps or blowers to accelerate drying, as these may cause excess evaporation of oils and perspiration.

6. Allow items exposed to freezing temperatures to warm up before attempting to process them.
7. Chemical processing or instrumental techniques should be used under the supervision of laboratory personnel, or only after proper training and experience.

D. Collection of Fingerprint Evidence Not Processed at the Scene

1. Items transported to the laboratory

Smaller items not processed by the investigator may be submitted to the laboratory for processing and lifting of latent fingerprints. Bring to the laboratory any item which requires chemical processing, such as paper materials, or evidence which will require alternate light examinations, such as use of the laser. In addition, any object which requires multi-disciplinary examinations should be submitted to the laboratory for these procedures.

1. In all cases, package physical evidence to minimize movement of the object and to immobilize it during transport.
2. Evidence to be processed at the laboratory should be packaged in a manner which avoids friction on the print-bearing surface; abrasion by movement within the packaging could alter or destroy any fingerprints which are present on the item. It is advisable to avoid simply placing the article in a plastic bag as this can also be a source of friction. Figure 15.4 shows the proper packaging of fingerprint evidence (in this case, a knife) for transport to the laboratory.
3. Place latent fingerprint lifts in an appropriately labeled envelope for submission to the laboratory.

2. Post-mortem fingerprints

1. To obtain fingerprints from a deceased person, the investigator must first dry the fingers and palms of the cadaver.
2. The fingers are then inked directly, using an ink roller or ink pad.
3. The investigator then presses each finger into the "fingerprint spoon," (curved metal plate capable of holding a fingerprint card), and releases.
4. Palm prints are taken by inking the palms in the same manner and then rolling a large cylindrical object, such as a beaker or bottle, wrapped in plain bond paper secured by elastic bands, over the palms of the cadaver.
5. If fingers have begun to decompose, as with "floaters," consult examiners at the forensic science laboratory, medical examiner's office or

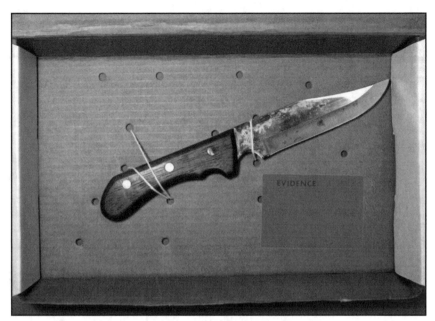

Figure 15.4 *A knife secured and packaged to prevent movement, which could result in loss of, or damage to, physical evidence.*

members of an identification unit as to other methods which may be used to obtain the fingerprints.

15.3 Laboratory Examination of Latent Prints Evidence
A. Processing of Physical Evidence for Latent Fingerprints
Physical evidence submitted to the forensic laboratory can be processed by various methods, depending on the nature of the print and the substrate upon which it is deposited. In addition, photographic techniques may also be employed to enhance visible characteristics. Table 15.1 summarizes some of the common methods used to visualize latent fingerprints. The following describes some of the many methods available for processing in the laboratory.

1. Powder dusting
A powder of contrasting color to the surface being dusted is chosen. Impressions on objects such as metal, plastic, glass, tile and other non-porous surfaces are easily processed with various fingerprint powders. Occasionally, a magnetic fingerprint brush can be used to advantage. The powder is made of fine iron particles which can develop the latent fingerprints on certain surfaces better than traditional fingerprint powders.

Table 15.1
Methods for Visualization of Latent Fingerprints

Methods	Principle	Applicable Surfaces
Powder dusting	Adherence of inert material to fingerprint residues.	Smooth, nonporous surfaces such as metals, glass, plastics, tile, and finished woods.
Oblique lighting and photography	Natural residues of fingerprints.	Smooth and nonreflective surfaces.
Laser or alternate light source	Fluorescent material in fingerprint residues.	Smooth, nonporous, or lightly porous surfaces such as plastic and paper.
Physical developer	Salts in fingerprint residues.	Smooth surfaces.
Crystal (Gentian) violet	Fatty acids and lipids.	Sticky side of tapes.
Iodine fuming	Chemical interaction with fatty acids and lipids.	Smooth surfaces such as paper and human skin.
Ninhydrin	Chemical interaction with amino acids, peptides, and proteins of residues.	Absorbent surfaces such as paper and cardboard.
Super glue	Formation of polymers with amino acids and water.	A wide variety of smooth, nonporous, and slightly porous surfaces including human skin.
Small particle reagent	Fatty acids and lipids.	Nonporous and damp surfaces.
X-ray	Adherence of lead to residues.	Smooth surfaces such as plastic films, polyethylene, and paper.
Vacuum coating	Adherence of gold, silver, or cadmium to residues.	Heat stable nonporous surfaces.

2. Iodine fuming

Vapor from warmed iodine crystals dissolves in the skin oils in a latent print, yielding a yellow brown print. Photograph the developed latent prints immediately, or chemically fix for a permanent record, because they fade rapidly.

3. Ninhydrin and ninhydrin analogues

The ninhydrin reagent is sprayed on the medium and reacts with amino acids and peptides from body secretions, giving a violet color. Placing the object in a humid atmosphere, in the dark, enhances latent print development, which may require up to 48 hours to maximize the quality.

4. Physical Developer

Physical Developer is a complex reagent which uses a chemical couple to deposit metallic silver on a latent print and provides excellent development of certain types of fingerprints. It is one of the few reagents that sometimes work with currency, which is a very difficult surface on which to develop fingerprints.

5. Fluorescent reagents

DFO, Fluorescamine, o-Phthalaldehyde, and 1,2-Indandione reacts almost instantaneously with amines from body secretions, yielding highly fluorescent patterns. These reagents are useful when caused to fluoresce in the dark, thereby removing the interference from multi-colored background surfaces.

6. "Super glue" method

This process relies on the fumes of cyanoacrylic esters (so-called "super glue" is based on cyanoacrylate esters) chemically forming cyanoacrylic polymers in the presence of water and amino acid molecules present in the latent print. This polymer stabilizes the print and is usually white and fairly visible on most surfaces. "Super glue" fuming can also be followed by dusting with various colored or fluorescent powders or swabbing with solutions of fluorescent dyes to enhance visibility.

7. Alternate processing methods

Many laboratories now employ various techniques, relying on technological advances in instrumentation and illumination with great success.

- **Argon laser**. In the proper optical setup, various components of body secretions fluoresce and may be photographed. This technique is non-destructive, but expensive, and requires specialized equipment. Use of fluorescent powders and sprays produce much brighter fluorescence and allow visualization of even very weak prints.

- **X-ray detection**. Prints are dusted with lead powder, producing distinct images on photographic film when exposed to x-rays. This is useful on many objects and occasionally on skin.
- **Vacuum coating**. A metal vapor is produced in a vacuum chamber and allowed to deposit on an object thought to hold a latent print. Prints on paper, fabrics, and plastics have been developed in this manner.
- **Alternative light source illumination**. Use of various wavelengths of intense light to illuminate a latent fingerprint may enhance the print. Varying the wavelength and intensity of light and the filters used to view the print may reduce or eliminate background or contaminant interferences.
- **Special chambers**. These control vapor pressure and humidity and are used to make cyanoacrylate processing even more effective.

B. Development of Latent Prints on Skin

Prints on skin can be difficult to obtain, especially if the cadaver has been exposed to adverse environmental conditions.

1. Iodine-silver method

A thin, polished silver plate is pressed on an area which has been iodine-fumed and then exposed to light, which turns it black at ridge locations.

2. Cyanoacrylate fuming and laser/alternative light source detection

The areas of interest on the body are tented and fumed with super glue and then dusted with fluorescent powders, which are easily detected with alternate light sources.

3. Decomposed bodies

Some laboratories are equipped to make identifications of fingerprints from decomposed bodies. Silicone or glycerin may be injected into the fingers; in some cases, the skin is removed, mounted on a glass slide and photographed from the back of the skin, thus making the patterns visible. Ultimately, identifications are made in many cases, even with badly decomposed bodies.

C. Comparison of Fingerprints

Comparison of fingerprints for identification is based on the recognition of general patterns and minutiae (ridge ends and bifurcations). Figure 15.5 depicts an example of a fingerprint comparison chart.

A 1973 International Association for Identification (IAI) study concluded that no valid basis exists for requiring a predetermined minimum number of friction ridge characteristics to be present in two impressions in order to establish positive identity. The IAI has officially rejected the notion of "possible" or "probable" identifications of questioned fingerprints. In the August 1979, *Identification News*, the IAI reported the passage of Resolution VII, which states in part:

> Whereas the delegates of the International Association for Identification assembled in their 64th annual conference in Phoenix, Arizona, August 2, 1979, state unanimously that friction ridge identifications are positive, and officially oppose any testimony or reporting of possible, probable or likely friction ridge identification.

D. Fingerprint Classification Systems

The modified Henry System is the most common in use in the United States today. It is a ten-finger classification system which allows the examiner to locate a reasonable number of appropriate fingerprint cards with which to make the comparison, even with very large files.

E. Automated Fingerprint Identification Systems (AFIS)

Virtually every jurisdiction now has access to computer-based identification systems for the storage and retrieval of fingerprint files and the comparison of latent fingerprints with print records in these files. This has enormously increased the value of latent fingerprint evidence.

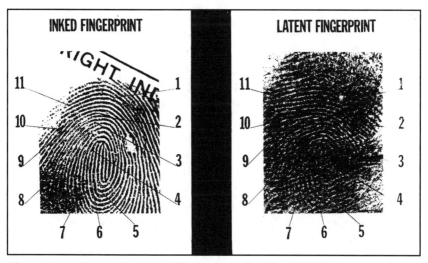

Figure 15.5 *Fingerprint comparison chart showing the points of comparison, which indicate a positive identification.*

1. Types of AFIS systems

a. Index systems. These systems store information such as MO (modus operandi), individual characteristics, fingerprint classifications and other information. Primarily, these systems serve as a computerized method of sorting information available to the examiner prior to a manual search of fingerprint files, thus eliminating some individual cards.

b. Ridge-angle systems. The angle of ridge flow at certain points on a ten-print card are stored. This information, combined with stored classification information, allows for comparison to and search of the reference file.

c. Encoded minutiae systems. Ten-print cards or latent fingerprints are scanned and the minutiae (bifurcations and ridge endings) of the print are mapped as to location and angle, and the data stored in a convenient format. Bifurcations are areas in the print where a single ridge splits into two ridges. Each result may be examined and edited, if necessary. The fingerprint(s) can then be compared against a stored file.

2. Use of AFIS

In addition to automating the classification and filing of ten-print cards, AFIS systems may have the following capabilities:

1. Search and comparison of ten-print card against known identification files.
2. Comparison of an unidentified latent print against a ten-print card in the file.
3. Search of a latent print against the unidentified or known latent prints on file.
4. Input into the file of unidentified latent prints.
5. Image enhancement to clarify the latent by background removal, "fill-in," or elimination of dust particles or other interferences in the latent fingerprint.

As AFIS systems have grown and developed interconnectivity, their value has increased enormously, and they have become a powerful investigative tool. Most modern AFIS systems "improve themselves" when an individual is arrested and fingerprinted for the second time and subsequent times. The AFIS system evaluates the quality of each print in the subsequent card, and if found to have superior clarity, will be substituted into the database.

Chapter 16

Firearms

Investigators often find firearms evidence, such as weapons, bullets, casings and impact or splatter patterns, at the scenes of violent crimes. This type of evidence may also be recovered during the investigation of other types of crime, such as a drug-related incident, robbery or burglary. Once firearm evidence has been located at a crime scene, personnel should follow procedures to ensure the safety of investigators and laboratory personnel, and to preserve any other types of physical evidence which may be present on the firearm as well as any firearms evidence.

16.1 The Nature of Firearms Evidence

Major components of a firearm and of ammunition are briefly described by the following sections.

A. Barrel

1. Rifled barrel

A rifled barrel is the hollow tube through which the projectile travels when exiting the weapon. A series of spiral (helical) grooves cut inside the barrel, leave raised areas called "lands"; these impress markings on the projectile (bullet) which can be used to associate a bullet to a particular barrel. Similarly the indented areas (grooves) in the barrel cause a raised area on the projectile which may also carry stria useful in association.

2. Smooth-bore barrel

No lands or grooves present in a smooth-bore barrel. Shotguns, very old weapons and homemade weapons (zip guns) may not have rifling.

3. Caliber

The gun barrel diameter measured, in hundredths of an inch, between opposite lands in a rifled barrel is called the caliber. In much of the rest of the world this distance may be expressed in millimeters.

B. Components of the Firing Mechanism

The firing pin, breechblock, ejector, and extractor often make characteristic marks on cartridge cases that can be compared with marks on test-fired cartridge cases to associate a cartridge casing to a weapon from which it has been fired.

C. Ammunition (See Figure 16.1)

1. Projectiles

The most common projectiles fired by a firearm are lead or lead alloy cylinders. Ammunition that produces pellets or slugs or nails or other objects as projectiles is also found at crime scenes.

2. Jacket

Some bullets are either completely or partially encased in a harder metal, usually copper or other metallic alloy.

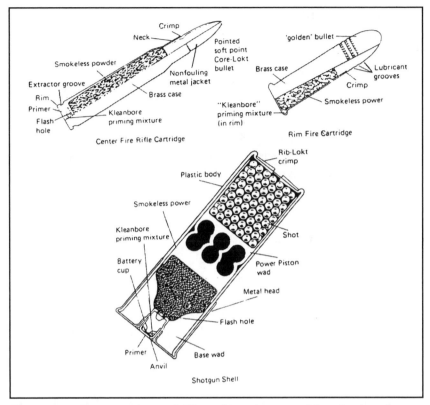

Figure 16.1 Cutaway views of rifle and handgun cartridges (top) and shotgun shell (below).

3. Cartridge case

The cartridge case contains the ignition system and powder and is usually made of brass or other corrosion-resistant alloy. Shotgun casings have a metal end fixed to a cardboard or plastic tube.

4. Primer

A shock sensitive chemical mixture which detonates when struck by the firing pin and ignites the powder.

5. Powder

The gases formed by the rapid burning of the powder force the projectile along its path through the barrel; smokeless powder (primarily nitrocellulose) is used in modern cartridges. See Chapter 18, *Gunshot Residue*, for further information about primer and powder compositions.

16.2 Collection of Firearms Evidence
A. Documentation

1. Photograph any located firearm as found at the crime scene and note the location of fired bullets on any sketches made of the scene (see Figure 16.2).
2. Take complete notes, including information on: the time the weapon was found, the condition of the weapon (i.e., safety on or off, hammer cocked, slide back, cylinder position jammed, and so forth), the position of any live rounds or cartridge casings near or inside the weapon, and all identification data on the weapon, including make, model, caliber and serial number.

B. Collection of Weapons

1. A firearm found at a crime scene may contain fingerprints. Bearing this in mind, handle only the weapon surfaces that normally would not yield fingerprints, such as checkered grips, edges of the trigger guard or knurled, finned or roughly machined surfaces manufactured into the weapon for the purpose of creating friction for gripping.
2. The investigator should also be alert for the presence of other trace evidence such as DNA from hair, blood, tissue, bone fragments, or paint, glass, fibers and other traces. Under no circumstances should the weapon be cleaned or wiped off, as it may destroy this trace evidence. If the investigator suspects that these materials may be present, he should communicate this fact on the examination request form or directly to those conducting the examination.
3. When, for safety purposes, the weapon is unloaded at the crime scene, the investigator should note the location of fired and unfired cartridges. Sketch the cylinder when dealing with revolvers, noting the type and condition of each chamber. In dealing with pistols and other weapons that load from a magazine, remember that removing the magazine may leave a cartridge in the chamber which must also be unloaded. It is not necessary to unload the cartridges from the magazine after it has been removed from the weapon. Remember that magazines and cartridges may also provide fingerprints.
4. Do not allow anything to be placed in the barrel which might damage the rifling on the inside of the barrel.
5. Since the identification data such as serial number, make, model, and caliber have already been recorded in the investigator's notes, it is not necessary to mark the weapon physically for identification. The excep-

tion to this would be if the serial number is defaced or is no longer clearly visible. However, attach a tag to the weapon containing such information as the case number, investigating officer, type of crime, and the location where it was collected.

6. If the weapon is to be transported to a laboratory, immobilize it to prevent friction from obliterating latent fingerprints which may be present, destroying other trace evidence or damaging the weapon itself. The most common method of doing this is to mount the weapon on cardboard with string. Special boxes for this purpose are also commercially available.

C. Collection of Bullets and Cartridge Cases

1. Do not mark cartridge casings and bullets in any way. Place in individual envelopes, mark with identification data, and seal. This protects the bullets or casings from scratching each other and thereby altering or obliterating the marks that the firearms examiner will examine for possible identification. Figures 16.3 and 16.4 show the proper packaging of firearms evidence.

Figure 16.2 *Spent bullets and casings were found at a shooting scene.*

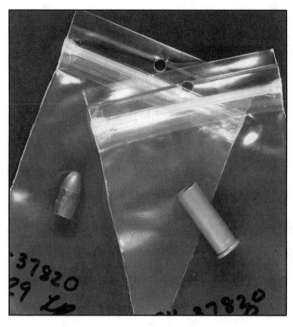

Figure 16.3
A bullet and a cartridge case packaged to prevent damage to markings.

2.   If any additional ammunition is found at the crime scene, collect it for use as a known standard.

D. Evidence Requiring Special Handling

1. Loaded firearms

If the weapon is not unloaded at the crime scene for any reason, the individual collecting the weapon should personally transport it to the laboratory at the first opportunity. Any packaging should bear the words, *"Caution: Loaded Firearm,"* in plain sight. Figure 16.4 is an example of an appropriately packaged weapon. Normally, loaded firearms are not accepted at the laboratory without prior clearance from appropriate laboratory personnel; the investigating officer should call before bringing such items for examination.

2. Weapons in water

In the event that the weapon is recovered under water, transport it to the laboratory as soon as possible before further deterioration from rust can occur. If it is not possible to transport the weapon during normal laboratory hours to receive immediate attention, follow special procedures to preserve the firearm from further deterioration. If the firearm is located in water, use a container with some of the water to keep the firearm submerged and out of the air. Rapid corro-

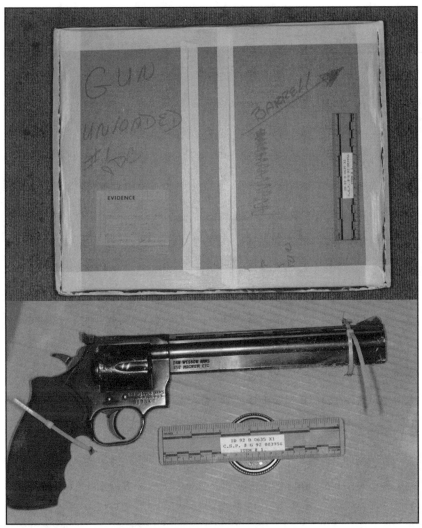

Figure 16.4 A firearm packaged and labeled for safety and to prevent loss or damage of physical evidence associated with the weapon.

sion will occur if oxygen from the air is allowed to reach the metal, which could adversely affect any comparisons of bullets or cartridge cases to the weapon.

3. Bullets

Spent bullets obtained from victims at autopsies must be gently removed from the body to prevent any damage to potentially useful marks. Even a slight pressure can mark the bearing surface and destroy microscopic stria (scratches).

If the projectile is embedded in bone, the bone should be cut out and then the bullet can be removed without damage.

4. Firearm adjustment or testing

Under no circumstances should any firearm mechanism be adjusted or manipulated in any manner except that which is necessary to unload and to make the firearm safe for transport. Do not test fire any firearm which is to be submitted for examination. It is important to submit firearms for examination to a local firearms laboratory. Even if the firearm is not pertinent to the case in question, because of extensive firearms databases it may be possible to associate it with another event.

16.3 Laboratory Examination of Firearms Evidence
A. Information Obtained from Firearms Evidence (See Table 16.1)

- **Bullets and other projectiles**—Caliber, manufacturer, type and make of weapon, pellet or shot size.
- **Cartridge or shotgun shell case**—Type of weapon, caliber, gauge of shotgun, whether factory or handloaded.
- **Weapon**—Manufacturer, functional characteristics.

B. Examination for Identification (Individualization)

It is the examination of the land and groove impressions found on the bullet, and the markings on a casing that produce the answer to the question, "Was a particular bullet or casing fired in/from a particular weapon?" The manufacturing process used to machine the rifling in a barrel, although within certain specified tolerances, produces unique barrels due to wear on the cutting tools, variations in the metal of the barrel and other variables. This, coupled with normal wear caused by the firing of the weapon, causes each barrel to mark any projectile it fires in a particular manner. The firearms examiner recognizes unique markings by examining the striations on the bullet caused by minute imperfections in the lands and grooves of the barrel. Similarly, the wear of the firing mechanism and other mechanical portions of the weapon produce individual markings on the cartridge casings that an expert can also examine and compare.

1. Bullet comparisons

Bullets are "test fired" from a weapon, usually into a water tank, to obtain projectiles characteristic of that weapon. These are compared to those found at scenes or in bodies.

Table 16.1
Information Obtained from Firearms Evidence

Characteristics for Bullet Identification
A. Manufacturer marks
    1. Shape (round nose, flat point, etc.)
    2. Weight (in grams)
    3. Caliber (diameter)
    4. Cannelures (grooves or crimps)
    5. Composition (lead, alloys, etc.)
B. Firearms rifling impressions
    1. Number (of lands and grooves)
    2. Width (of lands and grooves)
    3. Depth (of lands and grooves)
    4. Twist (direction of pitch—left/right)
    5. Pitch (angle of spiral from the horizontal)
C. Individual striations and markings
    1. Striations impressed by the barrel
    2. Striations due to wear and use
    3. Striations due to neglect and abuse
    4. Cone markings on bullet nose
    5. Results of misalignment

Characteristics for Cartridge Case Identification
A. Manufacturer markings
    1. Trademarks (manufacturer's name, headstamp)
    2. Shape (rimmed, rimless, straight, bottleneck)
    3. Caliber (usually on center fire cases)
    4. Composition (brass, cupronickel, etc.)
    5. Other markings
B. Individual mark impressions
    1. Firing pin impressions
    2. Breech face impression markings
    3. Extractor marks
    4. Ejector marks
    5. Marks from unusual models

a. Class characteristics. Caliber and type of bullet, metallic composition, weight, size and shape, and manufacturers' markings are important class characteristics.

b. Individual bullet characteristics. Striation marks resulting from the passage of the bullet over the individual weapon's lands and grooves as it is driven down the barrel are used for individualization; matching of patterns is done using a comparison microscope. Firearms examiners can often positively identify a particular weapon as having fired a particular projectile. Figure 16.6 shows an example of a comparison of two bullets that were fired from the same weapon, as it appears under the comparison microscope.

2. Cartridge case comparisons

Markings on an evidence casing as a result of firing in a weapon should be the same as on cartridge casings recovered from test firing that weapon. The markings on the evidence and test cartridges are also compared using the comparison microscope.

a. Firing pin impressions. The negative impression of the firing pin in the primer cup can vary in size, shape, impression and location, or may show imperfections from production or use. See Figure 16.7.

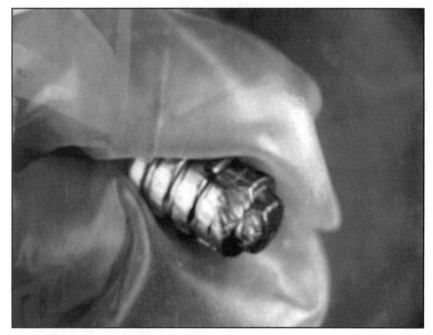

Figure 16.5 A spent bullet was recovered from victim's body by the medical examiner.

b. Breechface marks. When the shell or cartridge case is forced backward during the firing process, individual striations from the file or cutting tool used to machine the breechface are impressed into the head (breechface) of the cartridge case.

c. Extractor and ejector marks. The surface of the extractor and ejector mechanism may possess individual characteristics from manufacturing which will transfer to cartridge casings.

d. Chamber marks. The force of the explosion causes expansion of the case within the chamber, which may impress irregularities of that chamber onto the casing.

e. Miscellaneous markings. Individual markings due to scraping, scratching, and pressure, particularly in semiautomatic and repeating weapons.

Extensive collections of searchable cartridge case images, and sometimes bullet striation images, are maintained in many jurisdictions. A national interconnection between many of these image databases analogous to AFIS and CODIS is called NIBIN, and is now available in most forensic laboratories.

Figure 16.6
A positive match between a questioned bullet (left of vertical line) and a known test bullet (right of vertical line) as seen through a comparison microscope.

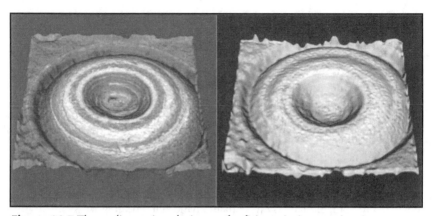

Figure 16.7 Three-dimensional views of a firing pin impression in a cartridge case using IBIS Trax-3D.

Chapter 17

Glass

Glass evidence is encountered in a wide variety of cases. For example, hit-and-run cases often provide windshield or headlamp glass as evidence; burglaries may involve window glass; and assault cases may involve bottle glass. Examination of penetrations (holes), bullet holes and breakage patterns in glass can have major value in incident reconstruction. The abundance of glass as evidence is attributable to several factors, including:

- Glass evidence is very common because it occurs in many varieties and has many uses.
- Although glass is very stable it is also normally quite brittle and easily broken, producing fragments of varying size.
- Small glass particles can transfer, and will often adhere to items of clothing without being noticed.

17.1 Nature of Glass Evidence
A. Stability
Glass is quite stable and is unaffected by common chemical, physical, and normal environmental conditions. Glass does not deteriorate or change from the time of deposit to the time of collection and laboratory analysis.

B. Composition
Glass, although mainly silicon dioxide, is produced in a wide range of compositions and by several different processes. There is also a range of chemical compositions within each type of glass, and manufacturing methods can also affect the composition of glass. This compositional variation is due to uncontrollable variations in the raw materials and the lack of homogeneity during the melting process. Other contamination of the molten glass during manufacture is also possible. Such compositional variations enhance the value of glass as physical evidence.

C. Patterns
Fracture patterns and fracture marks on broken glass often play a crucial role in reconstruction of events.

17.2 Documentation and Collection of Glass Evidence
A. Documentation of Glass Fracture Patterns

1. Photograph any glass fractures from both sides, both close up and from a sufficient distance to provide context. This will allow visualization of the whole pattern to determine the direction of force and sequence of fractures. Include a scale in some of the photographs.
2. Thoroughly document radial fractures, concentric fractures, rib marks, fracture distribution, and other patterns before collecting the glass evidence.
3. Broken glass may yield information about the direction and speed of a projectile and, in the case of multiple projectiles, the sequence of events.

B. Reconstruction of Glass Evidence
The possibility of a reconstruction to produce a physical match needs to be considered at the time of collection. These possibilities apply primarily to situations involving larger pieces, but this is occasionally possible even with relatively small fragments found on other evidence.

1. If pieces of glass large enough to contain fingerprints or blood or tissue are located at the point of entry of a crime scene, then examination of the glass for fingerprints or biological traces should be the first consideration.
2. If a physical match is possible, then the collection of fragments should be as complete and thorough as possible. In addition, conduct a detailed documentation of each piece of glass before moving the glass.
3. If samples are to be taken from a broken window, each of the major pieces should be individually identified, marked and documented prior to removal and packaging. Any notes and photographs should clearly show the orientation of each major piece, and the inside and outside should be labeled.

C. Collection of Glass Evidence

1. If the glass evidence is in small pieces, collect all pieces, as a physical match may be possible. If the article is large, collect known standards from the area of the break for possible future comparison to glass found on a suspect. Mark the known standards, if appropriate, to indicate

Figure 17.1 *Examination of point of entry in a break in.*

which side of the glass faced outside and which side faced inside. If fingerprints are not a consideration, package the glass by taping the pieces to a rigid surface, after cushioning to prevent further damage.

2. Plastic vials are suitable containers for collecting smaller pieces of glass. Only a single piece should be placed in a vial unless some means of keeping pieces separate is employed.

3. Very small pieces of glass are unlikely to break in transit and can be grouped together and submitted in druggist folds or plastic vials.

4. When clothing and other items are thought to possibly contain small glass fragments, technicians should submit them to the laboratory with minimum handling so that the trace evidence collection can be done under the best possible conditions. Individually wrap these items in clean brown paper, if possible, before sealing in a paper bag to prevent loss of small fragments of glass during transport or mixing of glass evidence from different items if more than one is placed in a larger container.

17.3 Laboratory Analysis of Glass Evidence
A. Types of Examinations Conducted

The forensic laboratory may carry out two major types of examination on glass. The first type determines whether the known and questioned samples could share a common origin (classification) and sometimes individualization by jigsaw match. Classification is usually done by determination of the physical, optical, and chemical properties of the glass. The second type of examination is reconstruction, which may provide useful information in the attempt to reconstruct the incident which caused the glass damage. In addition, never overlook the potential value of glass as a carrier of latent fingerprints. Any fragment of glass large enough to hold a latent print should be visually examined or processed for latent fingerprints.

B. Methods of Examinations

1. Macroscopic examination

The first stage in the laboratory examination of glass is a visual inspection to determine the gross characteristics of each sample. It may be possible to eliminate some samples from further consideration by determination of the basic properties of the glass, such as color, thickness, and texture. If samples cannot be eliminated, then consider the possibility of a physical match.

2. Physical match

Glass breaks in a random fashion, resulting in complex fracture surfaces that will often be unique upon careful examination.

Physical matching is the simplest comparison for determining commonality of origin with glass samples. There is a reasonable chance of success with a physical (jigsaw) match when the sample pieces are fairly large. However, if there are a large number of small pieces, then the chances of finding a physical match are greatly diminished.

To make a physical match, the known and questioned samples are brought into close proximity. The surface markings and the contours of the corresponding edges are examined. The fracture edges of glass samples are stable and often have a large amount of contour detail. Therefore, the overall contours of the glass, as well as the marks on the fracture surface, must correspond.

3. Glass chemical and physical properties

Glass is chemically complex and exists in many different formulations, with variations being present within a given formulation. Subtle differences in the chemical composition of a glass are reflected in the physical properties of the glass. Detection of slight differences in physical properties between glass samples is often easier than chemical analysis of the samples. The physical properties examined may be divided into two classes: optical and non-optical properties.

a. Optical properties. The way in which a substance interacts with light determines its optical properties. It is well known that glass will bend light that passes through it. The measurable property of glass resulting from this bending is called the Refractive Index (RI) of the glass. The methods used in the forensic laboratory to compare glasses take advantage of this important characteristic.

i. When the RI of a glass is exactly equal to that of a liquid in which it is immersed, the glass will become invisible. This effect is used by putting chips of the known and unknown samples side-by-side in liquids of the same refractive index. Their relative appearances are noted particularly when the RI of the liquid is close to that of one of the glass chips.

ii. It is possible to vary the RI of a liquid by heating it on a hot stage while observing the glass chips under the microscope. In this way an examiner may determine if the two chips have similar or different refractive indices. Only if the refractive indices are the same can the two glass chips share a common origin.

b. Non-optical properties. Three non-optical physical properties are used in comparing glass samples: hardness, density and chemical composition.

i. Hardness. The hardness of a material may be measured on several different scales. However, most glass samples fall within a narrow range and this is not a particularly useful means of comparison.

ii. Density. The density of a material is its mass per unit volume. The densities of two small fragments of glass may be compared by placing one of the fragments in a liquid having a density greater than the glass so the fragment will float. A liquid with a density less than that of the fragment is then added gradually, with mixing, until the fragment is suspended in the resulting mixture of liquids and shows no tendency to rise or sink. At this time, the other fragment is added to the liquid; if the second glass is from the same or a similar source it will behave similarly (i.e., be suspended).

iii. Trace element analysis. Because glass is made primarily from sand, the specific origin of that sand will affect its exact chemical composition. Several modern analytical techniques can measure concentrations of a large number of trace elements (20 or more) which commonly occur in glass. Examination of this trace element profile can very often differentiate glass samples whose other properties are identical. Where the elemental profile proves very similar, it adds considerable weight to the possibility of common origin.

C. Glass Fracture Patterns

When force is applied to glass, there is an initial stretching of the surface on the side opposite to the applied force. Once the elastic limit of the glass has been exceeded, radial cracks form, looking much like the spokes of a wheel. As the force continues to further deform the glass, concentric cracks begin to form on the same side as the applied force, since this surface of the glass has now been placed under tension. Thus, the surface opposite the force under tension breaks first. Note that the concentric cracks, being roughly circular in shape, have as their center the original point of impact. Generally, from glass patterns, a criminalist can make a number of determinations about the events that caused the fracture.

1. Determination of the direction of force

a. Crater at the point of impact. A projectile passing through or striking, but not penetrating through, the glass will leave a cone-shaped crater with the smaller diameter on the same side as the applied force and the larger diameter on the side opposite the applied force.

b. Radial crack edges. Examination of the edge surfaces (the area which was within the glass) of the various fractures will also yield information on the direction of force. The "Three R Rule" can be of assistance in this problem: "Radial cracks will have right angles on the reverse side of the applied force." If the observer looks at the edges of a radial crack, C-shaped lines will be seen, with one end of the "C" being at a 90-degree angle to the surface opposite the applied force. The converse of this rule is true when looking at the edges of the concentric fractures due to the physics involved in the actual fracture; that is, concentric cracks will have right angles on the side of the force.

c. "Blow back" effect. Small particles of glass will be sprayed back toward the direction of applied force in any glass fracture. These particles may be found in the hair or garments of the person breaking the glass and, as such, should be compared to the glass standards taken from the crime scene.

2. Determination of the sequence of multiple fractures

The order of occurrence can be determined by observation of the fracture lines. Once the initial fracture has been made, subsequent fracture lines will terminate at any original fracture lines they encounter. Thus, observation of these fracture endings will provide some sequence information. A series of glass fractures from which the sequence was determined is shown in Figure 17.2.

3. Direction of travel of the break

Examination of the edge of a broken piece of glass shows curved, rib-shaped lines which are perpendicular to the glass surface where the crack began and nearly parallel at the end of the crack. This can be used to determine whether the break was inward or outward, assuming that it is known which side of the glass was originally inside or outside.

Figure 17.2 Reconstruction of the sequence of bullet holes in a windshield. The sequence of shots fired through this glass was determined by examination of the fracture lines.

Chapter 18

Gunshot Residue

Synopsis
18.1 Source of Gunshot Residue
    A. Primer
    B. Propellant (Powder)
        1. Black powder
        2. Smokeless powder (virtually all modern cartridges use smokeless powder)
    C. Lubricants
    D. Metallic Materials
18.2 Collection of Gunshot Residue
    A. GSR Collection Kits
        1. Adhesive discs
        2. Swabs
    B. Gunshot Residue on Other Items of Evidence
18.3 Laboratory Analysis of Gunshot Residue
    A. Microscopic Analysis
    B. Chemical Tests for Nitrates and Nitrites
    C. Detection of Primer Residues
        1. Microchemical tests
        2. Atomic absorption (AA) or Inductively Coupled Plasma (ICP) Spectroscopic techniques
        3. Scanning electron microscope/energy dispersive x-ray analysis (SEM-EDX)
        4. Neutron activation analysis (NAA)
        5. Gas chromatography/mass spectrometer (GC/MS)
        6. High performance liquid chromatography (HPLC)
        7. Micellar electrokinetic capillary electrophoresis (MECE)
    D. GSR Pattern Analysis
        1. Direct contact
        2. Close range (1–6 inches)
        3. Medium range (1-$\frac{1}{2}$ to 4 feet)
        4. Long range (greater than 4 feet)
        5. Use of Greiss reagent and sodium rhodizinate reagent

When a firearm is discharged, it creates gases, soot, vaporized primer components and unburned or partially burned gunpowder, resulting from the detonation of the primer and the burning of gunpowder. Most of these materials are propelled forward with the projectile toward the target; at the same time, some of these materials are blown backwards onto the shooter. These materials constitute the major components of gunshot residue (GSR). If samples are collected from the hands or clothing of the shooter, before washing or loss by other means, GSR may be detected on these samples. They may also be found on a relatively close target surrounding a bullet hole. The detection of GSR may aid in the identification of a shooter or the reconstruction of a shooting incident.

18.1 Source of Gunshot Residue

Gunshot residue (GSR) can originate from the primer, propellant, lubricant and metals from the ammunition and barrel of a weapon. The following are the major sources of these residues.

A. Primer

Primers consist of four basic components which may have some of the following ingredients:

1. Initiating explosive—Lead styphnate, lead azide, diazodinitrophenol.
2. Oxidizing agent—Barium nitrate, calcium peroxide, magnesium peroxide and manganese dioxide.
3. Fuel—Antimony sulfide, calcium silicide, aluminum, titanium, zirconium and lead thiocyanate.
4. Sensitizing agent—Tetracene, powdered glass, titanium and calcium silicide.

B. Propellant (Powder)

1. Black powder

75 percent potassium nitrate, 15 percent sulfur, 10 percent charcoal.

2. Smokeless powder (virtually all modern cartridges use smokeless powder)

Nitrocellulose (single base); Nitrocellulose and nitroglycerin (double base).

C. Lubricants

Materials used to ease the bullet into or out of the casing, anti-friction agents to speed the bullet down the barrel, residues of gun oils and cleaning materials, and additives used in shaping and compounding the propellant.

D. Metallic Materials

Metal from barrel, projectile, bullet, jacket, and casing metals: lead, copper and trace elements such as zinc, antimony, arsenic, bismuth, and chromium.

18.2 Collection of Gunshot Residue
A. GSR Collection Kits

Two common methods for the collection of GSR are used, depending upon the method(s) of analysis that will be used. It is important to note that any activity such as rapid hand movement and especially washing removes gunshot residue from the hands. Thus, the investigator should conduct the collection of gunshot residue evidence as soon as possible after firing, and always before fingerprinting.

1. Adhesive discs

Adhesive discs are used to collect gunshot residue for analysis by scanning electron microscopy (SEM). Commercially available kits are sold which contain either two or four discs per kit.

1. Pat each hand and palm with the adhesive disc to collect particles of gunshot residue. Each hand should be patted until well after the adhesive properties of the disc appear to be lost. At this point no further sampling should be conducted with that disc.
2. The disc collection technique must be done before any other sampling technique in order to preserve the gunshot residue particles. Figure 18.1 shows a typical SEM collection disc and the collection of gunshot residue using one of these SEM discs.

2. Swabs

Swabs are used to collect gunshot residue for analysis by an Atomic Absorption Spectrometer (AA) or other elemental analysis techniques. Commercial kits are available that contain six or seven test tubes with swabs.

1. The test tubes should be labeled with various areas of the hand (left palm, left back, right palm and right back) in order for the investigator to use that particular swab and return it to the test tube after swabbing the corresponding hand area.
2. Gloves which are supplied with the kits must be worn by the individual conducting the test. The swabs are removed from the test tube and moistened with 5 percent nitric acid solution, which is also supplied.
3. The specific area of the hand is then swabbed. If any material such as blood is observed on the hand area to be sampled, swab the material and record this information on the data sheet provided.

Figure 18.2 shows the contents of a commercially available gunshot residue collection kit.

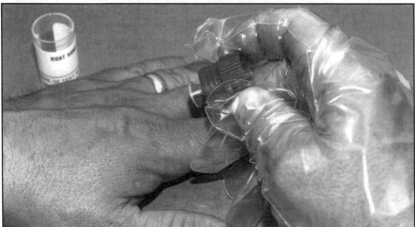

Figure 18.1 A gunshot residue evidence collection disc for SEM analysis (top) and the proper method for collection of GSR evidence using this disc (bottom).

B. Gunshot Residue on Other Items of Evidence

Other items of evidence, such as clothing, gloves, a towel or a vehicle, may contain GSR which the investigator or technician can collect and analyze.

1.   If the item is small, it is best to submit the evidence to the laboratory without sampling. Package items to limit their movement or possible loss of residue. Package clothing flat and wrap with clean paper. Take care to limit direct contact of the surfaces suspected of containing GSR with packaging.

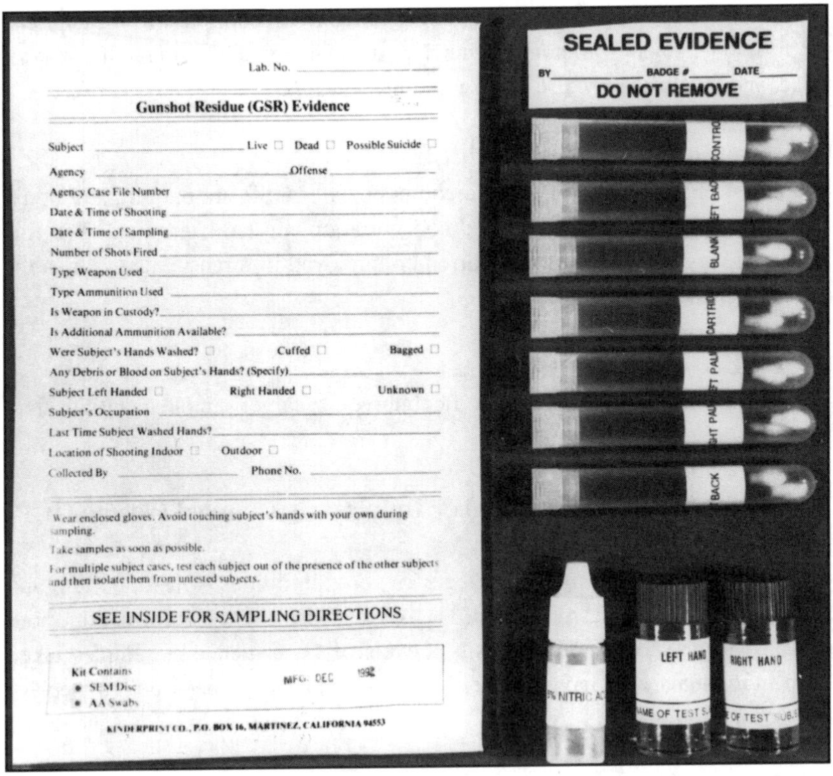

Figure 18.2 *A commercial kit for collection of gunshot residue from hands for elemental analysis examination.*

2. Sample large items which cannot be submitted using the available GSR collection kits, as described above. Since the commercially available kits have pre-labeled containers, it is important to remember to match the swab or disc with the specific origin being sampled.

18.3 Laboratory Analysis of Gunshot Residue
A. Microscopic Analysis
Examination for the presence of gunpowder particles, smudges, and burns around a bullet hole or in swabbings from the hands is aided by the use of low power magnification.

B. Chemical Tests for Nitrates and Nitrites
There are several reagents which react with nitrate or nitrite components of GSR to give a chromophoric (colored) pattern. This type of testing is useful for show-

ing the distribution of residue on clothing, or as a screening test to locate areas for further testing. Commonly occurring substances such as cigarette smoke, urine, and fertilizer may also react with these reagents.

C. Detection of Primer Residues

The major characteristic in organic components of GSR are barium, antimony, and lead, and their distribution and concentration can be determined. The following are some of the methods currently employed in forensic laboratories for detecting these components.

1. Microchemical tests

These tests may be highly specific, but require larger sample quantities than instrumental methods.

2. Atomic absorption (AA) or Inductively Coupled Plasma (ICP) Spectroscopic techniques

Atomic absorption method detects low concentrations of lead, barium and antimony on the samples submitted. The AA test does not give information about patterns of gunshot residue deposits. Levels of trace metals in samples taken from individuals who have not fired weapons must have been determined for proper interpretation of AA results.

3. Scanning electron microscope/energy dispersive x-ray analysis (SEM-EDX)

Gunshot residue particles can be identified by scanning electron microscopy by observing their nearly unique morphology. These particles are further analyzed by x-ray analysis for their elemental composition. The combination of a particle containing the elements of lead, barium and antimony with a distinct morphology confirms the presence of gunshot residue. This method can be time consuming and the cost of the instrumentation is high. Figure 18.4 shows a typical gunshot residue particle as seen using a SEM.

4. Neutron activation analysis (NAA)

Neutron activation analysis is an extremely sensitive instrumental method which requires the use of a nuclear reactor. The NAA technique can detect very low concentrations of metals, but it is now rarely used in the forensic field because of the equipment required and the complex test procedures.

Figure 18.3 *A forensic chemist conducts SEM-EDX analysis of GSR (gunshot residue) samples.*

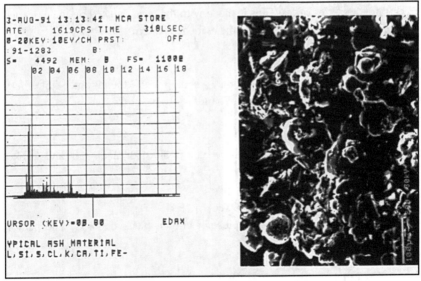

Figure 18.4 *Scanning electron micrograph of a gunshot residue particle (right) and elemental analysis of a particle (left).*

5. Gas chromatography/mass spectrometer (GC/MS)

This combination of instruments allows the separation and identification of the volatile components in gunpowder residues. Thermally stable organic components are analyzed by this technique.

6. High performance liquid chromatography (HPLC)

This technique can separate and identify organic components in GSR which would not pass through a GC/MS.

7. Micellar electrokinetic capillary electrophoresis (MECE)

This newer technique provides high component resolution on micro-samples of gunpowder and its residues. It has the advantage that it can be used for both inorganic and organic residues.

D. GSR Pattern Analysis

Gunshot residue pattern analysis is valuable in the reconstruction of shooting events, especially in distance estimation. Interpretations are dependent upon the weapon used, type and size of ammunition, whether an intermediate target was involved, and other factors. These GSR patterns are usually observed directly on the target clothing or the victim's body. It is also possible to transfer the patterns to filter paper or cleared photographic paper to make observation easier. For interpretation, a series of test fires is made with the weapon used on the evidence and these patterns are compared to the evidence pattern.

1. Direct contact

At contact range, soot deposits are visible around the entrance hole. Very little or no unburned powder will be found.

2. Close range (1–6 inches)

Residues are deposited around the bullet hole with black soot and smoke. The pattern is small and dense.

3. Medium range (1-$\frac{1}{2}$ to 4 feet)

Scattered gunshot residue is present without black deposits. The pattern spreads out as the distance increases.

4. Long range (greater than 4 feet)

Gunpowder residue is usually not found on the target when the barrel to target distance is greater than 5 feet. Figure 18.5 shows an example of some gunshot residue patterns produced by test firing under laboratory conditions.

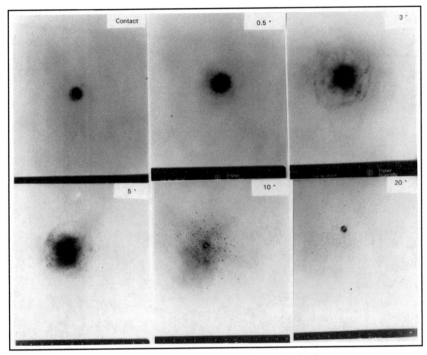

Figure 18.5 *Gunshot residue patterns which resulted when a weapon was test fired at various distances from the target: contact, 0.5 inch, 3 inches (top right panel), 5 inches, 10 inches and 20 inches (bottom right panel).*

5. Use of Greiss reagent and sodium rhodizinate reagent

Use of color-producing reagents on close and medium range targets allows one to visualize both the unburned power portion of the pattern and the lead particles in the pattern and makes estimation of distance more reliable.

Chapter 19

Hair

Hair evidence is among the most commonly gathered types of physical evidence and may be found in a wide variety of cases. Hairs may be of particular interest in cases known to involve personal contact, such as sexual assault, pedestrian-motor vehicle accidents, and homicides. In addition, hairs may also be an important piece of associative evidence to prove or disprove an event or an alibi.

19.1 Characteristics of Hairs
A. Nature of Hair

Hair is produced by cells within the skin hair follicle and becomes a non-living substance as it reaches the surface of the skin. During the formation and growth of hair certain characteristic areas are developed which are useful for comparison. Figure 19.1 shows diagrammatic views of a human hair.

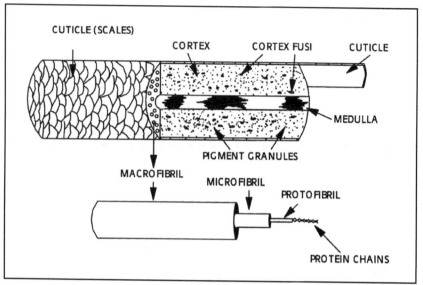

Figure 19.1 *Cutaway diagram of the structural components of a human hair.*

B. Microscopic Characteristics of Hair

1. Cuticle

The cuticle is a layer of scales that covers and protects the hair shaft; the cuticle forms various patterns, including:

- **Coronal** (crown-like). Scales appear as stacked cups; this type is seldom found in human hairs.
- **Spinous** (petal-like). Triangular-shaped and frequently protruding from the shaft.
- **Imbricate**. Flattened, overlapping scale, the usual type in human and some other animals.

2. Medulla

The medulla is the central core of the hair which was produced by cells in this central area. The medulla is described by one of the following forms:

- **Absent**. There is no medulla visible in the hair
- **Fragmented**. The medulla appears in small sections of irregular size.
- **Discontinuous**. Segments of the medulla are longer but spaces are present between the segments.

- **Continuous**. There are no breaks in the medulla as it moves from root to tip of the hair shaft. There are several other forms, including amorphous, serial, vacuolated, and lattice which are more common in animal hair.

3. Cortex

The main portion of the hair, the cortex, is made of elongated cells, and often contains many inclusions, such as:

- **Cortical fusi**. Irregularly shaped small air spaces, normally near the root, but may also be present throughout the hair shaft.
- **Pigment granules**. These small, solid structures vary in density, size, and distribution within a hair, and give it its characteristic color.
- **Ovoid bodies**. Large solid structures which are spherical or oval in shape.

19.2 Collection and Preservation of Hair Evidence
A. Collection of Evidentiary Hair Samples

Individual hairs may be picked up with the fingers or tweezers; however, this task may also be accomplished through the use of vacuum sweepers, lifting tape, or hair-fiber collectors.

The hair is then placed in a paper that is folded in the druggist fold, which in turn is placed in a suitable secondary container, properly labeled with location and identification data, and sealed. The druggist fold is prepared as follows:

1. Place the article of evidence in the center of the paper.
2. Fold paper lengthwise twice in non-parallel folds one from either side, so that the flaps overlap.
3. Fold over ends, tucking the smaller end inside of the larger end.
4. Place the resultant packet in a conventional envelope and seal. Label the envelope appropriately.

B. Collection of Known Hair Standards

Proper collection of known hair standards is important to obtain a representative sample of hairs for comparison purposes.

1. Comb the sample area gently to remove all loose hairs. Package and label these loose hairs.
2. Pull the hair standards so as to include the root. Take head hair samples from various parts of the head, such as the crown, neck, sides, and front. Collect a minimum of four to five hairs from each location (at least 20 total).

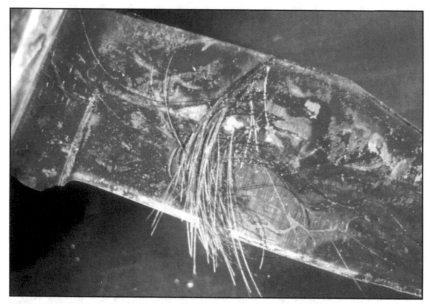

Figure 19.2 Hairs on a bloody knife found at a homicide scene.

3. A less-preferred method of obtaining samples is to cut the hairs as close as possible to the skin or scalp. If this is the method of collection, make a notation on the package that the hair represents the entire visible shaft, so the examiner will know that these are representative of the length of the hairs collected. Most hair examination experts are not comfortable making comparisons of hairs without roots.

19.3 Laboratory Examination and Comparison of Hairs
A. Identification

Hair-like fibers are first examined to determine if, in fact, these materials are hairs. Hair experts carry out examination of the gross macroscopic and microscopic characteristic structures of hair to reach this conclusion. This is usually done with the aid of a stereomicroscope.

If the hair is animal in origin (non-human), it may be useful to determine the type of animal from which the hair originated. Laboratory analysis and comparison to known standards must be carried out to make this determination.

If the hair is human, using microscopic examination of the detailed structure, examiners can sometimes determine race, somatic origin, and if the hair is from a hair piece.

B. Microscopic Examination and Comparison of Hairs

The structural characteristics of hair lend themselves to comparison. Table 19.1 lists some of the parameters and terminology used for microscopic studies of hair. Microscopic examination of hairs does not provide a positive means of individualization, but can greatly narrow the pool of potential donors and can essentially exclude a possible donor. Careful comparison must be done using a comparison microscope.

C. Instrumental Techniques

1. Neutron activation analysis (NAA)

Trace elemental analysis of the hair shaft is possible using neutron activation analysis (NAA), but results are difficult to interpret. At one time, it was thought that NAA might provide an objective analytical tool for hair individualization, but the distribution of trace elements was found to vary with time, greatly reducing its value. NAA is rarely, if ever, done today.

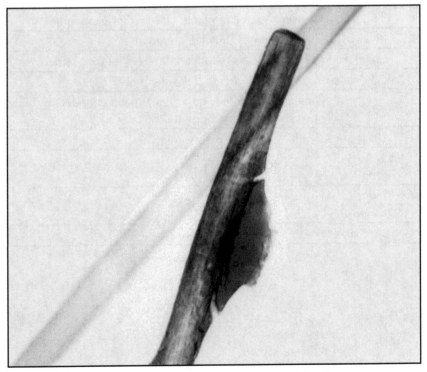

Figure 19.3 Photomicrograph of hair fragment with blood crust.

Table 19.1
Properties for Comparisons of Human Hairs

Scale Pattern	coronal; spinous; imbricate
Medulla	absent; fragmented; discontinuous; continuous
Medulla Pattern	uniserial; multiserial; vacuolated; lattice; amorphous
Diameter	constant; varies; range
Length	fragment; segment
Color	white; blond; light brown; brown; black; dark brown; gray; red
Reflectivity	opaque; translucent; transparent; clear
Tip	cut; broken; split; pointed; round
Root	normal; stretched; absent; bulbous; germ; follicular
Special Configuration	straight; curved; wavy; curly; kinky
Cross Section	polygonal; flat; oval; round
Pigment	absent; granular; chain; clump; dense; opaque
Cortical Fusi	absent; few; bunched; abundant
Cuticle	ragged; serrated; looped; layered; narrow; wide
Cortical Pigment	central; peripheral; one side; root
Damage	bleached; dyed; length of treatment; curled; cut; crushed; broken; burned
Race	White; African, East Asian
Body Area of Origin	head; pubic; body hair; beard
Special Characteristics	disease
Genetic Markers	ABO; isoenzymes; DNA

2. Pyrolysis GC

Efforts to individualize hairs by thermal decomposition and then separation of the products by gas chromatography have been made, but have yet to yield conclusive results. In addition, this method is a destructive technique.

D. Genetic Markers in Hairs

1. ABO grouping of hair

The ABO blood group substances are present in hair, but at very low levels. Absorption-elution methods have been used for the detection of blood group antigens in hair shaft samples with limited success. Hair roots, when present, give more reliable results.

2. Sexing of hair

Two methods have been used for determining the sex of the donor of a hair. Barr bodies and Y chromosome fluorescence have been used for sex determination of hair root sheath cells. Currently, examiners can detect X and Y chromosome-specific DNA sequences using molecular biology procedures, but this analysis requires hair root sheath cells.

3. DNA analysis

Besides X and Y chromosome analysis, full DNA STR profiles can be obtained from hair root sheet cells. The analysis of mitochondrial DNA (mtDNA) obtained from the hair shaft and telogen hair roots has been quite successful in DNA laboratories that have developed that capability. This technique is now mainstream in many forensic DNA laboratories. Although mitochondrial DNA has several limitations and has much less individualization information than nuclear DNA, it is a fully independent technique and, therefore in combination with microscopic hair comparison, provides much improved discrimination power. Each technique has been shown to sometimes differentiate hairs that the other cannot differentiate. Further, mitochondrial DNA can be successfully obtained in many cases where the entire hair (root to tip) is not available. A significant limitation on use of mitochondrial DNA is the fact that it is maternally transmitted and different individuals related on the maternal side will have non-distinguishable mtDNA.

Chapter 20

Imprint and Impression Evidence

Imprint or impression evidence is formed when an object comes in contact with another object or surface capable of recording a recognizable pattern. These contact markings can then be examined for the identification of class characteristics and the comparison of such class characteristics and individualizing characteristics if they exist.

Imprint and impression evidence, in addition to being used for identification purposes, is often useful in crime scene reconstruction, particularly blood spatter patterns, and in generating information about both the sequence of events and the identity of a suspect. The commonly encountered types of impression/imprint evidence are footprints, footwear (shoe) impressions, and tire tracks. Other forms of impression/imprint evidence such as fingerprints, toolmarks, and cartridge/bullet striations are addressed in separate chapters.

20.1 Nature of Imprint and Impression Evidence

The terms "imprint" and "impression" have sometimes been incorrectly used interchangeably. While both are produced by an object coming in contact with a receiving surface, imprints and impressions are different. Generally, the nature of the pattern evidence produced determines the type of marking, and can be divided into the following two categories:

A. Imprint (Residue) Prints

Residue prints are two-dimensional imprints found on hard and usually flat surfaces. The imprint of an object such as a shoe or tire is formed by residue deposited by the object itself or removal of material from the surface. These residues may be visible or made visible by enhancement techniques. An exact imprint pattern of the object in question may be left behind after it has contacted a medium such as soil, grease, blood, or mud and may be either a positive or a negative image. Shoe imprint on window sills, and bloody fabric impressions on car bumpers are common examples of two-dimensional imprints.

B. Impression Prints

Three-dimensional patterns or indentations which are produced when an object (e.g., shoe, tire, or tools) passes into a softer medium such as mud, wet sand, or snow are called impression prints. When an object is forced into soft media, the pattern produced may be a detailed three-dimensional impression of the object.

20.2 Collection and Preservation of Imprint or Impression Evidence
A. Documentation of Imprint and Impression Evidence

Before the collection of any imprint or impression evidence, thoroughly document and photograph these patterns. Whenever possible, take photographs with and without a scale and close-up and context pictures as well.

1. The camera must be set up so that the film plane is parallel to the plane of the surface containing the impression or imprint, that is, the lens is pointing straight at the print. In addition, position the camera directly above the center of the print to avoid distortion. A tripod is strongly recommended for this procedure.
2. Carefully focus the camera to ensure that all of the pertinent details necessary for the examination are recorded.
3. Set lighting at an oblique angle to enhance and highlight the detail of the print. Proper lighting is critical; if possible, take pictures with lighting from several different angles.

4. Take additional photographs after moving the light source 90 degrees to the next compass point until one full orbit of the imprint has been completed. It is absolutely essential to include a scale in the field of view of the camera. (Position the camera so that both the impression and scale take up the entire field of view.)

Pay special attention to the side walls of an impression, as these areas often aid in the examination for class and individual characteristics.

B. Collection of Residue Imprint Evidence

1. Movable or removable objects

It is preferable that the investigator obtains the entire object bearing the impression or imprint and, if the article is small enough, package the evidence in a manner which preserves the print intact. If the imprint is on a surface which can be cut out, remove the imprint area along with a small surrounding portion of the substrate. Package the evidence to avoid damage to the imprint.

2. Large items or immovable evidence

Two-dimensional imprint evidence is often deposited on surfaces which cannot be transported easily, such as footprints on permanent fixtures, footprints in dust on a floor, or some toolmarks. In addition, objects too large or cumbersome to move, or any imprint where movement may result in the destruction of the evidence, require an alternative method of evidence collection. In these situations, there is no alternative but to use enhancement and lifting techniques, after careful photography for documentation. Several procedures have been used, depending on the nature of the imprint and the substrate on which it is deposited:

a. Electrostatic lifting. The electrostatic technique is widely used for lifting dust-residue prints. It works best when the material of the imprint is dry and light. The electrostatic dust print-lifting apparatus consists of four basic components: power supply, 120 VAC-120 VDC charger, metal ground plate and metallic lifting film. Figure 20.1 is a photograph of the electrostatic dust print lifter. An example of lifting a shoe print using this apparatus is shown in Figure 20.2. In addition to floors, dust prints can be lifted from movable objects such as cloth, bed sheets, pillow cases, cardboard, newspapers, magazines, and envelopes by the following procedure:

1. Turn the voltage adjust knob on the power unit to the "low" position.
2. Connect the ground lead to the metal ground plate.

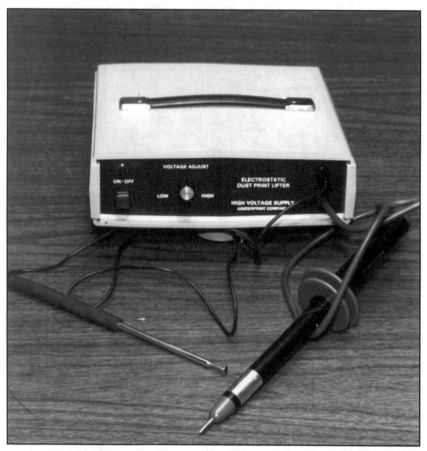

Figure 20.1 *The high voltage supply and electrode for the electrostatic dust print lifter.*

3. Place the objects bearing the residue prints on the metal ground plate, with the dust print away from the ground plate.
4. Cover the evidence with a sheet of lifting film with the metallic side away from the residue print.
5. Use a clean fingerprint ink roller to press and flatten the lifting film to the evidence surface.
6. Place a piece of heavy nonconductive type of board on top of the lifting film to ensure the tight contact between the lifting film and the residue print.
7. Turn on the power and touch the edge of the metallic film with the high-voltage probe for five to fifteen seconds, or until the lifting film has been "pulled down" to the surface.

Figure 20.2 *Use of an electrostatic dust print lifter.*

8. Disconnect the power and carefully remove the lifting film.
9. Photograph and preserve the residue print transferred onto the lifting film by covering it with a large, thin acetate plastic sheet.
10. When residue prints are found on objects not easily movable, such as doors, floor, carpets, large furniture, and cabinets, the ground lead should be connected to the ground. Dust prints found on metal objects such as safety deposit boxes, safes, and filing cabinets can also be lifted by the electrostatic procedure simply by attaching the ground lead and following the rest of the recommended procedure.

b. Gelatin lifter and adhesive tape lifting. Gelatin and adhesive tape lifting materials may prove useful when an electrostatic device is not available or is unsuccessful. Generally, use these methods only when the evidence cannot be removed from the scene. The principles and procedures are similar to those employed when lifting a latent print with fingerprint lifting tape. If the surface on which the print is deposited is at all unstable, the gel lifters greatly reduce lifting surface material along with imprint material.

c. Silicone rubber. Silicone rubber casting material may be poured over impressions and allowed to cure to recover an accurate three-dimensional rendering of the impression. This method is suitable for lifting prints from nonporous surfaces only.

d. Photographic imprint enhancement. Several nondestructive photographic enhancement techniques may be attempted:

- The use of filters to vary contrast.
- Digital imaging techniques—to improve contrast and bring out subtleties in pattern images. The vast array of digital image processing techniques now available can be used to clarify and improve visibility of such images.
- Alternate lighting techniques—oblique lighting, polarized light, UV light, IR light, and various wavelengths produced by an alternate light source. These lighting sources can also be used in combination with various filters.

e. Powdering. Fingerprint powders may be used to enhance residue imprint patterns, especially in situations such as when a wet shoe has tracked across a polished surface.

f. Chemical enhancement. The material picked up by a shoe to make the imprint often contains trace elements, minerals, and other compounds which may be made more visible after enhancement by certain chemicals. Examples of some of these enhancement reagents include:

- **8-Hydroxyquinoline** detects metal ions, including iron, aluminum, calcium, and magnesium. The reaction produces fluorescence, visible with UV illumination.
- **Iodine** detects organic matter, fatty acids, and oily material. The imprint appears yellow-brown. Unless fixed, the iodine will vaporize and the enhancement will be lost.
- **Ninhydrin** detects amino acids and peptides found in secretions, blood, and other body fluids, producing a purple color.

- **Amido black** produces a dark blue stain when blood is present.
- **Luminol** reacts with hemoglobin derivatives found in blood and luminesces. This testing must be conducted in the dark.
- **Bloody print enhancement reagent** combines a standard mixture used for highly sensitive screening tests for blood. The print turns a dark blue color with this extremely sensitive reagent. See Figure 20.3.

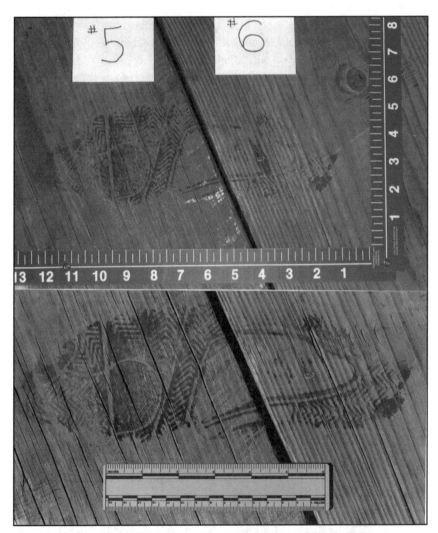

Figure 20.3 *Additional detail can be developed in a bloody shoeprint found at a homicide scene (top) by use of chemical enhancement reagents (bottom).*

- **Thiocyanate** is a chemical reagent used on dust prints where the dust is naturally rich in iron.
- **Bromcresolgreen** is a chemical reagent used with dust prints which have little iron.

C. Collection of Impression Evidence

The impression pattern itself must be recovered by making a positive image of the impression using dental stone or silicone casting material. This replica may yield class characteristics for identification, but will seldom yield the necessary detail for an individualized identification of a tire track or a shoe or boot impression. Silicone rubber casts of toolmarks, for example, can often produce a casting with enough detail to allow individualization. The procedure for making a plaster cast is as follows and is shown in Figures 20.4 and 20.5.

1. Examine the area to be cast and carefully remove large, loose articles of foreign matter without disturbing the surface of the impression.

Figure 20.4 *Preparations, including proper documentation, for the casting of a footwear impression found in soil.*

Figure 20.5 *Mixing and pouring of dental stone for a cast of the footwear impression shown in Figure 20.4.*

2.   If the material to be cast is easily moved and damaged, such as sand or soil, stabilize it by spraying lacquer, shellac, or hair spray onto a cardboard or paper held above the print at a 45-degree angle so that the sprayed liquid falls by gravity onto the print. Allow approximately 15 minutes for drying time.

3. Sprinkle talcum powder very lightly onto the print to facilitate separation of the dental stone cast from the impression upon completion. Alternatively, spray the print with light silicone oil.

4. Set up a physical barrier which will act as a dam around the impression. Commercially manufactured steel frames are available for this purpose. However, any object that will restrict the flow of the plaster and confine it to the immediate area of the print will suffice.

5. Prepare the dental stone in a rubber mixing bowl or strong plastic bag. If the dental stone is lumpy, sift it through a flour sifter or screen. Mix water with the dental stone material to produce a mixture which has the consistency of pancake batter.

6. It is important that the casting material not be poured directly onto the pattern area. Pour the dental stone (uphill from the impression when possible) by holding the bowl close to the print and deflecting the falling liquid off of the spoon or spatula just before the liquid reaches the impression. The pouring should continue around the area of the impression until the dental stone reaches a depth of 0.5 inch. Carefully control the flow of the dental stone into the impression.

7. When a depth of 0.5 inch is reached, place reinforcement in the form of screen or wire on top of the dental stone. The investigator must exercise caution so as not to press the reinforcements into the material to the point where they interfere with the impression being cast.

8. Continue the pouring as before until a thickness of 1 inch is reached. After allowing the cast to set for approximately ten minutes, scratch identification data into the top of the cast and then allow it to complete the setting process. After the cast has been allowed to set for 30 minutes, it can be removed from the impression. Make no attempt to clean the soil from the bottom of the cast at this time. A full 14 hours is required to complete the setting process. Efforts to remove soil may destroy the impression. The soil and debris which cling to the newly completed cast also make an excellent known sample for soil comparisons to material clinging to suspect shoes or tires.

9. There are special procedures for casting snow prints. Snow Print Wax® is a material suitable for coating footwear impressions in snow. This product is a rust-colored aerosol spray wax. First, photograph the snow print, since application of the wax is a delicate procedure. Next, apply the wax to the impression, forming a wax shell that preserves the detail of the footwear (see step 2 above). Then fill the Snow Print Wax® shell with dental stone to provide support for lifting the fragile impression. Do not touch the wax cast, as the detail can easily be destroyed or rubbed away. Hence, it is advantageous to photograph the finished product as soon as possible.

D. Collection of Known Standards

1. Shoes

Obtain footwear to be compared to any impressions or imprints as soon as possible to preclude additional wear markings from being developed on the shoes and possibly obliterating those present on the imprint or impression.

1. Standard inked imprints for laboratory comparison should not be collected in the field, but should be made at the laboratory after an examination for other potentially important physical evidence is made. Under no circumstances should an item of footwear be placed directly into an impression. To obtain useful control patterns, similar weight and directional forces should be used as were likely used in making the evidence pattern.
2. Package these items in paper wrapping or paper bags to prevent the possible loss of trace materials which may be present.

2. Tires

In the case of tires, the original impression was made with the weight of the vehicle bearing upon the tire. Thus, the investigator must try to duplicate this condition when making the known standard for comparison purposes. The following procedure is recommended:

1. Check the tires for the presence of any significant trace materials such as blood, soil, or fibers and collect these items prior to collecting imprint standards.
2. Jack the vehicle up so that the questioned tire clears the ground.
3. Ink the entire tread circumference of the tire with fingerprint ink or other suitable transfer medium.
4. Place approximately 10 feet of paper under the tire.
5. Lower the vehicle onto the paper and slowly drive or push it along the paper until the tire has completed at least one revolution.
6. Record identifying data on the paper, including which tire made the mark (position on the vehicle), and which side of the tire mark was facing inboard or outboard of the vehicle.
7. Repeat the entire process until all tires on the vehicle have been completed.
8. It is necessary to submit the known standards to the laboratory along with the cast or photographs of the tire impression. The submission of the actual tire, in most cases, is not necessary. Laboratories with forensic garages may be able to help obtain tire test impressions.

20.3 Laboratory Analysis of Imprint and Impression Evidence

Macroscopic and microscopic examination allow for the determination of class and individual characteristics of an impression. This determination can lead to identification of the type of object which made the patterns and, at times, the manufacturer. The comparison of impressions with known samples or other impressions may, in favorable cases, result in individualization.

A. Determination of Class Characteristics

Note general structural properties such as size, shape, pattern and design. If the imprint is a shoeprint, for example, determine the shoe size using standard footwear scales. Manufacturers often place characteristic patterns and logos on their products which may allow the examiner to identify the class or category of the object that produced the imprint. In the case of tire tread patterns, the manufacturer and model of the tire can often be determined from examination of photographs in the reference publication *Tread Design Guide,* published by Tire Guide or other available databases.

B. Determination of Individual Characteristics

Individual characteristics are those which are specific to a particular object. If such markings or characteristics are present and sufficiently well defined, they may enable the examiner to conclude that a particular object made the impression. Individual characteristics would include wear, damage, irregularities, and other accidental marks unique to a particular article as a result of its history. The exact location, size, and shape of each mark should be documented.

C. Comparison of Imprints or Impressions with Known Patterns

Imprints or impressions produced by known standards, such as submitted footwear evidence, are directly compared to the questioned patterns. When making an exemplar print or impression of the known for comparison, reproduce as nearly as possible the conditions present when the impression was generated. Pressure, angle of impact and nature of surface can all affect the observed impression or imprint.

The examiner compares class characteristics of the known and the questioned impression. If the two items demonstrate common class characteristics, a positive statement may be made concerning the similarity of the articles. It is also possible to eliminate a known as the source of an imprint/impression based on class characteristics.

If sufficient individual characteristics of the known and the questioned imprint agree and there are no unexplained areas of disagreement, one may conclude that the known produced the impression. As with comparisons of other types of physical evidence, no exact number of points of identification has been deemed necessary to declare a match. Extensive experience, however, is critical to reliable determinations. Figure 20.6 shows a charted comparison of a known and a questioned shoeprint.

When making comparisons of objects with casts, one must consider the shrinkage of the casting material. Charts and formulae exist to assist in these determinations.

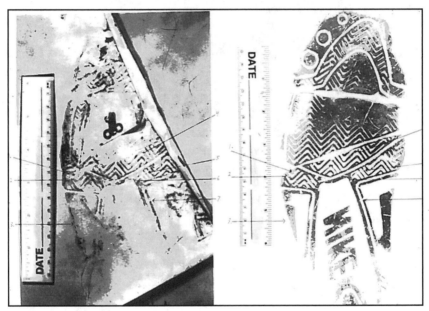

Figure 20.6 *A charted comparison between the imprint made from a suspect's sneaker (right) and the imprint found at the crime scene (left).*

Figure 20.7 *Area where a latent imprint was located on a truck which was suspected to be involved in a hit-and-run accident.*

Chapter 21

Paint Evidence

Investigators encounter paint and other protective coatings such as varnishes, lacquers and other films as evidence, with a high frequency, in connection with many types of crimes, including hit-and-run cases, burglaries and forced entries. Paint evidence may also be important in other types of cases. Paint may either be removed from an object, transferred to an object, or both during the same incident. The paint evidence is usually in the form of chips or smears. Automotive, architectural and specialty coatings can all prove to be excellent physical evidence. In the absence of jigsaw match or highly unusual layer structure, paint comparisons can, at best, prove possible common origin (classification).

21.1 Nature of Paint Evidence

A. Definition of Paints

The purpose of paint and other coatings is to provide protection or decoration for a surface, such as wood or metal. Paint is a suspension of white or colored pigments and a polymeric resin binder in a solvent carrier designed to make application of an even coating relatively simple. This suspension dries to leave a hard solid coating on the surface to which it is applied. The laboratory examination of paint evidence can determine the nature of the film forming polymer (binder), the pigment and some of the additives in the paint. The solvent carrier has usually evaporated by the time the paint becomes of evidentiary, and therefore forensic, interest.

B. Classification of Paints

Based on the suspension medium, paints may be classified in three general groups:

1. Drying oil types, for example, enamels and exterior building paints.
2. Solvent types, for example, spirit varnishes and lacquers.
3. Synthetic emulsion types or water-based paints (e.g., latex paints).

C. Pigment Classification

The most common inorganic pigments used in paints may be classified by color:

- White pigments—Titanium dioxide (most common), calcium carbonate, zinc oxide.
- Black pigments—Amorphous carbon, graphite, asphalt, bone black and ivory black.
- Blue pigments—Iron ferroferricyanide, cobalt aluminate, azurite, and ultramarine.
- Red pigments—Ferric oxide, antimony trisulfide, trilead tetroxide.
- Green pigments—Chromic oxide, copper basic carbonate, copper acetoarsenite.
- Yellow pigments—Lead monoxide, zinc chromate, lead chromate, cadmium sulfide, hydrated ferric oxide with clay.
- Brown pigments—Vandycke brown, hydrated ferric oxide and manganese dioxide with clay minerals.

In addition, many modern paints contain synthetic organic pigments in a great diversity of chemical types and colors.

21.2 Collection of Paint Evidence
A. Paint on Large Objects or a Vehicle

1. Photograph the area in question, for example, door frame or damage on car, both with and without a scale. Thoroughly document the location and appearance of the paint both close-up and in context.
2. If whole areas of paint are missing from door and window frames or parts of a vehicle, the entire part may be useful for attempting a physical match with paint chips. With this type of evidence, cut out the portions with the paint missing, if possible, and submit to the laboratory for analysis.
3. Collect large, loose deposits or chips of paint using tape to ensure getting intact pieces of the paint.
4. Obtain paint smears or other samples by chipping the sample, intact, to the underlying surface to ensure that full layer sequence is obtained. This chipping or scraping should include any underlying paint layers as well; for example, the under-layers of paint on the damaged vehicle. Collect the chips in paper, then fold in a druggist fold, place in a labeled envelope and seal. Use a clean, new razor blade or scalpel blade for each paint sample to avoid the danger of cross-contamination between samples.
5. Collect known standards for comparison or elimination adjacent to the area of interest, for example, the damaged area on a suspect vehicle in a hit-and-run case, to ensure that the paint types and layer structure are the same.
6. When toolmarks exist on the damaged object, collect known paint samples from areas immediately adjacent to the toolmarks without damaging the toolmarks.

B. Small Items of Physical Evidence

1. Paint chip evidence
Thoroughly search the scene for paint particles (chips) resulting from the impact between car and car, car and pedestrian, or other impact. If paint chips are found, package these in paper in a druggist fold and place in an envelope. Take extreme care during collection, packaging, and transport to prevent damage to the paint chips, especially if these are sufficiently large to be used for a possible jigsaw match examination.

2. Garments
Submit the outer clothing of a pedestrian victim to the laboratory so that the individual items of clothing may be examined for paint smears and particles.

Clothing of suspects in burglaries and forced entries may also have paint evidence. Make no effort to remove the paint before submission to the laboratory. Individually wrap clothing in paper, seal, label and submit to the laboratory. It is important to make sure that garments are thoroughly dry prior to packaging. Never package clothing in plastic bags.

3. Tools

In cases of burglary, forced entry to a building, safe or automobile, for example, a tool may have paint adhered to the end used to apply the force. Submit tools to the laboratory, with any paint smears intact. Never attempt to fit any tool to a toolmark; this could cause damage to the mark or transfer paint. Place the entire tool in a bag or other suitable container with the end covered and protected from paint loss or damage. Seal the package so that any paint that may fall off during transit remains in the container. Be sure to submit a control sample of the paint from the surface for comparison to any material found on the tool.

4. Projectiles

In some cases paint may be embedded in recovered fired bullets. This paint evidence may be used to establish that a bullet ricocheted off or passed through a painted surface. Place the bullet in a sealed container and make no attempt to remove the paint prior to submission to the laboratory. Take care to package the bullet so that movement does not damage it during transit, while in the package.

5. Paint smear evidence

In some cases when two objects come into glancing contact a smear of paint may be transferred from one to the other. Paint smears historically have been difficult to work with but with modern instrumentation even a very thin smear can be successfully analyzed.

C. Cases When No Suspect Vehicle is Available

In cases where there is no suspect vehicle, paint may, at a minimum, be useful in determining the color of the hit-and-run vehicle, and in some instances the make of the vehicle can be determined through laboratory examination. Further, examiners can sometimes match physical and chemical composition of paint recovered at the crime scene with that from the suspect's vehicle, even when the vehicle is located much later. Further, there are several automobile paint databases that can be searched for information that can narrow the search for a suspect vehicle.

1. Collect known specimens from the hit-and-run vehicle. These especially should include paint in the area of any damage to the vehicle.

2. If investigators note scrapes containing other paint material, collect these too for comparison as possible transfers from other involved vehicles.

21.3 Laboratory Analysis of Paints and Coatings
A. Macroscopic Analysis

1. Physical characteristics

Physical characteristics such as color, layering, weathering, inclusions and texture are useful in characterizing paint evidence.

2. Layer structure

In some instances, vehicles and residences that have been painted and re-painted many times may have so many layers of paint that, if all the layers match, the probability of the known and questioned samples sharing a common origin may be very high. The presence of two or three consistent layers adds weight to the evidence of possible common source.

3. Control samples

Different areas of the object in question may not be painted with the same type of paint as the area of interest, or may have additional layers due to repair. It is therefore extremely important to collect known samples as close to the damaged area as possible.

B. Physical Match of Paint Chips

If paint chips are sufficiently large, it may be possible to fit them physically into the damaged area of the paint, for example, on a damaged vehicle. This jigsaw puzzle-type match is a positive individualization and shows that the paint chip originated from that painted surface.

C. Microscopic Examination

1. Layer structure

In cases where the paint samples contain multiple layers of paint (virtually all automotive coatings), microscopic examination may determine that the number of layers and color sequence of layers, pigments, pigment distribution, and other information, such as contaminants, are consistent.

2. Further testing

Comparison of these characteristics between a questioned and known sample may be sufficient to show possible common origin without using chemical testing. However, in situations where only one or two layers of paint are present, additional testing is necessary.

D. Microchemical tests

1. Type of tests
Each layer of a paint chip may be tested microchemically for solubility and color change with various reagents. As shown in Table 21.1, these tests will show characteristic reactions for some common paint binder types.

2. Chemical properties
Chemical properties such as solubility and resin composition can indicate the type of paint and identify the pigmentation and type of fillers used during the manufacturing process. Known and questioned samples may be compared by examination of physical and chemical properties.

Figure 21.1 *Edge on view of a multilayer paint chip, viewed through a stereomicroscope.*

Table 21.1: Common Solubility Tests on Paints

Type of Paint	Trichloromethane	DPA	Acetone
Enamel	-		-
Acrylic Lacquer	+	-	+
Nitro Lacquer	-	+ (blue)	+
Latex	+	+	s.+

E. Instrumental Methods

The organic and inorganic composition of paints can be analyzed by several instrumental methods.

1. Microscopic-FTIR

The microscope sampling attachment for most FTIRs makes possible analysis of samples as small as about 5 microns. Examiners use this technique to determine the major organic components of each paint layer, that is, the basic resin of the binder, and sometimes inorganic or organic pigments and additives. The availability of microscope sampling devices for FTIR has greatly improved the quality of information from even very tiny paint chips or paint smears.

2. SEM-EDX

Scanning electron microscopy with energy dispersive x-ray analysis (SEM-EDX) can provide forensic chemists studying the morphology of a paint sample with a simultaneous elemental analysis of the sample. Figure 21.2 shows a multilayer paint chip as seen under the SEM and the EDX elemental analysis of one of the paint layers present.

3. Visible microspectrophotometry

The visible spectra of the pigments present in a paint sample can be obtained on microscopic size samples. A visible microspectrometer allows examiners to obtain CIE color coordinates and Munsell coordinates and to carefully compare the color of samples. It provides an excellent confirmation of an examiner's visual judgment and can sometimes differentiate colors that the examiner cannot distinguish.

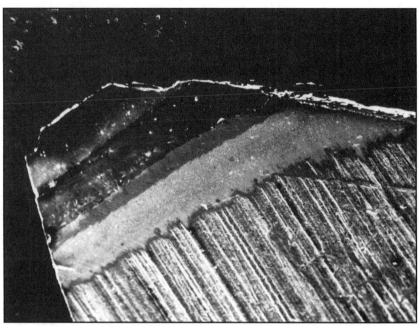

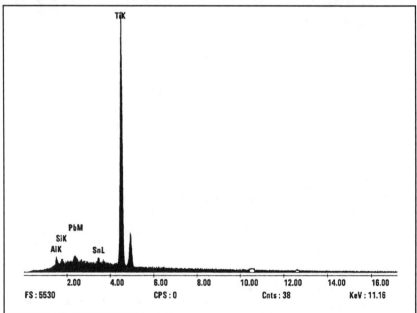

Figure 21.2 A multi-layer paint chip as seen on the scanning electron microscope (top) and the EDX analysis of one of these layers indicating elemental composition (bottom).

Chapter 22

Pattern Evidence

Pattern evidence occurs as a result of physical contact between two objects, one of which causes or transfers a pattern in blood, oil, bruising or other medium, onto the other object. There are a variety of physical patterns commonly found at crime scenes. Most of these physical patterns are in the form of imprints, injuries, indentations, striations, markings, fractures or depositions. Pattern evidence at crime scenes is extremely valuable in the reconstruction of events. It can be used to prove or disprove a suspect's alibi or a witness' version of what took place, to associate or dissociate the involvement of persons or objects in particular events, or to provide investigators with new leads to aid in investigation of the incident.

Pattern evidence may contain both class and individual characteristics and can thus be used for identification, individualization, and reconstruction.

Figure 22.1 *Bloodstain patterns found at a crime scene included medium velocity castoff bloodstains (left). Contact-transfer bloodstains, blood smears, blood dripping and vertical drop blood patterns were noted in another area of the same apartment (right).*

22.1 Pattern Evidence and Interpretations

The interpretation of pattern evidence should be made with extreme care. Examiners must often conduct controlled laboratory experiments to help validate interpretations and results obtained from examination of pattern evidence. If any questions arise during examination, consult a more experienced examiner. The following are some general descriptions of the types of patterns commonly encountered at crime scenes and on other items of physical evidence.

A. Bloodstain Patterns

Reconstruction from bloodstain patterns has long been a neglected area, but is now receiving more recognition.

Reconstructions of a criminal incident or at least a portion of an incident are often made possible by careful documentation and examination of bloodstain patterns. Correct interpretation must be based on detailed measurements and analysis of the blood patterns. Actual experimentation and objective evaluation are essential for further interpretation. Bloodstain patterns are often at least as valuable as the serological analysis of the blood in reconstructing events and solving a case.

Much can be learned from a careful examination of bloodstain patterns and study of fluid dynamics; some examples are given below:

- Approximate speed of blood droplets at impact.
- Approximate direction of travel of blood droplets.
- Approximate distance between the source of blood and the target surface.
- The approximate angle of incidence of blood droplets on a surface.
- Positions of persons involved from radial spatter patterns.
- Arc patterns from swinging (cast off) motions.
- Interpretation of patterns from arterial spurts.
- Determination of blood trails and their directions.
- Interpretation of blood flow patterns and pools.
- Interpretation of contact transfer, wipe and swiping patterns.
- Reconstructions of shootings from blood patterns.
- Estimation of elapsed time since blood was deposited.
- Falling, projected or impact pattern differentiation.

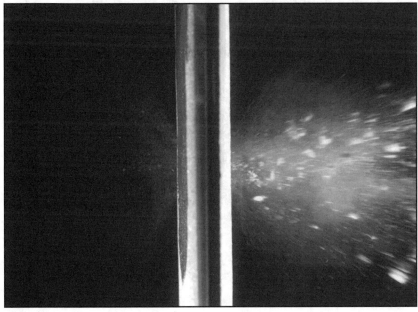

Figure 22.2 *High-velocity blood spatters commonly produced by a gun shot.*

- Reconstruction of sequences of events.
- Determination of geometric and spatial relationships.
- Estimation of the total amount of blood present.

B. Glass Fracture Patterns

Broken glass at crime scenes can sometimes aid in reconstruction, provide information about the events which took place, and assist in proving or disproving an alibi or a witness' statement.

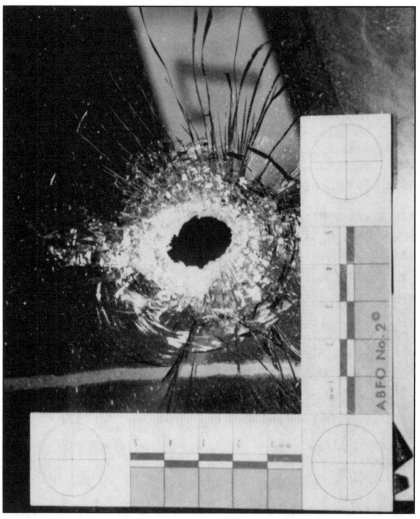

Figure 22.3 *Glass fracture pattern at a shooting scene showing typical radial and concentric fractures.*

The use of glass fracture patterns in crime scene reconstruction relies on careful observations and detailed studies of radial and concentric fracture lines. Examiners obtain other useful information by the analysis of rib or hackle marks, spatial relationships of glass fragments, stress cracks and the condition of any melted glass. At the scene, carefully preserve the glass fracture pattern to prevent further damage to the glass and to eliminate the chances of creating post-incident damage. (See also Chapter 17.)

The most common types of information that can be gained by studying glass fracture patterns are:

- Direction of application of impact force,
- Approximate force of impact,
- Approximate angle of impact,
- Determination of whether a window was broken inward or not,
- Determination of the cause of glass fracture,
- Determination of the sequences of shots from multiple bullet holes in glass,
- Determination of the direction of a shot,
- Determination of the angle of shots from bullet holes in glass,
- Determination of the type of projectile used from holes in glass,
- Estimation of fire temperatures from the degree of melting of glass or glass fragments,
- Determination of fire direction from melted glass, and
- Determination of the cause of breaks from examinations of glass fractures.

C. Fire Burn Patterns

Fire burn patterns often provide information on the various factors that could have led to the fire and its development.

A detailed study of the burn patterns generally helps in determining the point or points of origin, direction of fire travel, and the degree of damage caused by the fire. It may also provide clues pointing toward possible arson.

Every fire forms a set of patterns that is determined chiefly by the configuration of the environment, the availability of combustible material and oxygen, and the type and intensity of the fire. From the study of a fire pattern, and a determination of any deviations from normal or expected patterns, an experienced investigator can reconstruct a fire scene and determine the possible cause of the fire.

The following is a partial list of common patterns found at fire scenes:

- Inverted cone or "V" burn pattern (shown in Figure 22.4)

- Multiple origin burn patterns
- Low burn pattern configurations
- Depth of charring patterns
- Direction of charring patterns
- Trailer patterns
- Smoke stain patterns
- Material melting patterns
- Concrete spalling patterns
- Alligatoring patterns

Figure 22.4 A typical V-type burn pattern at an arson scene.

D. Furniture Position Patterns

At an indoor crime scene, the position and condition of furniture often yields information about the events that caused the pattern, their sequence, and possible actions of perpetrators and victims. Displaced or broken furniture can indicate whether or not a struggle took place. Patterns of disarray deviating from ordinary or expected furniture placement or condition may further reveal actions taken by suspects. Absence of particular favorite pieces of furniture may indicate premeditation of the fire.

E. Projectile Trajectory Patterns

Studies of bullet trajectories combined with knowledge of scene geometry, witness' statements and other physical evidence can assist in reconstructing a shooting incident. In addition, studies of projectile trajectory patterns can assist in locating and recovering bullets or cartridge cases for analysis. (See Chapter 16.)

Correct interpretation of projectile trajectory patterns can help in establishing the following information:

- Direction of the projectile
- Position of the shooter and the target
- Possible estimation of distance between gun muzzle and target
- Number of shots fired
- Possible sequence of multiple shots
- Possible angle of shots
- Determination of entry and exit holes
- Determination of primary and secondary projectiles
- Possible projectile deflections (ricochet)
- Existence of or position of intermediate targets

Figure 22.5 depicts the determination of bullet trajectories in the reconstruction of a homicide case.

F. Track-trail Patterns

Shoe imprint and footprint trails are often found at crime scenes. Proper interpretation of these patterns can yield information about how many persons were present at a scene, whether they were moving about, the nature of the movement (walking, running), the direction of travel, and whether heavy objects were being carried or dragged. Some of these patterns can give class characteristic information about the individual responsible for producing them, such as shoe size, stride length, sex, weight, or any abnormalities in movement or gait. Typical footprint impressions found at a crime scene are shown in Figure 22.6.

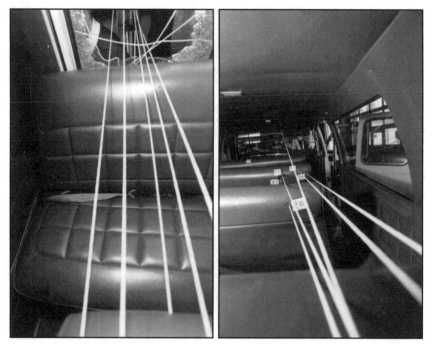

Figure 22.5 *Determination of bullet trajectories of multiple gunshots into a vehicle.*

G. Tire and Skid Mark Patterns

Tire or skid mark patterns are often seen at outdoor crime scenes, and can provide important reconstruction information. The value of skid mark patterns in traffic accident reconstruction is well known and documented. However, the use of these patterns in crime scene investigation and reconstruction is often neglected. These markings can yield information about the number and type of vehicles involved, the possible speed of travel, direction of travel, whether or not brakes were applied, and whether any turns were made.

H. Modus Operandi Patterns

These patterns are more subtle, and require careful observation as well as extensive knowledge of criminal behavior and of the crimes previously thought to be committed by an individual. MO patterns can tie apparently unrelated crimes together at the early investigative stage. These patterns include the type of the crime committed, the type of victim targeted, and other information, such as methods used to gain entry to a premises, types of weapons used, types of force used, types of language used, the sequence of actions followed by a criminal, types of prop-

Figure 22.6 *Multiple footwear impressions found at a homicide scene.*

erty taken, types of disguises, types of vehicles used or routes taken, and types of materials left behind at the scene. The FBI has developed a national database of such patterns. It is available to state and local agencies as well (VICAP).

I. Clothing or Object Distribution Patterns

This type of pattern can be subtle or, at times, very obvious. Detailed observation, documentation and correct interpretation of these patterns can be valuable in scene reconstruction. Some examples of the types of information these patterns can yield are:

- Whether a criminal ransacked a scene
- Proof or disproof of an alibi
- Direction and route taken by a criminal
- Physical contact between two persons or two vehicles, or between a person and a vehicle
- Disturbances of expected patterns at a scene
- Possible information about the sequence of events
- Powder residue patterns (muzzle-to-target distance)
- Indication of where latent fingerprints might be found

J. Gun Powder Residue Patterns

In the investigation of shooting cases, gun powder residue patterns sometimes play an important role in deciding the answers to questions such as: whether the case represents a homicide, suicide or accidental death; the muzzle-to-target distance; the trajectory of the fired bullet; whether a suspect recently discharged or handled a weapon; the maximum distance from victim to perpetrator; and the relative locations of, and relationships between, multiple targets.

K. Material Damage Patterns

The type and degree of damage to a victim's or suspect's clothing often can yield information on the type and direction of the force that caused the observed damage. The damage patterns on motor vehicles involved in traffic accidents and the location of such damage will provide information on the exact location of the contact between two vehicles or a vehicle and a body and the type of force that caused the damage. Other material damage patterns that can be valuable for crime scene reconstruction include broken knives, damaged weapons, and indentations on walls or doors.

L. Body Position Patterns

A victim's body position at a death scene is extremely valuable information for reconstruction. Whether or not the body has been moved can also sometimes be determined by careful examination of the location and the position of the body. The body position can also help to determinate if the manner of death was suicide, accidental death or homicide.

22.2 Documentation of Pattern Evidence

The recognition of pattern evidence at crime scenes requires careful observation and a systematic, meticulous approach in analyzing the crime scene.

A. Recognition and Documentation

Once investigators have located and recognized a certain pattern, they should document the pattern by description and photography. Dimensions and scale are important, and should be included in the descriptive and photographic documentation. The investigators should note and describe in detail the shape and size of each pattern. "Over-documentation" of a pattern is preferable to a lack of information, especially in cases where the pattern is transient or may be altered by other testing.

B. Interpretation

Investigators should carry out a careful and detailed study, keeping any preliminary interpretation within the boundaries of scientific and logical principles. Unless these interpretations have been verified by independent evidence, they should not be considered as final conclusions.

22.3 Collection of Pattern Evidence

The recognition of pattern evidence at crime scenes requires careful observation and a systematic, detailed approach in analyzing the crime scene. Pattern evidence generally is found at the scene on two categories of physical evidence: patterns deposited on movable objects, and those present on immovable surfaces. The recognition and proper documentation as described in Section 22.2.A, above, are critical first steps.

A. Patterns on Movable Objects

After detailed documentation of the item of physical evidence and the patterns on the item at the crime scene, collect the object itself and submit it to the laboratory for further analysis. Allow any wet stains present on the item to dry before packaging the item for transport and make sure that packaging will protect the pattern while it is in transit.

B. Patterns on Immovable Objects

Gather careful measurements, detailed descriptions, and other documentation. Then collect a sample of the material comprising the pattern, such as a bloodstain, paint, oil and so forth, by cutting, tape lift, or scraping. Again, over-documentation is preferable to under-documentation.

C. Preliminary Interpretation of Pattern Evidence

Any preliminary interpretation of pattern evidence found at a crime scene or on other items of physical evidence should be kept within the boundaries of scientific and logical principles. Unless these interpretations have been verified, they should not be considered final conclusions. A careful and detailed study must be carried out by trained personnel prior to drawing any final conclusions, and all relevant information should be utilized in developing a reconstruction.

Chapter 23

Plastics

Much of the modern world is made of various plastics that can, therefore, be important as physical evidence in many cases. Plastic evidence can be found in hit-and-run cases, for example, a part of the bumper or grill. Plastic bags often are used in the course of various crimes, such as homicides where the victim or bloody clothes are found in bags at the crime scene or at a secondary scene. Plastics are widely used in household products and building materials that may be important evidence in a particular case.

23.1 Nature of Plastics
A. Definition of Plastics
Plastics are synthetic materials composed of very large organic molecules known as polymers; polymers are composed of repeating subunits, monomers, which have been chemically linked, and often cross-linked, to form the plastic. Some polymers are natural materials, such as cellulose (building block of vegetable fibers); other plastics are totally synthetic, such as polyethylene, polyester and polystyrene; and some may be composites of natural and synthetic materials.

B. Types of Plastic Evidence
Articles composed of plastic represent a wide range of possible evidence types.

The most commonly encountered plastic materials submitted as physical evidence include:

- Plastic bags—Plastic bags of all shapes and sizes very often important physical evidence
- Plastic films—These include garbage bags, food bags, plastic sheets and plastic film wrapping.
- Plastic utensils and objects—The remains of tools, toys, containers, cooking utensils, electrical parts, household goods, office supplies, and other manufactured goods composed of plastic.
- Plastic tape—Materials such as surgical, electrical, household, office, and transparent adhesive tape.
- Other—Buttons, packaging materials, pieces of automobiles, and many other categories of articles can be composed in part by, or completely of, plastic.
- Synthetic fibers are polymers that could be considered plastics and are very common as evidence. They are discussed in Chapter 14, *Fibers*.
- Automotive plastic—Because significant amounts of plastics are used in many automotive applications they can often become physical evidence.

23.2 Collection of Plastic Evidence
A. Packaging
Place small items of plastic evidence in a paper envelope with proper label and seal. Place larger items in paper bags or wrap with paper and seal.

B. Other Evidence
The investigator should be alert to the presence of fingerprints, imprints or other trace evidence such as hair, blood, glass and fibers in cases where plastic has been involved in the commission of a crime; consider the presence of these materials when collecting and packaging the plastic evidence.

23.3 Laboratory Examination of Plastics
A. Physical Match
Since plastics often fracture with the generation of complex surfaces like glass, jigsaw matches of broken plastic are quite common. Pieces of a lens from a turning signal light can be physically matched with another portion of the object that was the source of the plastic. Such a physical match could prove that the questioned sample originated from the known specimen.

B. Macroscopic Analysis

Macroscopic analysis can determine the physical characteristics of the plastic, such as color, thickness, elasticity and hardness.

C. Microscopic Examination of Striations

Various striations and extrusion markings are formed during the manufacturing of plastics. Examiners can compare these class characteristics and individual markings on plastic bags and other similar types of plastic with known samples. Positive results indicate the two plastic bags could have come from the same source. Individualization is sometimes possible if markings such as scratches or pigment patterns can be shown to be continuous between a questioned sample and a known.

D. Microchemical Solubility and Color Tests

The use of screening tests can help determine the chemical nature of plastic materials used to manufacture an object. Various solubility schemes for testing of plastics have been developed. Some plastics will react with chemical spot test reagents as well, and this can be useful in screening what type of polymer might be present.

E. Instrumental Analysis

As with other synthetic evidence, forensic scientists conduct instrumental analysis on plastics to determine the chemical composition of the material. Many different instruments are used; for example, FTIR and x-ray fluorescence are used to identify the type of plastic and the type of filler used in the plastic. If two plastics have similar composition by instrumental analysis, this indicates they could have had a similar origin. More complete analysis is also possible using modern chromatographic and spectroscopic techniques, and can often differentiate similar types of plastics from minor components or other subtle differences.

Chapter 24

Semen

Semen is the most commonly encountered body fluid, other than blood, in the forensic laboratory and is usually associated with sexual assault cases. Semen can also be important evidence in homicide, burglary and paternity cases.

24.1 Nature of Semen Evidence
Semen is the physiological fluid that is released when the male ejaculates. It is a heterogeneous mixture that contains both fluid and cellular components.

A. Cellular Components
Spermatozoa, the male gametes, are produced in the testis and mixed with other components of semen upon ejaculation (see Figure 24.1). The normal adult male will produce from 60 to 100 million spermatozoa per milliliter of semen. Rela-

tively small numbers of epithelial cells from the lining of the male reproductive system are also found in ejaculate.

B. Seminal Fluid

The average volume of an ejaculate is approximately 3 milliliters. However, the volume of ejaculate is variable based on factors such as the time since last ejaculation, metabolic factors, and physical or physiological conditions. Most of the ejaculate volume is contributed by accessory glands: prostate, seminal vesicles, Cowper's glands, and glands of Littre. Each of these contributes identifiable materials into the seminal fluid mixture.

1. Testis

In addition to spermatozoa, the testes also are the source of glyceryl-phosphoryl choline, fructose, Na^+, K^+, and the isoenzymes PGM, ESD, and PEPA.

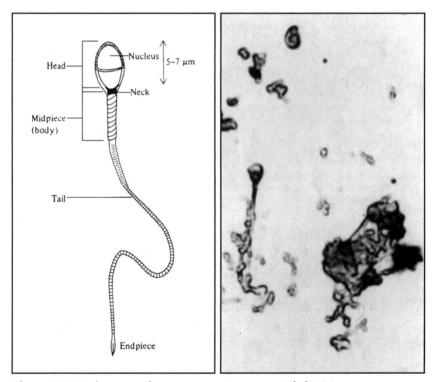

Figure 24.1 *A diagram of a mature spermatozoon (left). A photomicrograph of spermatozoa extracted from a vaginal swab obtained from a sex assault evidence kit (right).*

2. Prostate gland

Acid phosphatase, p30, citric acid, amylase, Ca^{2+}, Zn^{2+}, Fibrinolysin-splitting enzyme, and markers including LDH, PGM, Gm and Km are among the materials from the prostate portion of the ejaculate.

3. Seminal vesicles

The major portion, approximately 65 percent, of semen comes from the seminal vesicles. Fructose, albumin, lactoferrin, spermine, choline, transferrin and several inorganic ions can be identified from these structures.

4. Cowper's glands

This gland contributes amylase, proteinase, plasminogen inhibitor, and lysozyme.

24.2 Collection of Evidence Containing Semen
A. Clothing

1. Any garments suspected of containing seminal stains should be air dried at room temperature before packaging.
2. Individually package garments in separate paper bags or wrap in paper, being careful not to lose trace evidence, such as hairs, fibers, soil, and glass, which may loosely adhere to the surface of the clothing. If a seminal stain pattern is present and visible, wrap the clothing flat in paper to prevent damage to the pattern.
3. Place identification labels on the outside of the bag or package.

B. Sexual Assault Evidence Kit

1. Sexual assault evidence kits should be collected as soon as possible after the incident. The samples are collected by hospital staff, who should follow the standard collection protocol, which is usually provided as part of the kit. Figure 24.2 shows the contents of a sex crimes evidence kit; these materials are listed in Table 24.1.
2. Any items that are placed in the kit that may contain body fluids should be air dried before packaging. The kit is then sealed and placed in a refrigerator (not frozen) until delivery to the laboratory.
3. Deliver to the laboratory as soon as possible.

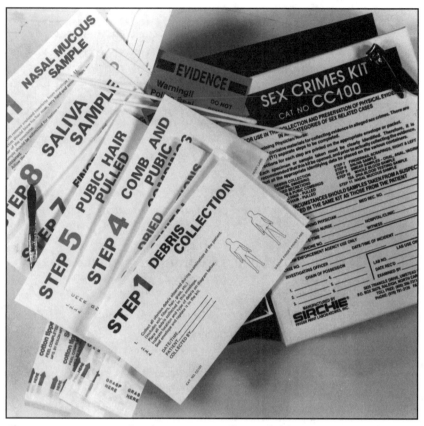

Figure 24.2 *An example of a commercially available sex crimes evidence collection kit.*

Table 24.1
Contents of a Typical Sexual Assault Evidence Kit

Known Sample from Victim	**Questioned Samples from Victim**
Whole blood sample	Vaginal smears and swabs
Saliva sample	Oral smears and swabs
Pulled pubic hairs	Anal smears and swabs
Pulled head hairs	Pubic combings
DNA control samples	Fingernail scrapings
	Genital swabbing
	Debris collection
	Dried secretions
	Nasal mucous

C. Condoms

1. If condoms are recovered from the scene, place these in a sterile plastic or glass specimen jar. Never package condoms in paper or envelopes.
2. Do not attempt to remove contents from the condom or to air dry this sample.
3. Label appropriately and refrigerate or freeze until transported to the laboratory.
4. Never place in, or in contact with, the sexual assault evidence kit.

D. Liquid Semen

1. Liquid semen should be collected in a clear syringe or disposable pipette and placed in a sterile test tube or specimen jar.
2. Keep the specimen refrigerated or frozen and transport to the laboratory as soon as possible.
3. Never place the semen specimen in the sexual assault evidence kit.
4. Alternately, collect the semen onto a sterile cotton gauze or cloth and air dry before placing in an envelope. Label the envelope and refrigerate or freeze until transported to the laboratory.

E. Large Items of Physical Evidence

1. If the item can be cut, remove the suspected semen by cutting around the stain after it has air dried and been thoroughly documented as to location. Package the cutting in an appropriately labeled paper envelope. Also cut a control sample of the material from an area near the stain.
2. If the stain is on a hard, nonabsorbent surface that cannot be submitted to the laboratory, such as a floor or counter, document the size, condition, and location of the sample. The stain may then be scraped onto a clean paper. Use a druggist fold and seal the resulting paper package in an envelope. Label appropriately.
3. If the stain is in a location or on a surface with a texture that cannot be scraped or cut, moisten a sterile swab or gauze with saline and remove the stain onto the swab after careful documentation of the evidence in its original condition. Use a minimum amount of liquid when collecting the sample. Swab vigorously on the suspected stain area. If it is a large area, use more than one swab. Air dry before packaging in paper and then in an envelope. A control swabbing should also be collected from a nearby area. Label the envelopes appropriately.

24.3 Laboratory Examination of Semen Evidence
A. Macroscopic Examination

Seminal stains produce either a whitish or yellowish, crusty residue. Using an ultraviolet wavelength light source or alternate light source may help to locate these stains, since components of semen often fluoresce when illuminated with these lights. This is particularly helpful with large items such as bedding, carpeting or car seats. The pattern of the seminal deposit may be more distinct when examined by such light sources.

B. Chemical Tests

Once a stain is located, the laboratory tests for the presence of acid phosphatase can be conducted. The suspected area is either swabbed or a small sample is cut and tested directly. Acid phosphatase is an enzyme found in high concentrations in semen, but since it is also found in other body fluids and substances, this test is only an indication of the possible presence of semen (screening test).

Chemical tests for other components of seminal fluid, such as spermine or choline, have also been developed. These tests detect biochemicals found in high concentrations in semen, but should not be considered as a positive means of identification of semen.

C. Confirmatory Tests for Semen

These tests confirm the presence of semen and rely on the identification of components unique to this body fluid. Since a sexual assault can occur without an ejaculation, it is important to note whether or not the suspect ejaculated, or if he wore a condom. This information is critical to the interpretation of laboratory findings. Also note the recent, previous sexual activity of the victim, as this may affect the laboratory interpretation of test results.

1. Microscopic

Spermatozoa are the male reproductive cells found exclusively in semen. A sample of the suspected stain is extracted in saline and this extract is then examined microscopically for spermatozoa. Sometimes a chemical stain is used to make recognition easier. The recognition of spermatozoa from their morphology is positive identification of semen.

2. Human seminal fluid protein (p30)

Tests for human seminal fluid protein are conducted when no spermatozoa are identified in the suspected semen stain extract. Since sperm cells are quite fragile, an intact sperm may be difficult to locate. In addition, vasectomized males and individuals who are aspermic due to various physiological conditions do not have spermatozoa in their semen. The presence of the seminal protein p30 (medically tested for using the PSA test) in an extract from a suspected semen stain can be detected by immunological methods. This test then positively identifies that the body fluid is semen. A simple card with stabilized test reagents referred to as an ABACard can quickly and easily indicate the presence of this material.

D. ABH Antigenic (Blood Group) Substances

If known saliva and blood samples are submitted from the suspect and the victim, then the questioned samples from the case can be tested for antigenic substances. Approximately 80 percent of the population are secretors and 20 percent are nonsecretors. The body fluids of secretors contain detectable levels of the antigenic substances associated with ABO typing. These substances can be determined and a suspect can be included or excluded as a possible donor of the seminal material from the blood group information developed.

E. DNA Testing

The genetic material from the male is found in the heads of the spermatozoa. This genetic material is the basis for the individualization of a semen stain by DNA analysis. In addition, in many cases the DNA from spermatozoa can be separated from the DNA of other nucleated cells in the sample, allowing for differentiation of victim and suspect DNA in a mixture stain. For a more detailed discussion of the DNA analyses conducted on seminal stains, refer to Chapter 11, *DNA Analysis.*

Figure 24.3 Intact spermatozoa.

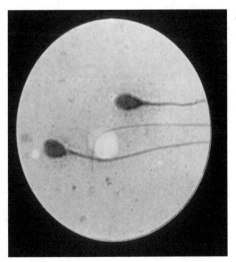

Chapter 25

Serial Number Restoration

Serial number restoration can be attempted on any stamped metal impression that has been altered or obliterated. This is not limited to firearms, but can also be successful on the metal identification tags found on a multitude of electronic devices and computer accessories, automobile parts, boats, airplane engines, and various appliances. Many manufacturers of fine jewelry and watches will also stamp serial numbers on their items. Serial number restoration is usually done by etching with an acid reagent. The stamping process deforms the crystal structure of the metal in the area that was stamped. As a result, the deformed areas react with the etching solution more rapidly than in undeformed areas. The possibility of success is largely determined by how the serial number was altered or obliterated (defaced) and how forcefully it was initially impressed. The deeper the defacing process has damaged the metal, the less likely the restoration process will be successful.

25.1 Collection of Evidence
A. Nature of Evidence
Due to the nature of the processes involved in raising serial numbers, submit items for restoration to an experienced laboratory for testing.

1. Small items of physical evidence, such as weapons, should be submitted to the laboratory intact.
2. Large items may require disassembly or cutting out the area with the

obliterated numbers. The area of interest can then be submitted for possible number restoration.

B. Packaging

Avoid packaging and transport methods that could further damage the area of interest.

25.2 Laboratory Restoration of Obliterated Serial Numbers

A. Methods of Restoration

The method of restoration used by the examiner will depend on several factors, including the type of metal into which the serial number was stamped and the method used to obliterate the number. After documentation of the original condition of the obliterated marking (usually careful close-up photography), the examiner will try to determine which method is the best to use. The following are some common procedures used in forensic laboratories to restore obliterated numbers.

1. Chemical restoration

Chemical etching is the fastest method to restore an obliterated marking. Several chemical solutions are used for this procedure, depending on the type of metal and specific alloy being etched. Table 25.1 lists some types of metals and reagents commonly used for restoration.

1. After careful examination, the first step is usually to smooth the area to remove gross scratches. This is usually done with emery cloth or a fine grinding tool.
2. Moisten a swab with the test solution and swab the area of the serial number.
3. Observe the area using a stereomicroscope after wetting and after the etching reaction has begun.
4. If the area has been contaminated with welding, it may be necessary to use instrumental analysis, for example, SEM-EDX, to determine if the type of metal in the weld is the same as the general composition of the item.
5. The etching, and any adjustments in the etchant used, is done on a trial and error basis.
6. The process is done in steps with etching, cleaning and viewing—and then additional etching and viewing as needed. The intermediate steps should be photographed in case some parts of the serial number become visible before others.

Table 25.1
Some Reagents Used in Obliterated Serial Numbers

Metal	Reagent Mixture
zinc-based	$KMnO_4$ = 10 grams Ethanol = 50 milliliters Conc. HCl = 80 milliliters Water = 60 milliliters
aluminum alloys, brass	$FeCl_3 \cdot 6H_2O$ = 6 grams H_2O or 1M HCl = 94 milliliters
steel, cast iron	$CuCl_2$ = 30 grams Conc. HCl = 30 milliliters Water = 33 milliliters

2. Electrolytic method

Electrochemical etching techniques can also be used to try to restore the obliterated number. The type of solution used during this procedure also depends on the metal being analyzed. It is important to follow closely chemical or electrolytic etching, since overexposure to the etching process can etch away the restored serial number.

B. Results

The examiner photographs all results after treatment, every step of the way, to record the serial number as it reappears. Use of oblique lighting may assist in determining the restored number. Thoroughly clean any surfaces exposed to chemicals and oil the metal to preserve the serial number after restoration. Because of variations in the initial stamping process and differences in how much metal was removed in the obliteration process, the etching process may not reveal the entire serial number at the same time, and some numbers or letters may appear and then be etched away before the process is complete.

Chapter 26

Soil

Soil is present at most crime scenes in one form or another and is usually recovered from evidence collected at the scene as a heterogeneous mixture which may include dust, clay, sand, rocks, plants, and other trace material. Soil is usually associated with outdoor scenes, but it may also play an important role in the investigation of indoor crime scenes.

Soil may either be deposited at or carried away from a crime scene, or moved from one scene to another. It may be present on or in any object that comes in contact with it. Some of the most common objects upon which soil or dust is found include: shoes, clothing, automobiles, tools, or weapons.

26.1 Nature of Soil

Soil is a complex mixture of diverse materials in a wide range of grain sizes. It contains mineral grains, decayed and other organic matter, plant materials, insects, animal derived matter and man-made particles. In general, the following materials are important for the forensic examination of soil.

A. Inorganic Materials

These components are primarily mineral grains derived from rocks. These minerals may be part of the natural environment or the result of transport to the area of origin of the soil. Particularly in suburban areas materials used in maintaining lawns and flowerbeds may add components not found naturally in the area.

B. Organic Matter

Decayed or decaying organic material is derived from plant and animal sources.

C. Man-made Materials

These can include any material, but commonly encountered particles include glass, paint chips, asphalt, concrete, plastic, rubber, fibers, deposited fly ash from industrial sites and other trace materials.

26.2 Collection of Soil and Dust Samples

The proper collection and analysis of soil or dust is extremely important in the reconstruction of a crime or in the association of a suspect or a victim with a crime. The following is an outline of some important aspects of the collection of soil or dust evidence under a variety of conditions.

A. Documentation

Collect dust and soil samples only after the scene and item have been properly documented with the appropriate photographs, sketches, videotape, and notes.

B. Collection and Packaging

1. Any control soil sample should consist of approximately 4 tablespoons of material from each of several locations characteristic of the scene.
2. If the samples can be brought to the laboratory immediately, place them in individual glass containers, seal, and label. If immediate transport is not possible, spread the samples out on clean paper and air dry for at least 24 hours before packaging.
3. Do not package soil samples in plastic bags, paper envelopes, or other containers with openings from which the soil may leak.

C. Impression Evidence

1. If the soil sample is to be taken from an impression, collect it after a cast has been made. Remember, do not clean the soil from a cast since it may be the best soil sample.

2. Then collect the soil from each impression or area that has a different color or texture.
3. Take additional samples from the four compass points surrounding the area of interest at a radius of a few feet; take a second set at a radius of 25 feet. The purpose of the additional samples is to establish how variable the soil is in the general area of interest.

D. Soil on Clothing

1. If soil or debris is present on a victim's or suspect's clothing, pack these items with paper between any folds or layers to avoid transfer, and wrap in paper or place in bags so that no soil is lost.
2. As is usually the case with physical evidence, do not package items of clothing, including shoes, in plastic bags.

E. Larger Evidence

In cases where larger clumps of soil are present at the scene, such as motor vehicle hit-and-run cases, make every effort to preserve the condition of these materials. Package the soil clumps with cushioning to preserve their integrity for layer analysis.

1. If collecting known samples from a suspect vehicle, take samples from each of the fender wells, since the layering may vary considerably among these areas.
2. If excavating a gravesite or other type of scene where material from below the surface layers may have been transferred, the investigator should also take a soil core sample from this area. The core should be as deep or slightly deeper than the grave, and should be maintained intact.

26.3 Laboratory Analysis of Soil

Because of the wide variety of soil components, as well as the nearly limitless types of soil mixtures, it is normally impossible to individualize the source of a soil sample. In most instances, it is only possible to render an opinion as to whether known control and evidence soil samples could have had a common origin. The following are some of the methods used in the forensic laboratory for soil analysis. The first step in any soil analysis is usually drying the soil.

A. Macroscopic Examination

The questioned and known soils are examined at relatively low magnification using a stereomicroscope. Each sample is examined to determine the presence of any identifiable materials. The physical characteristics of the soil sample, such as color and texture, are also noted. Unusual vegetation or insect parts, any trace materials and man-made components, such as metal filings, fibers, plastic, and paint, which may be unique to the sample are isolated and analyzed separately.

B. Initial Comparison

The first and often only comparison in a soil analysis is comparison of the dry color. If the color does not match, further analysis is usually not necessary.

C. Separation of Soil Components

1. The examiner passes the soil mixture through a series of sieves to determine a particle size distribution (see Section E below).
2. The examiner may then analyze the physical, mineralogical, morphological, and chemical characteristics of each portion.

D. Density

A density gradient tube filled with liquids ranging from quite high at the bottom to much lower at the top can be used to generate a density gradient profile for each soil sample for comparison purposes.

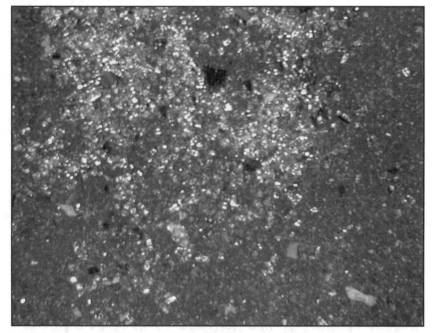

Figure 26.1 *Sieved trace particles from a shooting crime scene (right).*

E. Particle Size Distribution

Examination of a dried and gently broken up soil sample, using a series of sieves with decreasing screen size, yield a particle size distribution for that soil and then determines the percent composition by weight for each sieve portion. It has been found that this particle size distribution is a rather good discriminator of soils. Use of the polarizing light microscope (or petrographic microscope) allows for further comparison and identification of the mineral components of a soil sample. Emphasis is usually on sand grain size mineral particles and the high-density minerals usually give the most useful comparative information.

F. Instrumental Analysis

Identification of the inorganic materials in soil may be accomplished by use of atomic absorption spectroscopy, SEM-EDX or emission spectroscopy. Examiners may also use FTIR, GC and differential thermal analysis to analyze other organic and inorganic components of the soil.

Chapter 27

Tape

═══════════════════════════════

Tape is a common type of physical evidence encountered in criminal investigations. There has been an increase in the number of cases in which tapes have been used in the commission of crimes; therefore, investigators routinely submit tape evidence to forensic laboratories for examination. Tape is used in a variety of crimes such as homicides, burglaries, bombings and sexual assaults, to name a few. Criminals generally use tape to secure items such as an individuals' mouth for noise reduction or an individual's extremities to prevent escape, or wrap and protect objects such as explosive devices and marijuana bricks.

27.1 Nature of Tape Evidence

An enormous variety of tapes are manufactured for a multitude of purposes. Any of these can be encountered at a crime scene or otherwise employed in the commission of a crime. Black electrical tape, masking tape, duct tape, adhesive tape, construction tapes and scotch tape are most common. All tapes are composed of two basic components, ribbon and adhesive, but some specialty tapes may be more complex and have reinforcing layers for example.

243

A. Ribbon

The ribbon portion of tape can be composed of many types of material and varies in width and thickness. Generally, the ribbon portion of the tape is composed of paper, cloth or some polymeric material (plastic).

B. Adhesive

Vegetable, animal, or synthetic adhesives are used to attach the ribbon to the item being taped. A wide variety of adhesives are used which are carefully tailored to the particular application and therefore can be used to characterize the tape and differentiate it from other tapes.

27.2 Collection of Tape Evidence

1. Whenever possible, submit tape evidence to the laboratory as it is found. For example, do not remove tape from an inanimate object, such as a window. Rather, submit the item with tape in place.
2. If it becomes necessary to cut a portion of tape prior to submission, such as from the victim's wrists at autopsy, cut away from any tape ends already present. Clearly identify in some manner the cut ends made after the crime.
3. Make no attempt to separate tape or unravel balled-up tape at the time of collection. This can result in the loss of valuable fingerprint and trace evidence. Package the tape loosely in a bag or some other container to prevent loss of evidence and sticking of the tape to the packaging.

27.3 Laboratory Examination of Tapes
A. Trace Materials

The examiner should remove any trace materials from tape before any chemical testing or latent print processing. The tape can be submerged in liquid nitrogen in order to remove these trace materials and not destroy other potentially crucial forensic evidence. Careful picking with a probe or fine forceps will often suffice as well. Once these trace materials are removed, follow specific procedures for the examination of these types of trace evidence. In addition, pay special attention to preserving any latent fingerprints that may be on the tape surfaces. Physical and chemical characteristics of a tape sample can then be examined and compared to known sample tapes. Liquid nitrogen or some other solvents have been used to help unravel tape without losing other evidence.

B. Physical Match

In some cases with cut or torn pieces of tape, the edge of the tape piece can be compared to the cut or torn end on a seized roll of tape or other torn tape samples. The examiner should make macroscopic and microscopic examination of the ends of the two portions of tape for a possible physical match. A physical match can establish that the item of evidence came from the roll of tape, or that two pieces were removed from the same roll of tape in sequence.

C. Macroscopic Examination

If possible, the examiner should observe and compare physical characteristics of the tape, such as color of the tape and the adhesive, width, thickness, design, inclusions, texture, fiber counts (reinforced tapes) and gloss on the questioned item with the known tape sample.

D. Microscopic Examination

Microscopy can be used for more detailed examination of the morphology of a tape sample. In addition, polarized light microscopy can help in quickly comparing the tape components, and is especially useful when analyzing reinforced tapes, such as duct tapes, to identify the nature of the reinforcing material. Examination of fibers used to give strength to the ribbon of the tape can often give additional information for comparison.

E. Chemical Properties

It is possible to determine the solubility and composition of the adhesive and ribbon of the tape, usually through a combination of chemical and instrumental analysis.

F. Instrumental Analysis

Various instrumental analyses can determine the nature of the materials used to make both the tape ribbon and its adhesive.

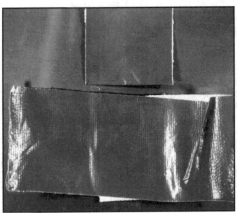

Figure 27.1 Two pieces of tape—the top one was recovered from the suspect's vehicle and the bottom one was found at the crime scene.

1. Fourier transform infrared spectroscopy (FTIR)

Analysis by Fourier transform infrared spectroscopy (FTIR) of the adhesive side, the backing side and any plasticizer used in the ribbon, will usually allow identification of the composition of each and allow comparison with known or other questioned sample. Black plastic electrical tape, for example, is commonly used as a means to hold together and insulate electrical components in an explosive device. Surprisingly frequently, much of the tape survives the explosion.

2. Pyrolysis GC

Pyrolysis GC can analyze and compare the composition of the tape layers. Since FTIR usually gives sufficient data and is nondestructive, it is more commonly used now than pyrolysis GC; however, both can give information useful for comparison.

3. SEM/EDX

Scanning electron microscope with an energy dispersive x-ray analyzer (SEM/EDX) can identify inorganic materials used as filler within the tape layers or trace amounts of materials adhering to the tape surfaces, in addition to giving a clearer view of the surface structure.

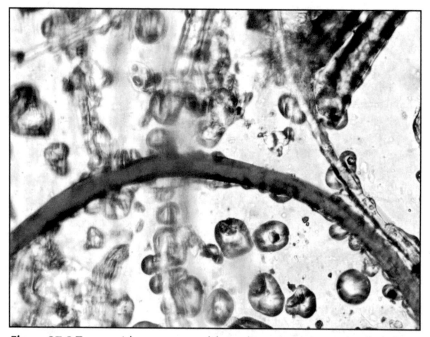

Figure 27.2 *Trace evidence removed from the tape and examined under microscope.*

Chapter 28

Toolmarks

A toolmark is any impression, cut, gouge, scratch, indentation or other marking left in or on an object by another object or instrument being forced into or moved across it. Forensic scientists often encounter toolmarks when examining manufactured materials or evidence to which mechanical force has been applied, such as a pried-open door.

28.1 Nature of Toolmark Evidence

Toolmarks usually are found in one of two categories: compression (indentation) marks and sliding toolmarks.

A. Compression Toolmarks

A compression toolmark results when force is applied between two objects in a roughly perpendicular direction. There is no lateral movement between the surfaces. In this instance, the harder material will mark the softer material in a three-dimensional replica of that portion of the harder material (usually the tool) that is making contact.

B. Sliding Toolmarks

A sliding toolmark will show striations caused by a lateral movement of one object across another. These striations result when the harder material is forced into the softer material from an oblique angle. The stria result from macro or micro imperfections in the contact area of the tool. Figure 28.1 shows typical toolmark evidence that might be submitted from a crime scene for laboratory examination.

28.2 Documentation and Collection of Toolmarks
A. Photo Documentation

1. Take overall photographs of the object containing the toolmark, both with and without a scale, to show the nature of the toolmark and its relationship to the scene. Include information that will specifically identify the top, bottom, inside, and outside of the submitted object.

2. Take a second set of photographs that will specifically show the toolmark detail. Because toolmarks are three-dimensional and photographs are only two-dimensional, examiners cannot usually make successful examinations from photographs alone. Therefore, wherever possible submit both the object marked and the tool for laboratory examination.

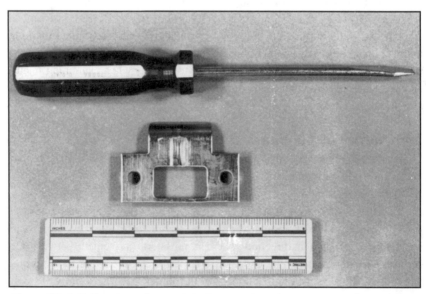

Figure 28.1 *Collection of materials for a toolmark comparison between this striker plate from a forced door and this screwdriver found in the possession of the burglary suspect.*

B. Written Documentation

Thoroughly document the item of physical evidence and the toolmark area with written notes, sketches and measurements.

C. Marking Toolmark Evidence

Wire, cable or objects of similar nature that may receive an additional cut from the submitting officer in order to detach them, must be clearly marked as to which end shows the suspect or evidence cut. This may seem elementary, but it is often impossible to properly orient objects once they are removed from their original positions. Notes taken at the scene should clearly reflect which end of the wire or cable was marked as the original cut.

D. Trace Evidence

The investigator should also be alert for the presence of trace evidence such as paint, glass, metal and blood that also may be present on the tool or in the toolmark and which may warrant analysis at the laboratory.

Figure 28.2 Forensic investigators check the point of entry and search for toolmark evidence on the screen.

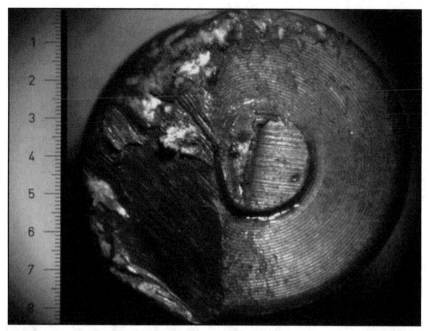

Figure 28.3 Photomicrograph shows the toolmarks on the metal surface.

E. Collection of Toolmark Evidence

1. Small items of evidence

a. By far, the best method for comparison of toolmarks is to secure the actual item containing the mark and to submit it to the laboratory along with the suspected tool. Take care to protect the working area of the suspect tool by wrapping it in paper or other cushioning material.

b. Under no circumstances should the investigator attempt to fit the tool into the mark; this may destroy the very evidence that the expert will examine. In addition, valuable trace evidence will be contaminated, transferred or lost by this action.

2. Large or immovable items

a. In dealing with large articles or articles not easily moved, the toolmark itself should be cut out of the object bearing the marking. This portion should be packaged and secured to prevent damage to the excised toolmark.

b. If it is not possible to remove the toolmark, the investigator has the option of making a high-resolution silicone rubber cast of the toolmark. Silicone rubber is recommended for such a replica, as it will reproduce the necessary detail for examination. *Note:* Plaster of Paris or dental stone are unsuitable for this type of casting, since they normally will not yield sufficiently detailed impressions, and will not be accepted for analysis at most laboratories. Silicone rubber kits are commercially available from forensic or dental supply houses; technicians should follow the individual kit instructions. The investigator may press the strings of an evidence tag into the edges of the casting material in a way that will not affect the area of interest and fill in the tag with the proper identification data.

28.3 Laboratory Analysis of Toolmark Evidence

Because of the complexity of toolmark comparisons, detailed comparison of a tool left behind at the crime scene with a toolmark at the scene probably is not justified unless the suspect tool or weapon can be associated with a suspect through investigation.

A. Class Characteristics

It is sometimes possible to determine general characteristics of a tool used at a crime scene from microscopic examination of the toolmark. Comparison of these characteristics to known tools associated with the case may lead to possible inclusion or exclusion of this tool as the source of a toolmark.

B. Comparison of Individual Markings

As with firearms evidence, the extended use of a tool will produce individual marks that are then reproduced in the softer substance when the tool is used. Using a comparison microscope, the examiner compares individual characteristics in a toolmark from the scene with toolmarks produced under controlled laboratory conditions. Depending on the type of tool and the object on which it was used, many test markings may be required to reproduce the angle or other conditions under which the toolmark was made. An example of a toolmark comparison is shown in Figure 28.4. These comparisons can show consistency (tool could have made the mark) or even in some cases individualization (this tool made the mark).

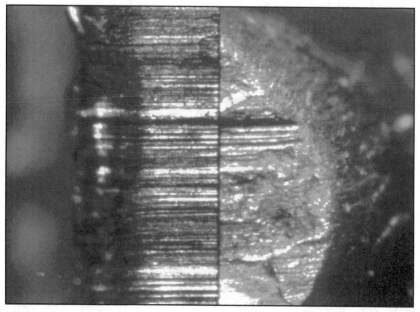

Figure 28.4 *A toolmark comparison made through the use of a comparison microscope. The test marking made at the laboratory (left) matches the striations found at the point of entry at a crime scene (right).*

Chapter 29

Voice Identification

In cases involving tape-recorded messages containing threats, obscene phone calls, wire taps, intercepted conversations, false alarms, or other criminal violations it may be helpful to conduct analysis and comparison of voices on the tape. These procedures are also often applied in investigations to analyze messages left on phone answering machines. The voiceprint or other more modern spectral analysis techniques can link a suspect to a particular recording, with the identification based on the analysis of unique patterns produced when an individual speaks a series of words. Today, only a few forensic laboratories conduct voiceprint analyses. Because of very active research in computer voice recognition for noncriminal applications, better tools for the investigator are now available and will continue to improve.

29.1 Principle of Voice Analysis
A. Voice Characteristics
The basic principle underlying voiceprint analysis is that each individual's voice has its own quality and characteristics. These characteristics arise from individual variation in the vocal mechanism.

B. Voice Spectrograms
Voice characteristics are recorded and transferred to a sound spectrograph. Voice spectrograms are produced by the voice spectrograph, which converts the sounds to a visual graphic display or voiceprint. The probability that voice characteristics and spectrograms will be exactly the same in two individuals is remote. This

is an old technology which will undoubtedly be replaced by newer computerized techniques.

29.2 Collection of Audio Samples
A. Questioned Samples
In the vast majority of cases, the only equipment needed to obtain the unknown sample (telephone calls) is a good quality recorder and an induction telephone pickup coil.

1. The victim can easily learn to activate the recorder as the telephone rings for each incoming call.
2. If the call is recorded by an automatic system, as is commonly found in 911 centers, police or fire departments, it becomes necessary to make a second or dubbed recording for laboratory analysis. The use of a second recorder and a patch cord attached directly between both recorders will accomplish this, thus eliminating any noise occurring in the environment of the recorders. This method will prevent the loss of significant information for identification.
3. Should there be an absence of jack outlets on the original recording machine, place the microphone for the second recorder in front of the speaker of the original recorder. This is the least desirable method, as the resultant tape will now contain any additional noise present in the recording site, and may lose information that was present on the original tape. Should this seem to be the only method available, consult the voice identification unit of the laboratory or agency for an alternate means of recording the sample.

B. Known Samples
Examiners use recordings of known origin for comparison to the questioned samples.

1. It is of primary importance that the text of both samples be identical. Random conversations will not be sufficient for comparison purposes.
2. The investigator should make every effort to duplicate the questioned samples as closely as possible regarding the context and conditions under which it was recorded, such as telephone, live conversation, or radio. Remember that while the quality of the evidence sample cannot be controlled, in many instances investigators can control the quality and the environment in which the known sample is recorded.

3. To ensure uniformity between the samples, make an effort to record them in surroundings that are free from other sounds which may mask the samples.

4. It is necessary in longer samples to have a transcription of the unknown sample. This will assist the investigator in obtaining a known sample and will also assist the voice identification examiner in examining the samples.

5. The investigator should make every effort to ensure that the suspect repeats the text duplicating inflection, speed, and, if possible, the emotion shown in the unknown sample. As reading out loud produces flat, robot-like samples, it is preferable that the investigator read the sample to the suspect, a phrase at a time, for repetition by that suspect.

6. Repeat the entire sample for the recording three times to provide a more natural sample of the suspect's normal speaking habits. It is perfectly permissible to have the investigator's voice on the tape as well as the suspect's voice.

7. Preface the tape with information containing the identity of the speaker, who is present, and the date and time of the recording. Known samples may be obtained either voluntarily or by court order.

29.3 Laboratory Comparison of Recordings and Spectrograms

By comparing voiceprints, an examiner may be able to make a determination as to whether a suspect made a particular phone call or recording. The examiner studies characteristic patterns on the spectrograph for groups of words or phrases. In order to draw a useful conclusion, an examiner must make a positive comparison of ten or more words or phonemes (the smallest units of spoken sound). Figure 29.1 shows two spectrograms produced when two individuals produced the same sounds. As with other comparisons used in forensic science, an exclusion can be as useful as an inclusion. Often the spectral analysis and other computer-based techniques can be made more reliable through the use of a human expert to aurally compare the recordings as well. In addition, modern electronic techniques can help to identify background noises or voices barely audibly to the human ear. This type of information can often be of considerable investigative value.

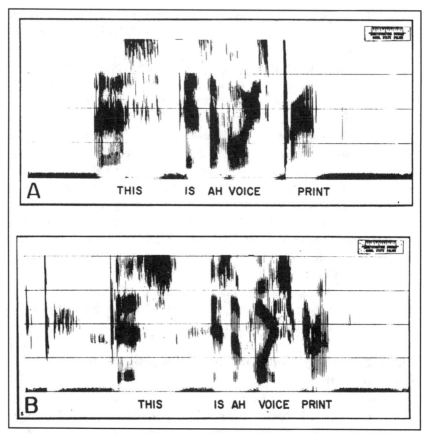

Figure 29.1 *The spectrograms produced when two individuals produced the same sounds: "This is a voice print."*

Part III
Legal Aspects of Forensic Science

Chapter 30

Proper Seizure of Evidence for Effective Utilization in Court

30.1 Introduction

Evidence used in court must have been legally obtained by law enforcement and its seizure should be well documented to help establish its admissibility. Compliance with the Fourth Amendment is one of the key requirements for admissibility of physical evidence. This chapter will discuss how to comply with Fourth Amendment requirements. A particular jurisdiction may have more stringent or somewhat modified rules. A jurisdiction can require an investigator to adhere to stricter standards than those required by the Fourth Amendment. Investigators must be aware of the specific requirements of their jurisdiction. This chapter will assist crime scene and fire investigators in performing their jobs in a legally satisfactory way. Some special attention and specific examples will highlight the unique problems of a fire scene search. Although it should be evident that a fire scene search is really just one type of a crime scene investigation, it is important to recognize some of the special problems that come up in the context of a fire scene search.

The Fourth Amendment protects persons from unreasonable searches and seizures. The first step in an analysis under the Fourth Amendment is to decide whether the Fourth Amendment even protects the particular property involved. If it does not, there is no need to obtain an administrative or search warrant. If the Fourth Amendment does apply under the circumstances, this section will discuss some of the essential elements in obtaining a warrant to search the property, and some of the alternatives to seeking a warrant.

If a warrant is required, it must specify, or "particularize" the items to be seized. This particularity requirement will be discussed later. In addition, the proper procedure for handling and preserving evidence for presentation in court will be discussed.

30.2 When Does the Fourth Amendment Apply?
A. The Fourth Amendment
The Fourth Amendment provides:

> The right of the people to be secure in their persons, houses, papers, and effects, against unreasonable searches and seizures, shall not be violated, and no warrants shall issue, but upon probable cause, supported by oath or affirmation, and particularly describing the place to be searched, and the persons or things to be seized.

This is, of course, part of our Federal Constitution and the states are bound by it as well. The states are free to provide additional protection in their constitutions or by law, as indicated above.

B. Reasonable Expectation of Privacy
The central question in deciding whether or not the Fourth Amendment applies to a piece of property (which can be a building, an article of clothing, a motor vehicle,

or any personal possession) is whether or not there is a reasonable expectation of privacy in the property. The United States Supreme Court has emphasized that the Fourth Amendment protects people, not places. Therefore, an analysis of whether or not Fourth Amendment protection applies to a crime scene must be guided by the Court's definition of when someone has a reasonable expectation of privacy.

In *Katz v. United States*, 389 U.S. 347 (1967), the United States Supreme Court ruled that this reasonable expectation of privacy test determines whether or not the Fourth Amendment applies. In his concurring opinion, in *Katz,* Justice Harlan gave a practical, utilitarian approach to defining a reasonable expectation of privacy: 1) Has the person exhibited an actual, subjective expectation of privacy? 2) Is the person's expectation of privacy one that society will recognize as objectively reasonable? If the answer to both of these questions is "yes," and there is a subjective expectation of privacy which is objectively reasonable, then the Fourth Amendment applies.

Discussions about whether the Fourth Amendment applies to property sometimes use the terms "open fields" and "curtilage." In *Oliver v. United States,* 466 U.S.170 (1984), the United States Supreme Court ruled that the Fourth Amendment does not protect open fields but does apply to the curtilage (the area adjacent to the home and associated with the intimate activities of the home). The most difficult question which arises in this context is whether an area is an open field or is curtilage.

In *United States v. Dunn*, 480 U.S. 294 (1987), the United States Supreme Court outlined several factors to help guide investigators in deciding whether property is an open field or curtilage. Perhaps the most significant factor is whether the property is being used for activities associated with the intimate and daily activities of the home or home life, for example, children's toys, a clothesline, lawn furniture, a swimming pool. Additional factors include: the distance from the house itself, whether the property is within a fenced-in area around the house, and finally, whether the defendant has done anything to protect the privacy of the house. If the property is considered "curtilage," the Fourth Amendment applies. If, on the other hand, the property is an open field, because there is no reasonable expectation of privacy, the Fourth Amendment does not apply and no warrant is needed to enter onto the property.

C. Abandoned Property

The Fourth Amendment does not apply to abandoned property. When an individual abandons property, he gives up any reasonable expectation of privacy which he may have had. This reasoning explains why when a person puts his garbage out at the curb for collection, no search warrant is needed to go through his garbage bags. In *California v. Greenwood*, 486 U.S. 35 (1988), the Court held that there is no reasonable expectation of privacy in garbage left at the curb for pick-up. The court did not, however, address whether or not there is an expectation of privacy in garbage left on the curtilage, as opposed to garbage left on the public sidewalk. Therefore, it remains an open question whether the Fourth Amendment protects garbage found within the curtilage.

D. Importance of Knowing When the Fourth Amendment Applies

The importance of knowing when the Fourth Amendment applies and when it does not cannot be overemphasized. When the Fourth Amendment does apply, investigators must either obtain a warrant, or be sure that they fall within one of the narrowly defined situations where they are excused from obtaining a warrant.

E. Sanction for Failing to Comply with the Fourth Amendment

Failure to comply with the requirements of the Fourth Amendment can result in suppression of the evidence. In *Mapp v. Ohio,* 367 U.S. 643 (1961), the United Sates Supreme Court applied the Exclusionary Rule to evidence illegally seized by state or local law enforcement. The main purpose of the Exclusionary Rule is to deter illegal police misconduct. The reasoning underlying the rule is that if police misconduct is punished by the exclusion of evidence then police will be deterred from acting improperly. In the years since the adoption of the rule, the Supreme Court has carved out some exceptions to the suppression of improperly seized evidence. The good faith exception recognizes that excluding evidence seized in good faith, though perhaps improperly, does not deter noncompliance with the Fourth Amendment. In *Massachusetts v. Shephard*, 468 U.S. 981 (1984), the Supreme Court held that where the police act in good faith, and the judge or magistrate makes the mistake, there will be no exclusion of evidence. In *United States v. Leon*, the Court held that where police have a good faith belief that probable cause exists and had drafted a thorough warrant, the good faith exception can save an otherwise invalid warrant. Some states have refused to follow *Leon*, reasoning instead that no search should be allowed on less than probable cause.

Other exceptions to the exclusionary rule are the independent source doctrine and the inevitable discovery doctrine. *Murray v. United States,* 487 U.S. 533 (1988*); Nix v. Williams*, 467 U.S. 431 (1984).

30.3 Situations When a Search Can Be Performed Without a Warrant

This section discusses those situations most common to crime scenes and fire investigations where property may be searched and seized without a warrant.

Warrantless searches are considered unreasonable unless they fall into one of the narrowly carved-out categories of exceptions which the Supreme Court has created. The exceptions which most often apply in crime scene and arson investigations are described below.

A. Consent

Consent, when freely and voluntarily given, is one of the well-recognized exceptions to the warrant requirement. It is important to understand that a free and voluntary consent to search is more than just a mere acquiescence to the investigator's wishes. The burden of proving that consent has been freely and voluntarily given is on the prosecution.

Challenges to a consent search: the two most common challenges to a consent search are that it was not voluntary, or that the person giving the consent did not have the authority to do so.

1) The consent was not voluntary: The United States Supreme Court has set forth a number of factors that it will examine in deciding whether consent is voluntary. In *Schneckloth v. Bustamonte*, 412 U.S. 218 (1973), the following factors were among those considered important: the defendant's age, education level, intelligence, lack of advice concerning constitutional rights, length of detention, physical punishment, and the nature and extent of the questioning. The investigator must keep these factors in mind and be prepared to meet this burden of proving a free and voluntary consent. 2) The authority of the person giving consent: This was addressed in *United States v. Matlock*, 415 U.S.164 (1974), where the Supreme Court held that: "The consent of one who possesses common authority over premises or effects is valid as against the absent, non-consenting person with whom that authority is shared."

In *Matlock*, the United States Supreme Court ruled that a woman had the authority to consent to the search of the room which she shared with her boyfriend, the defendant. The Court, however, emphasized that not everyone with joint property interests has common authority over property. For instance, a landlord's right of entry under a lease does not give common authority to consent legally to a search of rented premises. Likewise, a hotel clerk cannot consent to the search of a rented room. The *Matlock* decision does recognize that cohabitants assume the risk that one of them may permit shared areas to be searched. The situation sometimes arises where one cohabitant consents and one does not. In *Georgia v. Randolph*, 547 U.S. 103 (2006), the Court held that evidence could not be admitted against a cohabitant who is present and objects to a search.

It is important to recognize that, while consents are extremely useful, and perhaps the most expeditious vehicle for compliance when the Fourth Amendment applies, they can be withdrawn or limited at any time before the search is completed. Sample consent to search forms should be developed in each jurisdiction to ensure that a valid consent can be proven.

B. Exigency

Exigent or emergency circumstances have been recognized in some situations as exceptions to the warrant requirement.

1. Fire scene searches

It is uncontroverted that "a burning building clearly presents an exigency of sufficient proportion to render a warrantless entry 'reasonable.'" *Michigan v. Tyler*, 436 U.S. 499 (1978). In the *Tyler* case, which involved an arson at a furniture store, the United States Supreme Court also held that officials may remain on the scene of the fire for a reasonable time after it has been extinguished to determine its cause. The Court stated that this reasonable time is allowable because "prompt determination of the fire's origin may be necessary to prevent its recurrence as through the detection of continuing dangers such as faulty wiring or a defective furnace. Immediate investigation may also be necessary to preserve evidence from intentional or accidental destruction." The Court recognized in *Tyler* that what is a reasonable time may vary widely depending on the nature and circumstances of a particular fire or a particular building. As a result, in the *Tyler* case, the Supreme Court found that the entries on the same day as the fire were just a continuation of the initial entry, and that evidence was properly seized. Entries occurring after that day were not justified by the initial exigency and the evidence was therefore suppressed.

In *Michigan v. Clifford*, 464 U.S. 287 (1983), the United States Supreme Court ratified its earlier holding in *Tyler*, that firefighters and fire investigators may make a warrantless entry into a building while the fire is burning and for a reasonable time thereafter. The Court recognized that the Fourth Amendment does apply to a building even though it has suffered fire damage, although the Court peripherally noted that some fires may cause such extensive destruction that no reasonable expectation of privacy remains in the property. In discussing the question as to whether or not there was a reasonable expectation of privacy, the Court in *Clifford* observed, "We frequently have noted that privacy interests are especially strong in a private residence." This should serve as a caution to investigators that any court is more likely to find a reasonable expectation of privacy in a private residence than with other types of property interests.

In *Clifford*, the United States Supreme Court went on to discuss the type of warrant needed to enter a house after a fire has been extinguished and a reasonable time has expired. The Court held that, where the purpose of the search is to determine the cause and origin of a fire, an administrative warrant is proper. The scope of such an administrative warrant is limited, however, to the finding of the cause of the fire. In other words, once fire investigators have discovered evidence which gives probable cause to believe a crime has been committed, they must cease their activity, because to do otherwise would exceed the allowable scope of an administrative search.

Once fire investigators have fulfilled the mandate of the administrative search warrant, which is to find the cause and origin of the fire, they must obtain a conventional search warrant based on the probable cause that they have developed. They may, of course, seize the evidence which they found during the course of their legitimate activities under the plain view doctrine. As the Court stated: "The plain view doctrine must be applied in light of the special circumstances that frequently accompany fire damage. In searching solely to ascertain the cause, firemen customarily must remove rubble or search other areas where the cause of fires is likely to be found. An object which comes into view during such a search may be preserved without a warrant."

In *Clifford*, the Court suppressed all evidence which was found in the Cliffords' house and which was seized without a warrant. The only item of evidence which was not suppressed was a Coleman fuel can that had been left by firefighters in the Cliffords' driveway before they left the premises. Because fire investigators entered several hours after this time without an administrative warrant, the Court held that their entry was a violation of the Fourth Amendment.

In order to obtain an administrative warrant, the Supreme Court in *Clifford* set out the following requirements: 1) Investigators must establish that a fire of undetermined origin has occurred; 2) The scope of the search must be reasonable and must not unnecessarily invade the victim's privacy; 3) The administrative warrant will be executed at a reasonable, convenient time; and 4) In some jurisdictions, the administrative warrant will contain a description of the investigative efforts which already have been undertaken, and may properly include a description of the owner's or occupant's efforts to secure the property since extinguishing the fire. The fire investigator should also be aware that in situations where there is a homicide or where there is danger to human life, the United States Supreme Court's decision in *Mincey v. Arizona,* 437 U.S. 385 (1978) may apply.

2. Other crime scene searches

In *Mincey v. Arizona*, 437 U.S. 385 (1978), the United States Supreme Court held that when police officers come upon the scene of a homicide and "they reasonably believe that a person within is in need of immediate aid, they may make a prompt warrantless search of the area to see if there are other victims or if the killer is still on the premises." In other words, the Supreme Court has authorized investigators at the scene of a homicide to make a *victim-suspect* search. The Court also authorized that any item which the police officers see in plain view during the course of these legitimate emergency activities may be properly seized.

Once police officers have ascertained that there is no suspect and have rendered any necessary aid, they are required to secure and obtain a search warrant, which has come to be known as a *Mincey* warrant. This is because in *Mincey*, the Court held that a "warrantless search must be strictly circumscribed by the exigencies which justify its initiation...." Some investigators may be inclined to minimize the need for a Mincey warrant by assuming that there is no possible perpetrator who possesses a reasonable expectation of privacy in the crime scene. Investigators may assume too quickly that a total stranger committed the crime. This is a very dangerous assumption, especially in light of the Supreme Court's decision in *Minnesota v. Olson*, 495 U.S. 91 (1990), where the Court held that an overnight guest has a reasonable expectation of privacy in the host's premises.

C. Automobile Exception

Another long-standing and well-recognized exception to the warrant requirement is the automobile exception or car doctrine, which was first enunciated in *Carroll v. United States*, 267 U.S.132 (1925), when the United States Supreme Court allowed the search of mobile vehicles, which are located in a public place, and for which the investigator has probable cause to believe contain criminal evidence.

In *California v. Acevedo*, 498 U.S. 807 (1990), the Court expanded the *Carroll* doctrine to allow the search of a closed container found in a car. The investigators had probable cause to believe that narcotics were in a package in the trunk of the car, and the Court held that the package could be searched without a warrant. This case made clear that investigators may search a closed container for which they have probable cause, and answered the long-standing constitutional law question about searches of containers which officers have probable cause to believe contain contraband. This case did not address the question of the propriety of forcing open locked containers.

D. Inventory Searches

Another exception to the warrant requirement of the Fourth Amendment is an inventory search pursuant to a standardized routine investigative procedure. In *Colorado v. Bertine*, 479 U.S. 367 (1987), the Court held that routine inventory searches are proper, and may even include the opening of closed containers as a reasonable part of an inventory search. In *Florida v. Wells*, 495 U.S.1 (1990), the United States Supreme Court clarified that the forcing open of locked containers may be made part of a routine inventory procedure. It is necessary that the inventory procedure be properly drafted to cover locked containers in order to take advantage of *Wells*.

E. Plain View

The essential elements of the plain view exception to the warrant requirement are:

- The investigator is where he has a legal right to be (whether by warrant, consent, or exigency); and
- The investigator has probable cause to associate the item with criminal activity.

In *Horton v. California*, 496 U.S.128 (1990), the United States Supreme Court eliminated what had been a long-standing third requirement: that the item be discovered inadvertently.

It is important to keep in mind that once an investigator's justification for being on the premises has lapsed, the plain view doctrine is no longer available to justify the search for and seizure of evidence. For instance, if an investigator has made entry onto a fire scene under the justification of an administrative warrant, and that investigator has developed probable cause to believe a crime has been committed, the authority of the administrative warrant has expired and the plain view seizure would not be constitutional at that point.

F. Search Incident to Custodial Arrest—Stationhouse Searches

When a defendant has been taken into lawful custodial arrest, her person and the area within her immediate control are subject to search incident to this arrest. A search incident to an arrest is another well-established exception to the warrant requirement. *Chimel v. California*, 395 U.S. 752 (1969).

When the defendant is stopped in a car, and placed under custodial arrest, this exception has been expanded to include a search of the passenger compartment of a motor vehicle and open or closed containers within that passenger compartment. *New York v. Belton*, 453 U.S. 454 (1981). The holding in *Belton* was significantly restricted in *Arizona v. Gant*, 129 S.Ct. 1710 (2009) when the Supreme Court held that:

Police may search a vehicle incident to a recent occupant's arrest only if the arrestee is within reaching distance of the passenger compartment at the time of the search or it is reasonable to believe the vehicle contains evidence of the offense of arrest. When these justifications are absent, a search of an arrestee's vehicle will be unreasonable unless police obtain a warrant or show that another exception to the warrant requirement applies.

Justice Alito wrote a strong dissent in *Gant* challenging the decision's assumption that the right to search incident ends when the arrestee is in handcuffs, use of a standard of "reason to believe" rather that probable cause, and limitation of searches to evidence of the crime of arrest.

In addition, the Court has ruled that the taking of a defendant's clothes at the time of his custodial arrest is a normal incident of such a custodial arrest. *United States v. Edwards*, 415 U.S. 800 (1974). The stationhouse seizure of an arrestee's clothing subject to a lawful custodial arrest and within a reasonable time after that arrest can yield valuable forensic evidence. This stationhouse seizure of clothing is an area of the law where many local jurisdictions have seen fit to impose stricter, and sometimes unusual, requirements on investigators. As with all areas of constitutional law, it is important to coordinate investigative search policies with the investigator's local prosecutor.

G. Caretaking Search

In certain limited circumstances the Supreme Court has recognized the existence of a caretaking search. In *Cady v. Dombroski,* small town police were allowed to search a car for a gun they thought an off-duty police officer had left in the vehicle. At least one state has restricted the use of items found during a caretaker search and has required a warrant for the forensic examination of evidence seized under the caretaking exception. This warrant requirement for laboratory analysis of caretaking evidence is currently limited to Connecticut. *State v. Joyce*, 229 Conn. 10 (1994).

H. Stop and Frisk

In *Terry v. Ohio*, 392 U.S.1 (1968) the Supreme Court recognized the necessity for police to perform investigative detentions on less that probable cause and to frisk suspects for weapons. Other evidence may properly be seized during the course of a stop and frisk if the contraband nature of the article is immediately apparent to the investigating officer upon a frisk of the subject. This is called the "Plain Feel Doctrine" and is the touch corollary of the plain view doctrine, which is discussed above. *Minnesota v. Dickerson*. 508 U.S.366 (1993).

30.4 Search Warrant Must Particularize the Items the Investigator is Requesting Permission to Seize
A. Description of Things to Be Seized

The Fourth Amendment requires that a search warrant particularly describe the things to be seized.

If the description of the items to be seized is too general, the court may not allow the evidence. "The property must be identified sufficiently to prevent a mere roving commission." *United States v. Scharfman*, 448 F.2d 1352, 1354 (2d Cir. 1971). In order to be confident of compliance with the Fourth Amendment's particularity requirement, investigators should be as specific as possible in describing items to be seized, and avoid broad generalities. The application in support of the search warrant must provide probable cause to believe that the item particularized will be found at the location to be searched.

B. Examples of Particularizing Items

1. Items from a fire scene

A sample list of particular items, for which there is often probable cause to search and seize in a possible arson case, includes the following:

1. Ignitable materials (with a more particular description if there is probable cause for a specific item such as gasoline or kerosene)
2. Samples of burned material
3. Materials capable of absorbing ignitable materials
4. Containers capable of holding ignitable materials
5. Chemicals
6. Trailers used to help the spread of fire
7. Timing devices (which should be particularized according to what is known by the investigator)
8. Cigarettes or cigars
9. Samples of building materials
10. Samples of charred cloth, carpeting or other material
11. Evidence concerning circuit breakers or fuses which may have been altered
12. Samples of electrical wiring and outlets
13. Control samples
14. Evidence of moved or altered property
15. Evidence of altered sprinkler systems
16. Ignition devices (with as specific a description as possible)
17. Body fluids, including blood, saliva, semen, sweat, urine, articles of clothing containing same, and items containing trace evidence of same
18. Articles that may contain the perpetrator's fingerprints, footprints, or toolmarks
19. Door and window locks, or glass for evidence of forced entry

This list is, of course, not exhaustive, and is offered as an illustration of the types of descriptions that will usually comply with the Fourth Amendment.

2. Examples of *Mincey* warrant items

The following is an example of a particularized description of items to be seized under a *Mincey* warrant. Of course, depending on the particular facts of a given situation, the items to be seized should be added to or deleted from the list:

1. Blood and blood-like substances
2. Semen
3. Saliva
4. Physiological fluids and secretions
5. Hair
6. Fibers
7. Fingerprints
8. Palm prints
9. Footprints
10. Shoe prints
11. Weapons and firearms including pistols, rifles, revolvers, shot guns, hatchets, axes, knives, cutting instruments, and cutting tools
12. Blunt force instruments
13. Projectiles
14. Ammunition
15. Bullet casings and fragments
16. Dirt, dust and soil
17. Paint samples
18. Glass and plastic fragments
19. Marks of tools used to gain access to locked premises or containers
20. Items containing traces of any of the above-mentioned articles

This list is for illustrative purposes and is not exhaustive. If an investigator has probable cause to believe that different items containing evidence may be found in the place to be searched, those items should be included in the list of items sought.

30.5 Effect of *Daubert versus Merrill-Dow*

In *Daubert v. Merrill-Dow Pharm. Inc.*, 509 U.S. 579 (1993), the United States Supreme Court initiated a major change in the way courts decide the admissibility of expert scientific testimony. The Court indicated that the trial judge was to have a gatekeeper role in insuring that scientific evidence was reliable and relevant before being admitted. This role included not only a determination of whether the expert was properly qualified, but also whether the findings were the result of the proper application of that expertise. A few years later in *General Electric Co. et al. v. Joiner*, 522 U.S. 136 (1997), the Court reinforced the importance of the trial judge's role by indicating that appellate courts should only reverse trial court determination of admissibility or exclusion of expert testimony where there was "clear abuse of discretion."

A controversy arose in the federal courts over whether *Daubert* should apply only to "scientific experts" or to "technical experts" as well. This was settled in *Kumho Tire Company, LTD., et al., v. Patrick Carmichael, etc., et al.*, 119 S.Ct. 1167 (1999). Kumho clearly set out the Supreme Court's determination that the mandates of Daubert applied to "technical experts" as well as well as "scientific experts."

The importance of this line of decisions, to those involved in the interpretation of physical evidence, was emphasized in *Michigan Millers Insurance Corp. v. Jannelle R. Benfield*, 140 F.3d 915 (1998), where the U.S. 11th Circuit Court of Appeals upheld the striking of the testimony of the insurance company's arson expert because "he could not rationally explain how he came to his conclusion" and he "failed to perform any tests or take samples." This case makes it clear that those who are doing reconstruction based on evaluation of crime scene information and evidence must be able to convince a trial judge that their determination is based on solid information and well-grounded interpretation, not just on extensive experience. The experts in *Kumho* and *Michigan Millers* both had extensive experience in their respective technical fields but failed to convince the judge that their testimony was "reliable." Although this line of cases is binding only on federal courts, the great majority of states accept the *Daubert* reasoning in whole or to a large extent in their courts. In 2000, the Federal Rules of Evidence were amended to incorporate the *Daubert* decision. The goal of the decision and the rule is to eliminate "junk science" from the courtroom.

In early 2009 the National Academy of Science released a report entitled "Strengthening Forensic Science in the United States: A Path Forward." The report has created controversy and generated discussion about the status of forensic sciences and the need for scientific validation of tests and opinions. Combined with *Daubert*, it is a wake-up call that the admissibility of forensic evidence is dependent on the use of scientific method and that opinions from experts will not be automatically allowed by the courts.

30.6 Professional Handling of Evidence
A. Documentation of the Chain of Evidence
Once the items have been seized and property inventoried, chain of custody must be fully documented. Each jurisdiction should develop or use a form which documents the chain of custody of every piece of evidence seized, and which speci-

fies the officer who seized it, and every subsequent individual who has custody or control of the item. It is also critical that the chain of custody document note whenever evidence leaves police custody, for example, when evidence is turned over to the laboratory or a defense expert. The investigator should be able to reconstruct at a later date to whom the evidence was given at the laboratory as well as from whom it was retrieved, and the date on which all of these activities were performed.

B. Packaging of Evidence

It is also important that the investigator make sure that the evidence is properly packaged according to the recommendations of the forensic laboratory for its safekeeping and preservation. Obviously, this is most critical at the time of initial seizure and transportation to the laboratory; however, it is also important that the evidence be safely packaged and preserved upon its return from the laboratory.

When investigators introduce evidence in court, it should be professionally packaged and presented. Torn paper bags or cardboard grocery boxes make a very poor and unprofessional appearance to a jury. Investigators should be aware of this, and strive to keep and present their evidence appropriately. If it is necessary to repackage evidence for any reason, the original packaging must be included in or securely attached to the new package.

30.7 Conclusion

This chapter has provided basic guidance to the crime and fire scene investigator. Since many jurisdictions have additional, and sometimes unique, legal requirements for the search, seizure, and handling of evidence, it must be emphasized that this chapter only outlines the initial threshold to ensure admissibility of evidence. All investigators should review local law and policy with their own prosecutor's office to ensure that their activities are proper.

I, _____, having been informed of my
constitutional right not to have a search made of my premises without
a search warrant and of my right to refuse to consent to such a
search, do authorize _____, or his designee, to
conduct a complete search of my premises known as _____
_____, for the purpose of establishing the cause and origin
of the fire which occurred on my premises on _____
_____. I am aware that the search is being conducted for possible
evidence of arson and I agree to allow the above-named person or
his designee to take photographs of the premises, to remove papers,
letters, materials, or other property, knowing they may be submitted
for examination and analysis and/or testing.

I am aware that the above-named person or his designee will
be on the premises for a period of time and I have no objection to
their entering and remaining on the premises for a number of days.

This written consent is being given by me voluntarily and
without threats or promises of any kind.

I know that I can refuse to give this consent to search and I am
waiving that right by signing this consent.

Signed _____
Dated _____

WITNESSED:

_____

_____
(date)

_____
(location)

Figure 30.1 *A recommended Consent to Search form.*

I, _____, having been informed of
my constitutional right not to have a search made of the premises
hereinafter mentioned without a search warrant and of my right to
refuse to consent to such a search hereby authorize _____
_____, and _____, (name of officers)
_____
(titles of officers and names of departments) to conduct a complete
search of my premises located at _____.
     These officers are authorized by me to take from my premises
any letters, papers, materials or other property which they may desire.
     This written permission is being given by me to the above-
named persons voluntarily and without threats or promises of any
kind.

Signed _____

Witnesses:

_____

_____

Figure 30.2 *Consent to Search form.*

Appendix A

Preparation of Common Test Reagents

A.1 Blood Screening Test Reagents

Phenolphthalein Solution

Stock:

Phenolphthalein	2 grams
Potassium hydroxide	20 grams
Distilled water	100 mL

Reflux the stock mixture with 20 grams of powdered zinc for two hours until the solution becomes colorless. The stock solution should be stored in a dark bottle and refrigerated with some zinc added to keep it colorless.

Working solution:

Phenolphthalein stock	20 mL
Ethanol	80 mL

Ortho-tolidine

o-tolidine	1.6 grams
Ethanol	40 mL
Glacial acetic acid	30 mL
Distilled water	30 mL

Leucomalachite Green

Leuocomalachite green	0.1 gram
Sodium perborate	3.2 grams
Glacial acetic acid	66 mL
Distilled water	33 mL

Luminol

Solution I:	3-Aminophthalhydrazide (luminol)	0.1 gram
	Distilled water	50 mL
	Ethanol	20 mL
Solution II:	Sodium carbonate	0.5 gram
	Sodium perborate	0.7 gram
	Distilled water	30 mL

Immediately before use, mix solutions I and II.

A.2 Acid Phosphatase Reagents

Substrate solution:	Calcium-2-naphylphosphate*	200 milligrams
	Sodium acetate	2 grams
	Glacial acetic acid	1 mL
	Distilled water	to 100 mL
	(*Calcium -naphthyl phosphate)	
Color reagent:	Fast blue B salt	2 grams
	Distilled water	100 mL

Filter the color reagent solution after dissolving the Fast Blue B salt in the distilled water. *Note: These acid phosphatase reagents should be prepared freshly, shortly before use. They do not have very good storage or shelf life.*

A.3 Bloody Print Enhancement Reagent

Solutions:

Acetate buffer:

Sodium acetate	10 grams
Glacial acetic acid	86 mL
Distilled water	100 mL

Collodion solution:

Ethanol	65 mL
Collodion	15 mL
Tetramethybenzidine	0.4 gram
Sodium perborate	0.3 gram

Mixing instructions:
Color stock solution:
Add the 0.4 grams tetramethylbenzidine to 20 mL acetate buffer. Mix thoroughly until the powder is dissolved. Filter the solution into a small brown bottle for storage.

Working color solution:
Add 4 mL color stock solution to 80 mL Collodion solution. Mix well until no undispersed color stock solution is noted at the bottom of the bottle.

Perborate solution:
In a capped test tube add the sodium perborate to 3 mL acetate buffer. Shake vigorously for several minutes to dissolve the perborate.
Immediately prior to use, add the perborate solution to the working color solution. Shake well to mix thoroughly.

Spraying instructions:
Spray the surface lightly several times. Color development should begin within 60 seconds, but may take a few minutes to develop completely. Photograph any prints which develop, since the print will fade with time.
Remove the developed print, when feasible, in the most appropriate manner as indicated by the size of the imprint and the material on which it is deposited. Re-development of most prints can be conducted at a later date, if necessary.

Appendix B

The Druggist Fold

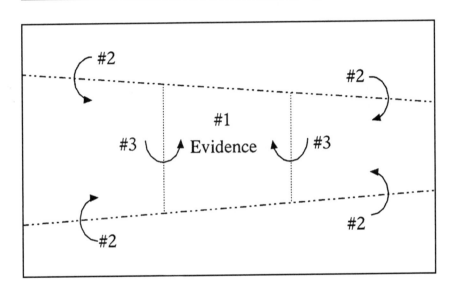

1. Place the article of evidence in the center of the paper.

2. Fold paper over lengthwise twice in nonparallel folds so that the flaps overlap.

3. Fold over the ends, tucking the smaller end inside the larger end.

4. Place the resultant package inside a conventional envelope, seal and label.

References

Abbott, John Reginald. *Footwear Evidence*. Springfield, IL: Charles C. Thomas. 1964.

Bennett, Wayne W., Hess Matison, and Karen Matison. *Investigating Arson*. Springfield, IL: Charles C. Thomas. 1984.

Bevel, Tom, and Ross M. Gardner. *Bloodstain Pattern Analysis with an Introduction to Crime Scene Reconstruction*. Boca Raton, FL: CRC Press. 1997.

Beveridge, Alexander. (Editor) *Forensic Investigation of Explosions*. Taylor & Francis Books Ltd. 1997.

Blaker, Alfred A. *Handbook for Scientific Photography*. Boston, London: Focal Press. 1989.

Bodziak, William J. *Footwear Impression Evidence*. Boca Raton, FL: CRC Press. 1990.

Bodziak, William J. *Tire Tread and Tire Track Evidence*. Boca Raton, FL: CRC Press. 2008.

Butler, John M. *Forensic DNA Typing, Second Edition*. Maryland Heights, MO: Academic Press. 2005.

Carroll, John R. *Physical and Technical Aspects of Fire and Arson Investigation*. Springfield, IL: Charles C. Thomas. 1979.

Catts, E. Paul, and Neal H. Haskell. (editors) *Entomology and Death: A Procedural Guide*. Clemson, SC: Joyce's Print Shop, Inc. 1990.

Cheskin, Melvyn P., Kel J. Sherkin, and Barry T. Bates. *The Complete Handbook of Athletic Footwear*. New York, NY: Fairchild Publications. 1987.

Cowger, James F. *Friction Ridge Skin*. New York, Amsterdam, Oxford: Elsevier. 1983.

Davies, Geoffrey. (Editor) *Forensic Science.* Washington, D.C.: American Chemical Society. 1986.

DeForest, P.R., R.E. Gaensslen, and Henry C. Lee. *Forensic Science—An Introduction to Criminalistics.* New York, NY: McGraw-Hill Inc. 1983.

Di Maio, Dominick J. and Vincent J.M. Di Maio. *Forensic Pathology.* Boca Raton, FL: CRC Press. 1989.

Di Maio, Vincent J.M. *Gunshot Wounds.* New York, Amsterdam, Oxford: Elsevier. 1985.

Douglas, John E., et al. *Crime Classification Manual.* New York, NY: Lexington Books. 1992.

Duckworth, John E. *Forensic Photography.* Springfield, IL: Charles C. Thomas. 1983.

Eckert, William G. and Stuart H. James. *Interpretation of Bloodstain Evidence at Crime Scenes.* New York, Amsterdam, London: Elsevier. 1989.

Farley, Esq., Mark A. and James J. Harrington. *Forensic DNA Technology.* Boca Raton, FL: CRC Press. 1990.

FBI. *Handbook of Forensic Science.* FBI Laboratory. 1978.

FBI. *The Science of Fingerprints.* FBI. 1984.

Field, Annita T. *Fingerprint Handbook.* Springfield, IL: Charles C. Thomas. 1959.

Fisher, Barry A. J. *Techniques of Crime Scene Investigation, Seventh Edition.* Boca Raton, FL: CRC Press. 2004.

Fitch, Richard D. and Edward A. Porter. *Accidental or Incendiary.* Springfield, IL: Charles C. Thomas. 1968.

Gaensslen, R.E. *Sourcebook in Forensic Serology, Immunology, and Biochemistry.* Washington D.C.: U.S. Department of Justice. 1983.

Gaensslen, R.E. and Henry C. Lee. *Procedures and Evaluation of Antisera for the Typing of Antigens in Bloodstains.* Washington D.C.: U.S. Department of Justice. 1984.

Gaensslen, R. E. Howard A Harris, Henry Lee. *Introduction to Forensic Science & Criminalistics.* Columbus, OH: McGraw-Hill Higher Education. 2008.

Geberth, Vernon J. *Practical Homicide Investigation.* New York, Amsterdam, Oxford: Elsevier. 1983.

Goddard, Kenneth W. *Crime Scene Investigation.* Reston, VA: Reston Publishing Co. 1977.

Gray, Henry. *Anatomy.* Philadelphia, PA: Running Press. 1901.

Grieve, M., and J. Robertson. (Editors) *Forensic Investigation of Fibres.* London: Taylor & Francis Books, Ltd. 1999.

Heard, Brian J. *Handbook of Firearms and Ballistics.* Hoboken, NJ: John Wiley & Sons. 2008

Hedge, John. *The Photography Handbook.* New York, NY: Alfred A. Knopf. 1987.

Hilton, Ordway. *Scientific Examination of Questioned Documents.* Boca Raton, FL: CRC Press. 1982.

Inman, Keith, and Norah Rudin. *An Introduction to Forensic DNA Analysis.* Boca Raton, FL: CRC Press. 1997.

Jungreis, Ervin. *Spot Test Analysis Clinical, Environmental, Forensic, and Geochemical Applications.* Second Edition. John Wiley & Sons. 1996.

Kennedy, Patrick, M. and John Kennedy. *Explosion Investigation and Analysis.* Investigations Institute. 1990.

Kind, Stuart and Michael Overman. *Science Against Crime.* London: Aldus Books. 1972.

Kirk, Paul L. *Fire Investigation.* New York, London, Sydney, Toronto: John Wiley & Sons, Inc. 1969.

Lee, Henry C. and Robert E. Gaensslen. (Editors) *Advances in Forensic Science, Volume I.* Foster City, CA: Biomedical Publications. 1985.

Lee, Henry C. and Robert E. Gaensslen. (Editors) *Advances in Forensic Science, Volume II.* Chicago, London, Boca Raton: Year Book Medical Publishers, Inc. 1989.

Lee, Henry C. and Robert E. Gaensslen. (Editors) *Advances in Fingerprint Technology.* Boca Raton, FL: CRC Press. 1991.

Lee, Henry C., et al. *Crime Scene Investigation.* Taoyuan, Taiwan: Central Police University. 1994.

Lee, Henry C., et al. *Physical Evidence in Criminal Investigation*. Westbrook, CT: Narcotic Enforcement Officers Association. 1991.

Lee, Henry, Timothy Palmbach and Marilyn T. Miller. *Henry Lee's Crime Scene Handbook*. Maryland Heights, MO: Academic Press. 2001

Li, Richard; *Forensic Biology*. Boca Raton, FL: CRC Press. 2008.

Luntz, Lester L. *Handbook for Dental Identification*. Philadelphia and Toronto: J.B. Lippincott Co. 1973.

MacDonell, Herbert Leon. *Bloodstain Pattern Interpretation*. 1983.

McDonald, James, A. *Close-up and Macro Photography for Evidence Technicians*. PhotoText Books. 1992.

McDonald, Peter. *Tire Imprint Evidence*. Boca Raton, FL: CRC Press. 1989.

Menzel, E. Roland. *Fingerprint Detection with Lasers*. New York and Basel: Marcel Dekker, Inc. 1980.

Miller, L.S. and A.M. Brown. Criminal Evidence Laboratory Manual. Ohio: Anderson Publishing Company. 1990.

Morse, Dan, Jack Duncan, and Stoutamire (editors). *Handbook of Forensic Archaeology and Anthropology*. Tallahassee, FL: Florida State University Foundation. 1983.

Noon, Randall. *Introduction to Forensic Engineering*. Boca Raton, FL: CRC Press. 1992.

O'Connor, John J. *Practical Fire and Arson Investigation*. New York, Amsterdam, London: Elsevier. 1987.

Olson, Robert D., Sr. *Scott's Fingerprint Mechanics*. Springfield, IL: Charles C. Thomas. 1978.

Redsicker, David R. *The Practical Methodology of Forensic Photography*. New York, Amsterdam, London, Tokyo: Elsevier. 1991.

Robertson, J. (Editor) *Forensic Examination of Human Hair*. London: Taylor & Francis Books, Ltd. 1999.

Robertson, James; *Forensic Examination of Fibers, Second Edition*. Boca Raton, FL: CRC Press.. 2002.

Rynearson, Joseph M. *Evidence and Crime Scene Reconstruction*. California: J.M. Rynearson. 1985.

Saferstein, Richard. *Criminalistics: An Introduction to Forensic Science*. Englewood Cliffs, NJ: Prentice-Hall, Inc. 1990, 1987, 1981, 1977.

Saferstein, Richard. *Forensic Science Handbook*. Englewood Cliffs, NJ: Prentice-Hall, Inc. 1982.

Saferstein, Richard. *Forensic Science Handbook, Volume II*. Englewood Cliffs, NJ: Prentice-Hall, Inc. 1988.

Saferstein, Richard. *Forensic Science Handbook, Volume III*. Regents/Prentice-Hall. 1993.

Siljander, Raymond P. *Applied Police and Fire Photography*. Springfield, IL: Charles C. Thomas. 1976.

Spitz, Werner U. and Russell S. Fisher. (Editors) *Medicolegal Investigation of Death*. Springfield, IL: Charles C. Thomas. 1976.

Swanson, Charles R., Neil C. Chamelin, and Leonard Territo. *Criminal Investigation*. New York, NY: McGraw-Hill, Inc. 1992.

The Home Office (Scotland Yard). *Fingerprint Development Techniques*. United Kingdom: Home Office. 1988.

Vandiver, James V. *Criminal Investigation*. Metuchen, NJ: The Scarecrow Press, Inc. 1983.

Walls, H.J. *Forensic Science*. New York, NY: Praeger Publishers. 1974.

Weston, Paul B. and Kenneth M. Wells. *Criminal Evidence for Police*. Englewood Cliffs, NJ: Prentice-Hall, Inc. 1986, 1976, 1971.

Weston, Paul B. and Kenneth M. Wells. *Criminal Investigation*. Englewood Cliffs, NJ: Prentice-Hall, Inc. 1990, 1986, 1980, 1974, 1970.

Yinon, Jehuda. *Forensic Applications of Mass Spectrometry*. Boca Raton, FL: CRC Press. 1994.

Zonderman, Jon. *Beyond the Crime Lab*. John Wiley & Sons, Inc. 1990.

Zuckerman, A.A.S. *The Principles of Criminal Evidence*. Oxford: Clarendon Press. 1989.

About the Authors

Dr. Henry C. Lee is one of the world's foremost forensic scientists. Dr. Lee's work has made him a landmark in modern day forensic sciences. He has been a prominent player in many of the most challenging cases of the last 50 years. Dr. Lee has worked with law enforcement agencies from 46 countries in helping to solve more than 8,000 cases. In recent years, his travels have taken him to the United Kingdom, Bosnia, China, Germany, Singapore, Croatia, Brunei, Thailand, the Middle East and other locations around the world.

Dr. Lee's testimony figured prominently in the O. J. Simpson, Jason Williams, Peterson, and Kennedy Smith trials, and in convictions of the "Woodchipper" murderer as well as thousands of other murder cases. Dr. Lee has assisted local and state police in their investigations of other famous crimes, such as the murder of JonBenet Ramsey in Boulder, Colorado, the 1993 suicide of White House Counsel Vincent Foster, the kidnapping of Elizabeth Smart, the death of Chemdra Levy and the reinvestigation of the Kennedy assassination.

Dr. Lee is currently the director of the Forensic Research and Training Center and Distinguished Professor in Forensic Science of the University of New Haven. He was the Chief Emeritus for Connecticut State Police from 2000 to 2010, the Commissioner of Public Safety for the State of Connecticut from 1998 to 2000, and served as that state's Chief Criminalist from 1978 to 2000. Dr. Lee was the driving force in establishing a modern state police communication system, community-based police services, a sex offender and DNA database, major crime investigation concepts and advanced forensic science services in Connecticut.

In 1975, Dr. Lee joined the University of New Haven, where he created the school's Forensic Sciences program. He has also taught as a professor at more than a dozen universities, law schools, and medical schools. Though challenged with the demands on his schedule, Dr. Lee still lectures throughout the country and worldwide to police, universities and civic organizations. Dr. Lee has authored hundreds of articles in professional journals and has co-authored more than 40 books, covering such areas as: DNA, fingerprints, trace evidence, crime scene investigation and crime scene reconstruction. He is the author of multiple bestsellers, such as *Famous Crime Revisited, Cracking Cases: The Science of Solving Crimes, Blood Evidence*, and *Cracking More Cases*. In addition, his textbooks, including *Forensic Science Today, Physical Evidence in Forensic Science* and *Henry Lee's Crime Scene Handbook* have been widely adopted in the medical-legal and forensic professions. He has appeared on many TV shows and movies. His new television series, *Trace Evidence—The Case Files of Dr. Henry Lee*, has received high ratings and been showing around the world.

Dr. Lee has been the recipient of numerous medals and awards, including the 1996 Medal of Justice from the Justice Foundation, and the 1998 Lifetime Achievement Award from the Science and Engineer Association. He has also been the recipient of the Distinguished Criminalist Award from the American Academy of Forensic Sciences, the J. Donero Award from the International Association of Identification, and in 1992 was elected a distinguished Fellow of the AAFS. He has received the ACFE Lifetime Achievement Award, American College of Forensic Examiner, in 2000, Medal of Honor by Ellis Island Foundation in 2004, Congressional Recognition for Outstanding services by the U.S. Congress in 2004, Presidential Medal of Honor, by Croatia President in 2005, Medal of Service, Ministry of Interior, Taiwan, ROC, 2006, and Gusi Peace Award from the Philippines in 2008.

Dr. Lee was born in China and grew up in Taiwan. Dr. Lee first worked for the Taipei Police Department, attaining the rank of Captain. With his wife, Margaret, Dr. Lee came to the United States in 1965, and he earned his B.S. in Forensic Science from John Jay College in 1972. Dr. Lee continued his studies in biochemistry at NYU where he earned his Master's Degree in 1974 and Ph.D. in 1975. He has also received special training from the FBI Academy, ATF, RCMP, and other organizations. He is a recipient of 20 honorary degrees: Doctorate Degrees of Science from University of New Haven, University of Connecticut, Honorary Doctorate of Law from Roger Williams University School of Law, Mitchell College, American International University and Taiwan Scientific Technology University, Honorary Doctorate Degree in Human Letters from the University of Bridgeport, St. Joseph College, Armstrong University, in recognition of his contributions to law and science, etc. Dr. and Mrs. Lee have been married for 49 years and have two grown children: a daughter, Sherry, and a son, Stanley, as well as three grandchildren: David, Rachel and Alex.

Dr. Howard A. Harris is currently a Professor in the Forensic Science Department at the University of New Haven. His educational background is in chemistry (A.B. Western Reserve University, M.S. and Ph.D. Yale University) and law (J.D. St. Louis University). He was admitted to and has maintained his membership in the Missouri Bar. Dr. Harris was a research chemist for seven years before entering the forensic field as the Director of the New York City Police Department Police Laboratory. After holding that position for twelve years, he moved upstate to become the Director of the Monroe County Public Safety Laboratory in Rochester. He held that position for eleven years before taking early retirement to make a career change to academics. He assumed his current position at the University of New Haven in the fall of 1996. Dr. Harris is a past president of the American Society of Crime Lab Directors and a past chair of the criminalistics section of the American Academy of Forensic Sciences. Dr. Harris and his wife, Carolyn, have one daughter and two grandchildren.

Index